Date of Conviction	Term of Transportation	What Ship	Casualty
21 April 1784	7 Years	Scarborough	
23 Febry 1785	7 Years	Scarborough	
24 May 1784	7 Years	Charlotte	
		Friendship	
13 Janry 1784	7 Years	Lady Penrhyn	
5 March 1785	7 Years	Lady Penrhyn	
8 March 1786	Life	Alexander	Died 2d June 1787 at Sea
24 March 1784	7 Years	Alexander	
11 May 1785	7 Years	Lady Penrhyn	
5 April 1785	7 Years	Alexander	
29 June 1785	7 Years	Alexander	
5 April 1785	7 Years	Alexander	
21 April 1784	7 Years	Scarborough	
7 July 1784	7 Years	Scarborough	
20 March 1786	7 Years	Charlotte	
16 Feb 1785	7 Years	Alexander	
24 Mar 1784	7 Years	Alexander	
10 Decr 1784	7 Years	Alexander	Pardond 10 May 1787
11 July 1786	7 Years	Alexander	Died 7 May 1787
15 Septr 1784	7 Years	Scarborough	
20 Decr 1786	7 Years	Friendship	
		Friendship	
		Friendship	
9 July 1785	7 Years	Prince of Wales	
18 April 1787	7 Years	Prince of Wales	
13 Decr 1786	7 Years	Lady Penrhyn	
13 Decr 1786	7 Years	Lady Penrhyn	
4 Augst 1783	7 Years	Alexander	

G H I K L M N O P Q R S T V W X

Bound for Botany Bay

Bound for

BOTANY BAY

BRITISH CONVICT VOYAGES TO AUSTRALIA

Alan Brooke & David Brandon

the national archives

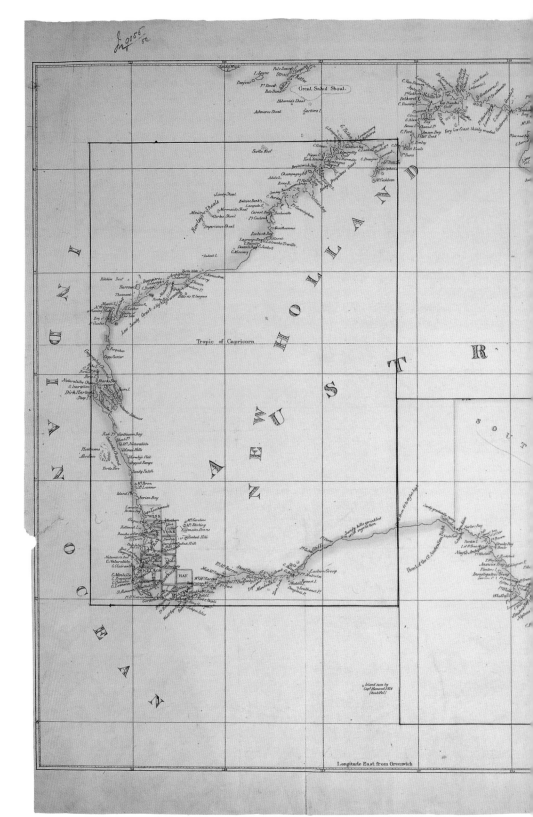

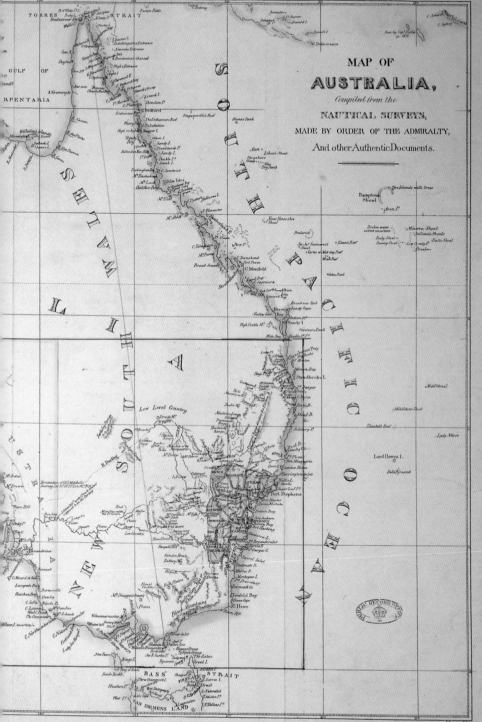

MAP OF
AUSTRALIA,
Compiled from the
NAUTICAL SURVEYS,
MADE BY ORDER OF THE ADMIRALTY,
And other Authentic Documents.

Ordered by the House of Commons to be Printed 14th July 1837.   J. Basire Lith.

First published in 2005 by

The National Archives
Kew, Richmond
Surrey, TW9 4DU
UK

www.nationalarchives.gov.uk

The National Archives (TNA)
was formed when the
Public Record Office (PRO)
and Historical Manuscripts
Commission (HMC)
combined in April 2003.

A catalogue card for this book is available
from the British Library.

ISBN 1 903365 78 3

Edited by Catherine Bradley
Book design by Ken Wilson
Printed in the UK by
Butler and Tanner, Frome, Somerset

ENDPAPERS
*A Home Office document showing details of convicts
embarked on the First Fleet in 1787 (HO 10/7).
They sailed on the first fleet for and Van Diemen's
Land. A comprehensive list of settlers and convicts
exist for the years 1787–1859.*

HALF TITLE
Convicts embarking for Botany Bay *by Thomas
Rowlandson shows convicts being taken to their
transportation ship. The corpses hanging from the
gibbet are a reminder of what the convicts' fates
might have been.*

TITLE PAGE
'Scenes On Board an Australian Emigrant Ship'
W.G. Mason (ZPER 34/14 p40)

PAGES 4–5
'Map of Australia / compiled from the / Nautical
Surveys / made by order of the Admiralty / And
other Authentic Documents.' (MPG1–476)
Issued by the Committee on Transportation, 1837
*An 1837 lithograph of a map of Australia, taken
from nautical surveys. Early explorers were expected
to make charts of the coast to assist later navigators
and settlers. At this time, Australia consisted of
Western Australia, New South Wales and South
Australia.*

Contents

Introduction

BEFORE STARTING RESEARCH for *Bound for Botany Bay*, we carried with us a host of preconceptions and prejudices concerning transportation. We shared the view that those responsible for law and order in Britain in the eighteenth and nineteenth centuries must have been cruelly vindictive people, happy to hang men, women and even young children for stealing objects of trifling value. Those who escaped execution faced a living death in desolate convict colonies on the opposite side of the world. These unfortunates were transported in ships amounting to floating hells in which they were systematically abused, physically and mentally. Unsurprisingly, convicts died in vast numbers of disease and neglect while at sea. The prisoners who survived to reach Australia had to eke out their sentences in chain gangs—breaking rocks and beaten constantly by spiteful guards for the slightest inattention or the merest hint of insubordination. Some convicts escaped from this torture to form robber gangs, which then terrorized evolving settlements. Such were the antecedents of Australia, or so it was easy to assume.

However, while researching and writing the book we found much evidence to contradict our perceptions concerning transportation. The judicial system in Britain in the period under review was characterized by elements of humanity as well as cruelty—but above all by flexibility mixed with pragmatism. Conditions on many of the early convict ships to Australia were indeed appalling, but they improved enormously over the years. As a result, large numbers of convicts not only survived the voyage but also completed their sentences, going on to make new and successful lives for themselves in Australia. Sometimes convicts were joined in later years by those they had been forced to leave behind in Britain.

In *Bound for Botany Bay* we have focused on the human side of transportation. It is hard to imagine the convicts' experience of leaving their native country, loved ones and all that was familiar; or how they handled the largely unknown hazards of a long sea voyage; or how they coped with the trauma of exile once they got there. Through contemporary documents we can approach the realities at first hand, from the discipline, health and food on board ships to the kinds of people sentenced to transportation and the reasons why it was instigated in the first place. In so doing, we hope to dispel one or two well-established myths about crime and punishment in eighteenth century Britain and specifically, about transportation itself. We have tried to ensure that, above all, this is a history of people—those who survived, those who died and those who were left behind.

There is no substitute for handling historical documents at first hand. To hold and read a letter written 150 or 200 years ago by a distraught wife or mother appealing to the Home Secretary for support so that she could go to Australia with her convicted but loved, husband, partner or, in some cases, son brings the past vividly to life. The hundreds of documents we have looked at illuminate the breadth of human experience—the desperately sad, the humorous, the pompous, the cringing and sanctimonious, the cruel and callous, the generous and humane. Some documents emphasize the sheer heroism or simple stoicism of individuals who found themselves in the dire circumstances of being transported.

We have examined hundreds of letters to the Home Secretary, many of which reflect the appalling privations that the transportation of a breadwinner could bring to his or her dependants.[1] Ann Flanagan, writing in 1837, for example, described her 'deplorable state' since her husband had been transported: 'I have been almost famished for want of food. My husband left me with one child, I have neither father nor mother, relatives nor friends to give me and my child any assistance whatever and I have nothing to get my bread with.' Sarah Smyth from County Monaghan similarly pleaded to be allowed to follow her husband. Smyth stated that neither she nor her three children had any support whatsoever except for what she earned daily; as a result, the family was ragged and half-starved.

A mass of records exists in the National Archives and they provide the names of convicts and the ships they sailed in, the crime of which they were convicted, the date of their conviction and embarkation, length of sentence, their age and the particular colonies to which they were sent. One particularly rewarding source of material can be found in the Judges Reports on Criminals 1783 to 1830.[2] They contain thousands of individual cases which deal with petitions for clemency and provide insights into the kinds of crime committed by those whose sentences had been commuted from death to transportation. These examples—rich in human interest—indicate a flexible attitude on the part of the judges: they were often willing to consider factors such as age, previous character, family circumstances and the social standing of those supporting the prisoner's appeal.

Such records cast valuable light upon the mechanism of mercy as it operated in the early eighteenth and early nineteenth century.

For example, Robert Stewart, a seaman, had been sentenced to seven years in 1792 at Bristol for stealing a silver watch and a tablespoon. He was recommended for clemency on grounds of his youth and the fact that it was his first offence. Interestingly, also offered in mitigation was information that he had formed an attachment to a young lady, only to find out that she was to be married to someone else. This had caused him to be 'deranged' and to act out of character.[3] In another case, a prisoner by the name of Larkin was convicted of stealing fowls and geese in 1790 at Southampton. The court considered him to be part of a gang which 'infested the town of Alton'. His grounds for clemency included his previous unblemished conduct in the militia. The judge recommended that he be made to enlist as a marine or in HM Navy.[4] William Davis, a Hackney coachman, was convicted in 1786 of stealing a pocket-handkerchief. He was considered by the judge hearing his case to be 'one of those bold, desperate pickpockets who at that Time infested and were a Terror to that part of the Town.' As mitigation Davis pleaded previous good behaviour on the hulk, plus the fact that this was his first offence and he had been drunk at the time of the crime.[5]

Families were often brought into the appeals, as they suffered severely from the loss of the breadwinner. George Morris was convicted at Shrewsbury in 1783 for stealing lead from a house. The grounds for clemency were that the house was uninhabited and ruined, that he had become very ill while lodged in a crowded gaol, his wife had died from contracting gaol fever while visiting him and all his children had contracted smallpox also while visiting him. In addition, it was stated that his family was now in a state of utter deprivation and Morris himself promised to be a good character in the future. The judge dodged the issue by passing on the sentence to the Home Secretary without any specific recommendation.[6] John Hack, a carpenter and joiner, was convicted at the Old Bailey in 1786 for stealing two gallons of rum shrub liquor. This was his first offence, and it was stated that he was of previous good character and had behaved well during his imprisonment. Also taken into consideration was the information that he had an aged mother, a wife and four children suffering severely as a result of his conviction, and that he had received an offer of employment from a respectable tradesman if he was released. It was recommended that he be released on condition of good behaviour for seven years.[7]

There are also interesting additional comments made by judges on the state of those brought before the court. In one case the judge reported on the problems of those discharged without conviction. He stated that they are 'turned loose, without Credit or Character, without—money—& almost naked, & probably at a Distance from their Friends and their Homes… They are thus forced to become Vagrants or Thieves.'[8]

The wealth of records also allow us to follow convicts from where they lived, through their trial and conviction to the voyage and their subsequent experiences in Australia. Richard Pinnuck from Enfield in Middlesex was one of over 200 boys who sailed on the *Elphinstone* in 1842 bound for Van Diemen's Land. He had had been convicted of theft at the Central Criminal Court and was then taken to the hulk *Euryalus* to await passage to Australia. As with many other convicts, we have Richard's physical details and we know how long he spent in the penal colony at Point Puer. We also know that, for example, he married the daughter of two fellow-convicts, but then left his wife to go in search of gold in Victoria.

Many of the most evocative records come from the surgeons who sailed on the convict ships. The journals they were required to keep provide a wealth of fascinating information and human interest. They chronicle the illnesses and daily sufferings of the convicts, as well as the deep levels of compassion shown by many of these surgeons whose job was not an easy or prestigious one. The surgeon Alick Osborne who sailed on no fewer than nine convict voyages said that most of the prisoners on his ship did not deserve the punishment inflicted on them. Thomas Logan, surgeon-superintendent on the *Albion* in 1828, appreciated the convicts' sense of delight at first seeing the coast of Australia. He wrote that they showed 'an animated eagerness to behold their future country… Fun and frolics arise out of the common hilarity.'

It became evident to us that the work of the surgeons who sailed in the convict ships has not received the attention it deserves. The surgeons' journals make it clear that although some voyages were blighted by epidemic disease, cruelty, depravity, mutiny and even shipwreck, such events were few and far between. Most convict voyages fell swiftly into a mundane and largely uneventful routine, punctuated only by salutations to occasional passing ships, landfalls, the appearance of such creatures as flying fish and dolphins and the celebrations that marked the crossing of the Equator. Mutinies, murders and untoward events were rare. Sometimes prisoners died; so too, occasionally, did members of the crew. Falling from the tops was a hazard common to all sailing ships.

Transportation entered deeply into the folklore and popular culture of the British Isles. Symbolized by the remoteness of Botany Bay, it became a pervasive theme of innumerable ballads and broadsides, as well as the writings of the literary elite. The practice was established well before the First Fleet sailed to Australia in 1787. Daniel Defoe, for example, transports his picaresque heroine Moll Flanders to the English colony of Virginia in the novel of that name, published in 1722. The French writer Abbé Prévost (1696–1763) likewise places the final stages of *Manon Lescaut* (1731) in the New World. His heroine Manon is deported as a prostitute to Bienville in Louisiana, where the French had established a penal colony of their own.

We also consider how and why transportation came about and why it was used so extensively between 1787 and 1868. It was in many ways a logical development within the evolution of English penal practice, the result of concerns in the seventeenth, eighteenth and nineteenth centuries that crime was getting out of control. For all that it was a flawed form of punishment, it unquestionably provided some convicts with the chance to make a fresh start in a land of immense promise well away from the criminal networks from which many of them came. The experience of being torn from all that was familiar to be forcibly transported across the world by sea could never be other than traumatic. The evidence, however, shows that the authorities went to lengths that surprised us to prevent arbitrarily cruel treatment of prisoners at sea, and to ensure that they reached the penal colonies in as healthy a state as possible. For many convicts, regular diet, medical care and clean surroundings actually provided them with the better conditions than they had ever previously enjoyed. Truth, when it emerges from the neglect of centuries, can sometimes be stranger than fiction.

1

The Beginning of Transportation

THE PRACTICE of sending convicts overseas began long before Botany Bay became a destination. Between 1614 and 1775, more than 50,000 men, women and children were dispatched from the British Isles to the English colonies in North America, providing a substantial part of the early white population. However, the nineteenth century saw a new era of forced migration in which convicts and bonded labour from India, France, Russia and Spain, as well as Britain and Ireland, were shipped without hesitation to other parts of the world.

An illustration of Tyburn gate and gallows in the seventeenthth century (WORK 16/376). Located close to where Marble Arch now stands, Tyburn was the most notorious site of execution in London from the twelfth century to 1783. Tens of thousands died there.

Over 162,000 British and Irish convicts were transported to Australia between 1787 and 1868. Such a massive movement of people involved 806 ships and countless associated individuals—magistrates and judges, turnkeys, constables and other law enforcers, a host of

The coffins   Javelin men.

government employees, private contractors and agents, merchant seamen and officers, guards and their officers, surgeons and, of course, the prisoners themselves. The human cost was high. Families were torn apart and cast into poverty; convicts, some no more than children, were thrust from everything familiar into a terrifying, alien world. The whole operation was a major undertaking for the British government, seeking to create an economic infrastructure and foster colonization on the far side of the world. Yet it was always a controversial procedure, drawing criticism from humanitarians and hardliners alike and subject to changing social attitudes and perspectives.

Why did the authorities decide to transport so many of the country's felons and other undesirables such a huge distance? Part of the answer lies with Parliament, which greatly increased the number of capital offences during the eighteenth century in an attempt to tackle the apparent increase in the levels of crime of all sorts. At the end of the sixteenth century, there were over 50 capital offences—two centuries later, there were more than 200. The loosely worded legislation of 1723, subsequently known as the 'Waltham Black Act', was aimed ostensibly at establishing the capital sanction for poachers and rustlers. However, it also imposed the death penalty on those apprehended merely for being armed and disguised on the open road, on heathland or in forests where there was game; for wounding cattle, for setting fire to crops and a host of other rural crimes. Sir Leon Radzinowicz, a Cambridge don and an authority on criminal jurisprudence, described this Act as 'a complete and extremely severe criminal code which indiscriminately punished with death a great many offences'[1], and noted its failure to consider either individual personalities or particular circumstances. Rushed through Parliament at the behest of the landowning class, particularly those who owned game preserves, it gave the State a formidably comprehensive capital statute with which to attack the perceived menace of rural anarchy.

Other new legal enactments which bore down heavily on the common people in the eighteenth and nineteenth centuries included the Riot Act, the Combination Act and the Workhouse Act. These were all part of a hardening of attitudes on the part of the governing classes, the result of their fear that crime and the common people were getting out of control. Some uttered darkly that hanging was too good for convicted felons and that it would be preferable for them to be broken on the wheel instead.

As it was, public hanging was intended to act as a deterrent, stark and visible evidence of the power of the State and its ability to bring those who broke the law to account for their crimes. The terror of capital punishment, epitomized by the procession to the gallows, was integral to its fascination. Nowhere was the sense of theatre stronger than in London, when prisoners were brought from Newgate prison and taken through the city streets the three miles to Tyburn, London's main execution site. The word 'Tyburn' became synonymous with a ravening, voyeuristic crowd; with the very public anguish of those who were close to the condemned; with the defiant hauteur of those felons who absolutely refused to be cowed by their imminent death; with the grotesque spectacle of the hanging itself, and the sight of the relatives of the deceased and the agents of the anatomists, sometimes fighting tooth and nail over the body.

The ritual of public hanging, however, was appropriated by the populace as a form of mass entertainment. Unpopular felons were subjected to verbal and sometimes physical abuse. Those favoured by the crowd, for whatever reason, were cheered, often showered with flowers or fruit and applauded if they went off to the scaffold with heads held high. On the scaffold, some entertained the crowd with jokes and ribaldry or launched into scathing attacks on the law, the political authorities or the fates that had conspired against them. Densely packed crowds jostled for the best view of the proceedings. Pickpockets prospered, oblivious to the death agonies of the felon—possibly convicted of precisely the same crime.

Much has been written about Britain's 'Bloody Code', complete with horror stories of how, for example, children aged 12 or less were dispatched to the gallows for shoplifting or were transported for crimes that nowadays seem trivial. Between 1660 and 1819, no fewer than 187 additional offences came to carry the death penalty. These included cutting hop bines, setting fire to coal mines, concealing the death of an illegitimate child, sending threatening letters, bigamy, consorting with gypsies, stealing a shroud from a grave and various other offences that to modern eyes do not seem to warrant the capital sanction. Private property had become sacrosanct, elevated in law almost to the level of a deity. John Locke in *Two Treatises of Government,* published in 1690, declared that 'Government has no other end but the preservation of property.' In order to safeguard wealth and property, governments from the sixteenth to the nineteenth centuries produced a penal code which, at first glance, was of fearsome severity. The classes that dominated Parliament used the criminal law and the creation of more and more capital offences to support a redefining of property and the purposes of government. The social historian Douglas Hay has described how the ruling elite 'set new standards of legislative industry' as they passed 'act after act to keep the capital sanction up to date, to protect every conceivable kind of property from theft or malicious damage.'[2]

Nowhere did the perceived threat from crime seem as serious as in London. The capital, expanding rapidly through internal migration, offered unique opportunities to the criminally inclined. Much of its large, rootless and volatile population was unskilled and consequently vulnerable to economic downturns and slumps. With few familial or other loyalties, many naturally turned to crime, at least when times were hard. The prisons of the capital, probably the most appalling in the land, were awash with a sea of desperate and despairing humanity.

The prison system was not reformed along more modern lines until the nineteenth century. Prior to that, gaols, such as the notorious Newgate, were incubators of crime in which prisoners were held, irrespective of age, crime or condition, to await trial, sentencing or punishment. In many prisons, those who had money could obtain tobacco, alcohol and all sorts of luxuries, indeed just about anything they wanted in order to make their stay more tolerable. For the rest, it was often a living hell. As Robert Hughes has said, 'The prison pickled the felon in evil, hardened him, perfused him with the hard salt of sin.'[3] The reformer John Howard, whose name is commemorated in the Howard League for Prison Reform, described the appalling conditions in his *State of the Prisons of England and Wales*, published in 1777:

> Convicts … are ironed, and thrust into close offensive dungeons, and there chained down, some of them without straw or other bedding; in which they continue, in winter, sixteen or seventeen hours out of the twenty four, in utter inactivity, and immersed in the noxious effluvia of their own bodies… Their diet is at the same time low and scanty; they are generally without firing; and the powers of life soon become incapable of resisting so many causes of sickness and despair… Certain it is that many of those who survive their long confinement, are by it rendered incapable of working. Some of them by scorbutic distempers, others by their toes mortified, or quite rotted from their feet, many instances of which I have seen.[4]

Between 1783 and 1785 alone, the Home Secretary received reports from magistrates in 35 localities about gross overcrowding, outbreaks of fever, attempted or successful riots and requests for assistance from the military. Significantly, these communications were laced with pleas for transportation (stopped after the American War of Independence) to be resumed as a matter of priority.[5] Specifically, the Gloucestershire reforming magistrate, George Onesiphorus Paul, pleaded with the Secretary of State to remove prisoners in Gloucester gaol awaiting transportation, noting that they 'are so numerous and so desperate that it is found impossible to ensure their safe custody.'[6] This is merely one instance from many regarding the dire conditions of the country's gaols.[7]

A London vagabond, 1815, from John T. Smith's Vagabondia, *1874. The capital's shifting population frequently resorted to criminal activity, and many beggars and vagabonds found themselves on the convict ships.*

The scale of the crime problem becomes apparent when we appreciate the inadequacies of law-enforcement agencies before the nineteenth century. As a result of these weaknesses, only relatively small numbers of those who offended were actually apprehended and brought to justice. In many cases, they were made an example of and dealt with ferociously. The elaborate rituals in which bewigged judges, wearing ermine-tipped scarlet robes, donned the black cap when death sentences were solemnly pronounced emphasized the majesty of the law; they sought to overawe those who offended against it. However, the courts also frequently practised what was sometimes called 'pious perjury'. This meant that the severity of the law might be lessened by juries in cases where prisoners had been charged with capital offences. If theft was involved, for example, juries sometimes deliberately undervalued the articles stolen so that the offence was no longer grand larceny, a capital offence, but petty larceny, which was a misdemeanour attracting a lesser punishment. Judges on their own initiative sometimes dismissed cases, and reprieves, even on the day set aside for the hanging, were by no means uncommon. A number of women avoided the death sentence by pleading 'benefit of belly'. This allowed them a stay of execution until after the baby was born, which usually meant that they were ultimately pardoned. Judges were capable of acting arbitrarily and subjectively, none more so than Judge Jeffreys. At the 'Bloody Assizes' in September 1685, Jeffries, hoping to win the King's approval sentenced 330 of the insurgents, who had supported the Duke of Monmouth in his rebellion, to the gallows and around 800 to transportation to the Americas.

An unpredictable, even capricious, mixture of terror with a degree of humanity and clemency by the judiciary added powerfully to its mystique. The fact that the court's decision might be unclear until the last minute ratched up the dramatic tension. Juries were often reluctant to convict where a penalty seemed disproportionate to the crime committed, and the courts increasingly imposed sentences other than hanging on convicted felons. These might involve detention with hard labour or transportation to the American colonies and the West Indies. Penal policy, especially in the eighteenth century, was characterized by a flexible, albeit inequitable, balance between deterrence by terror and practical humanitarianism. The harsh criminal code was thus unexpectedly tempered, if inconsistently so, by pragmatic 'acquittals and partial verdicts', resulting in 'falling rates of hanging and the elaboration of a number of alternative, non-capital punishments.'[8]

TRANSPORTATION BEFORE BOTANY BAY

In a sense, transportation was a logical development of the medieval practice of banishment—the imposition of involuntary exile to somewhere beyond the country's borders. Property was forfeit under such a sentence, and the subject faced enforced estrangement from an entire familiar world. It was dangerously close to a death sentence in the Middle Ages since penniless strangers were likely to be vulnerable everywhere.

The first known mention of transportation as a punishment probably dates back to Richard Hakluyt (*c.*1552–1616). An Elizabethan geographer, cleric and historian, he recommended despatching criminals to saw and fell trees and plant sugar cane in the American colonies in 1584. Transportation was to prove a far more institutionalized process than banishment, which simply abandoned the offender to fortune's whim. The State organized and supervised travel arrangements and retained some responsibility for the fate of the prisoners once they had reached their destination. Not least, a formidable penal apparatus was available if they escaped or if they returned home before their sentences were completed.

The Elizabethan authorities were apparently obsessed with the perceived threat posed by 'sturdy beggars and vagabonds'. The latter sometimes formed gangs that roamed around terrorizing and robbing countryside and town. Vagrancy, poverty, and joblessness were effectively lumped together as being virtually synonymous with criminality. Legislation passed in 1597–8 stated that 'incorrigible rogues' who refused to live within the law might be banished to distant parts or sent to the galleys, their lives forfeit if they ever returned to England. In 1615, the Privy Council ordered that those convicted of serious crimes could be dispatched to forced labour on plantations in the East Indies or the Americas. Little use was made of these initiatives, and between 1615 and 1640 only about 120 prisoners, who otherwise faced execution, were 'reprieved' by being transported.

For some in the seventeenth century, transportation seemed the ideal solution to the question of what to do with those they considered habitual criminals and idle ne'er-do-wells. There were those who argued that many of the poor and destitute people swarming London's streets were causing the diseases, some of them deadly, which were ravaging the capital. The best known was the Great Plague of London in 1665, but there were other major outbreaks of bubonic plague, for example in 1630, 1636 and 1647. Other epidemic diseases affecting the capital included smallpox and typhoid. It was suggested that the Corporation of London and other bodies such as the Livery Companies should raise funds to ship such individuals out to Virginia where they would be found useful employment and cease to pose problems of health, crime and anti-social behaviour, at least in the metropolis. Although money was raised, this scheme came to nothing.

CONVICTS IN THE NEW WORLD

During the Commonwealth, numbers of English capital offenders and many Irish political prisoners were dispatched to Virginia on the American mainland and to Barbados and Jamaica in the Caribbean. In 1655, formal permission was given for convicts who had received conditional pardons to be transported. Although at first it had no sanction in common law, transportation of this sort suited the authorities because it was an economical measure which enabled them to be seen exercising clemency while ridding the country, usually permanently, of many of those perceived as its most anti-social elements. In 1657 and 1662, acts were passed which targeted 'idle and wandering persons'. Those found guilty of minor misdemeanours had to give sureties of good behaviour, something like a modern parole; if they breached these, the offenders made themselves liable to transportation for seven years.

Others who were transported in the seventeenth century included religious recusants (dissenters who refused to submit to authority), Scottish Covenanters and various other political prisoners. Quakers were sent for transportation in the reign of Charles II (1660–85), but the authorities decided not to send them to Virginia or New England, where their views might have aroused some sympathy. Instead they were deported to the sugar plantations of the Caribbean, particularly Barbados.

In 1678, after the restoration of Charles II, Parliament officially approved the idea of sending convicts to serve their sentences in the American colonies of Virginia and Maryland, and in the West Indies.

Engraved for the Newgate Calendar.

Representation of the Transports going from Newgate to take water at Blackfriars.

This engraving of 1760 shows chained convicts walking from Newgate prison to the Thames at Blackfriars, where they would embark on a transportation ship. Such processions were familiar sights for Londoners.

These places were desperately short of manpower, and it was argued that using convicts as forced labour would help to harness their economic potential. The shipping of the convicts was managed by contractors, such as Stephenson and Randolf from Bristol, who recouped their costs by selling the prisoners to colonial employers. The convicts were auctioned to the highest bidder, for whom they had to work for the duration of their sentences as indentured servants, under conditions not very different from those of slaves. They were valuable commodities: in 1740, a healthy, strong convict could fetch up to £80 in the West Indies. Not all of them reached there, of course. After the 1745 Jacobite Rebellion, for example, several hundred captured Scots were brought to Liverpool to be shipped off to the plantations. Eight such prisoners were drowned when their barge overturned while they were being rowed out to the convict transports. They could not make any attempt to save themselves because they were handcuffed.

Transportation to the American colonies ceased for a while because it was decided that Britain could not afford to lose so many able-bodied people, especially young men. The practice was then resumed and given official sanction after the Transportation Act of 1718—a measure prompted by a growing public concern over an apparent crime wave and an inadequate penal system. This Act allowed the courts to sentence non-capital felons, meaning those who could claim benefit of clergy, to seven years' transportation. It also established a term of 14 years transportation for capital felons, those not eligible for benefit of clergy, where they had received a royal pardon. Benefit of clergy was an anachronistic practice which had originally given clergy the privilege of being tried in ecclesiastical rather than civil courts. This was advantageous as the former could not impose the death sentence. Over the centuries, the practice developed that any prisoner charged with a felony could plead benefit if he could prove that, like a clergyman, he could read.

The preamble of the 1718 Act made it clear that transportation was held to be a deterrent to crime, a punishment and a means of supplying the colonies with labour. The availability of an alternative sentence led to a substantial fall in the number of hangings. For example, of the 27 people convicted of offences for which they could plead benefit of clergy at the Old Bailey in 1719, 25 were transported. Some convicted felons were offered enlistment in the armed services as an alternative to hanging. It is interesting to muse on the fact that enlistment was clearly seen as a form of punishment. Although numbers of men evaded judicial death by enlisting, the naval and military authorities often found such recruits were of unsuitable calibre. They also believed that having criminals in the ranks deterred men of the right calibre from volunteering because they did not want to be associated with common malefactors.

By permitting the banishment of convicts to America for sale as servants, it was felt that they might be rehabilitated, or at least would be kept off England's streets. Scotland copied the English model and, in 1766, started deporting its own convicts to the Americas. Between 1718 and 1775, over 50,000 convicts were transported and this expedient became a key element in English penal practice. It was sufficient to account for a quarter of all British migrants to the colonies during the period and, excepting African slaves, comprised 'the largest body of immigrants ever compelled to go to America.'[9]

All the American colonies, except New England, received convicts, but they went in the largest numbers to Maryland and to Virginia where they provided unskilled field labour on the tobacco plantations. Up to 80 per cent went to the Chesapeake region, where they worked alongside slaves of African origin; the convicts were regarded as far more efficient labourers. It has been argued that most of those transported to America were convicted of serious crimes, were mainly young, male, single and poor, with minimal skills and often driven to crime by need. They came from most parts of Britain, although roughly half of those sold into labour in the American colonies were sentenced in courts in and around London. While England's capital in the eighteenth century saw the emergence of professional master criminals, such as Jonathan Wild, many of those woe-begone souls who were shipped to America were far more likely to be the victims of circumstances, who had offended out of desperation, rather than real Napoleons of crime.

Many American colonists disapproved of the convicts' presence, either on principle or because of the malign influence and activities of the worst characters among them. Although the burgeoning colonies had seen the establishment of new, hard-working, free migrant settlers, con-victs in penal servitude acting as servants generally worked hard and were treated badly. When convicts became free, some were able to marry, acquire property and ultimately gain a respectable foothold in the new society. Full integration into the developing colonial society could, how-ever, take generations.

From sporadic beginnings in the seventeenth century, England came to rely on the systematic deportation of large numbers of those consid-ered to be her more serious offenders over the next 250 years. This period coincided with Britain's greatest colonial expansion and rise to global domination, and with the era of the Industrial Revolution. It was a time of rapid population growth and widespread migration of mostly younger people to London and the developing industrial towns. This process in many ways destabilized society and caused widespread social disruption and misery; those in search of economic betterment often encountered conditions that were grossly overcrowded, filthy and insanitary. As indus-trial production spiralled, Britain became involved in a network of inter-national commercial and financial activity. This experienced economic cycles of booms and recessions which could neither be effectively pre-dicted nor controlled, but their effects hit the poor and powerless hardest of all. The engines of economic growth exacerbated the differences between rich and poor. They increased the opportunities for criminal activity and also, in periodic downturns, resulted in unemployment, poverty and deprivation. It was the conjuncture of these processes that caused considerable numbers to turn to crime.

THE END OF AN ERA

Hard labour in the colonies or in the houses of correction reflected a significant shift in attitudes to punishment for crime. It had become less a violent public spectacle and more part of a process defined in terms of labour and time. Whether at home or overseas, hard labour was believed to combine suffering for the criminal and retribution for society with the possibility of reforming his character.

Whether or not transportation to the American colonies formed an effective punishment was an object of debate. The notable prison reformers, Sir John Fielding and John Howard, both entertained optimistic views on the matter. It was believed that transporting felons to distant parts got them into the habit of working and away from the criminal networks that were a malign influence, especially in London. The lawyer Sir William Eden disagreed. He believed that the conditions for those who were transported were so inherently congenial that some convicts offended simply in the hope that they would be deported to the American colonies. He preferred the idea that convicted felons should work in England on beneficial public works under stringent discipline. Another suggestion from Eden was that the most dangerous felons, instead of being transported, should be exchanged for Christian slaves, who were eking out a miserable existence in such places as Tunis, Morocco and Algeria, often as oarsmen in corsair galleys.

Not surprisingly, after some years the colonists made it clear that they did not wish to be a permanent dumping ground for the Mother Country's convicts. It was said that the notoriety, real or perceived, of the convicts who were sent to the American colonies was deterring free settlers from moving there and, by 1770, Maryland was the only colony still accepting transported prisoners, due to a shortage of labour. The American colonies ceased to be a destination for English convicts when the former gained their independence in the 1770s. The successful defiance of the American colonists turned the world on its head as far as the English were concerned; they had to find an alternative destination, and quickly. Facing the pressures of overcrowding prisons, demands for penal reform and the dramatic loss of American colonies, the government was to respond by banishing its criminals elsewhere. As Robert Hughes wrote, 'The names of Newgate and Tyburn, arch symbols of the vengeance of property, were now joined by a third: Botany Bay.'[10]

While a new destination was sought, life—and crime—went on. Currently, offences for which transportation was a possible punishment were dealt with in two types of court. Less serious crimes were tried at Quarter Sessions before the magistrates of a county, riding or country town who originally met four times a year. More serious crimes were tried before judges at Assize Courts held in the county towns twice annually. In the case of London and Middlesex, they were held at the Old Bailey and were more frequent. After conviction and the receipt of a sentence of transportation, the prisoner was returned to the gaol in which he or she had previously been lodged. From the 1770s, these unfortunates might be dispatched for temporary accommodation in a prison 'hulk'—a superannuated wooden man-o'-war with its armament, rigging and other fittings removed. In some cases, convicts awaiting transportation, especially older prisoners, were 'temporarily' accommodated in hulks, but in fact remained in them until the expiry of their sentences. In later years, those sentenced to transportation almost always found themselves temporarily housed in a hulk while awaiting a convict ship.

HELL ON WATER

The hulks were moored on the River Thames and elsewhere, and the convicts were mostly employed in public building, dockyard or maintenance works. They worked under the supervision of contractors who looked after them in return for an annual payment for each convict.

From the start, government control of the hulks was considerably more rigorous than that applied to most English prisons. In the early days, most of the hulks were operated by Duncan Campbell, the contractor who had conveyed many of the convicts to the American colonies in the period 1758–75. However, it was soon discovered that far from being a cheap expedient, convict labour in the hulks was an expensive one. Issues of security meant that the prisoners actually worked shorter hours than free labourers and, as is inevitable with forced labour, they did as little work as they could possibly get away with and even that was usually performed grudgingly and often inefficiently.

Some of the hulks were based close to each other on the south bank of the River Thames at Woolwich and Deptford, downstream from London. They housed only male prisoners, many of whom suffered from hernias owing to the physically demanding nature of the work they had to do. Although detailed descriptions of conditions aboard two of the first hulks at these locations have not survived, they can be guessed at when John Howard, the prison reformer, reported that from a total of 632 prisoners admitted to one of the hulks, *Justitia*, between August 1776 and March 1778, 176 of them had already died.

In the sixteenth and seventeenth centuries, the rotting timbers of Sir Francis Drake's redoubtable little ship *Golden Hind,* in which he had circumnavigated the world, lay in the mud at Deptford, becoming a magnet for the attention of tourists. Now the same thing was happening to the decaying hulks at Deptford and Woolwich. Enterprising businessmen were soon running boat trips on the river for voyeurs prepared to pay good money to be rowed near the hulks. Fascinated by the rumours and reports, they sought to catch a glimpse of the horrific conditions in which the poor wretches aboard lived. Visits were also available to places from which the convicts could be viewed, busy or otherwise, at work.

The hulks had originally been intended as a short-term measure when the war with the American colonies started in 1775. They were a temporary expedient until such time as the rebels were defeated, whereupon they could be persuaded to resume taking English convicts. The plan foundered after the colonists won the war and wanted nothing more to do with these unwilling immigrants. In this situation, it is not surprising that the population of the hulks increased from 526 in 1779 to 1,017 in 1782 and 1,937 in 1783.

The hulks became full to bursting point and notorious for their living conditions; of all the places of confinement used in England, they were the most brutalizing and demoralizing. They were filthy, insanitary and overcrowded for much of the time. Hardened criminals lived cheek-by-jowl with bemused and terrified first-time offenders, among whom were children, some not yet in their teens. Bullying, violence and abuse were rife, vermin were everywhere and diseases such as dysentery, typhus, cholera and smallpox were rampant. Some idea of the conditions on board the hulks can be gauged by the records which show that on the hulk *Surprize*, at Cove near Cork, between 5 May and 31 December 1834, there were 747 'bowel affections'; 763 'catarrhal affections'; 1240 cases of 'the itch'; 392 of 'the cough'; 560 of 'feverish cold'; and 284 'herpetic eruptions'.[11] This source also provides information on the diet of the convicts, and the rules and regulations in force on *Surprize* and another hulk, *Essex*.

There was also considerable brutality. In 1847, it was revealed that an elderly man had been given 36 lashes of the cat-o'-nine-tails for being just five minutes late for the early morning muster. This punishment was particularly heinous because it was inflicted three months after it had been awarded because the overseer had in the meanwhile forgotten about it.

A nineteenth-century artist's impression of convicts on board a prison hulk (ZFER 34/8 p.125). This actual space between decks was even lower, and most prisoners would have been unable to move without stooping.

The hulks were grim places for all concerned, and it is not surprising that those employed in them tried to find a little light relief. This could lead to serious situations. An example is the inquiry into incidents aboard the hulk *Victoria* at Portsmouth in 1854, which culminated in the court-martial of Lieutenant Charles Knight of the Royal Marines. On the night of

A View near *WOOLWICH* in *KENT*, shewing the Employment of the *CONVICTS* from the Hulks.

This busy scene portrays convicts from the hulks moored on the Thames near Woolwich in Kent. They were put to hard labour, such as dredging the Thames or driving in posts to protect the riverbanks from erosion.

the 17 September, he brought two 'improper' women on board *Victoria* and then acted inappropriately, plying them with large quantities of drink and possibly taking sexual liberties. One of the women became so inebriated that she later fell and received injuries which proved to be fatal. It is probable that had she not died, the episode would have been regarded as a high-spirited and harmless jape, eliciting no more than a reprimand. The commanding officer of *Victoria* was ashore at the time and Knight, who was himself drunk, attempted to excuse his conduct by advancing the rather feeble excuse that the two women were his sisters. It was, of course, against the regulations to bring unauthorized personnel on board, let alone in such a drunken state, and completely unacceptable then to ply them with further drink. It was also not permitted for officers to have a 'run ashore' in civilian clothes. Knight was dishonourably dismissed.[12]

There were often disciplinary problems associated with the hulks. A letter from John Henry Capper, Superintendent of Hulks, dated 17 July 1832, raises the perennial conundrum of how to prevent the presence of hardened criminals 'polluting' other novice offenders. Capper writes:

> The great influx of youthful offenders matured in crime, who are daily
> received on board the Hulks from the several Gaols in Great Britain, make it
> advisable that a considerable number of Convicts should be sent to the
> Australian or other settlements during the present year; as it appears, judging
> from the report of their characters that, if discharged from any place of
> confinement in this country at the expiration of their sentences, there is but
> little hope of their pursuing an honest course of life.

He returns to the same theme in a number of other letters. [13]

Not all those concerned with the hulks publicly considered their task
to be a hopeless one as a number of letters, dated July 1832, from chaplains serving on board the hulks and addressed to Capper, indicate. From
a hulk at Devonport:

> The convicts on board this ship have conducted themselves in a very exem-
> plary manner during the half year terminating on the 1st July. The offences,
> considering the number of men and their previous habits of life, have been
> very few. During Divine Service, the behaviour of the prisoners is uniformly
> good, and they appear attentive and desirous to receive religious instruc-
> tions. Those who cannot read are regularly taught in the school, and with a
> few exceptions, are desirous to learn.

From the chaplain of the hulk *Canada*:

> It is gratifying to state that the convicts on board continue to behave orderly
> and submissive (with few exceptions), suited to their humiliating condition. I
> would hope some of them are sensible of the sinfulness of those habits to
> which they mainly owe their present troubles and privations: I allude espe-
> cially to the profanation of the Lord's Day and bad company, to which the
> prisoners generally attribute their present misfortunes… I should observe,
> that during the raging of the pestilence (cholera) there were among the con-
> victs some affecting instances of contrition…

The chaplain of *Euryalus*, moored at Chatham, writes:

> That the behaviour of every boy has been such as to merit commendation is
> more than I am able to state, but if a few have failed to profit by the advantages
> which they have enjoyed, a large majority have evinced that the labour which
> has been bestowed on them has not been in vain. I trust that many who have
> here learnt to read the Sacred Scriptures will derive from them a knowledge
> of the "great salvation" therein revealed, and imbibe those sacred principles,
> by the influence and operation of which, they will, when they regain their

liberty, be saved from the evil that is in the world; be furnished with an unfailing source of comfort; rendered in their humble station valuable members of society; and made faithful servants of their God and Saviour.

The chaplain of the *Ganymede* and *Discovery* hulks reports:

> The convicts ... have in general conducted themselves with great propriety and have particularly evinced a becoming fortitude and resignation under the fatal disease (cholera) with which it has pleased the Almighty so lately to afflict them. There are indeed a few who have been troublesome to those set in authority over them; but the promises they have made me as to their future conduct, lead me to expect that we shall hear no more complaints upon this subject.

Further evidence relating to cholera on the hulks appears in many National Archive documents.[14] Few submissions are as obsequious as that from the chaplain on the ironically named *Retribution* hulk at Sheerness:

> It would be painful to me to have occasion to vary the representation which I have for sometime past had the gratification of giving you in my reports of the good conduct of the prisoners on board the *Retribution*. Had there been any dereliction of their accustomed obedience to the laws of the ship, or any marked inattention at the seasons of Divine Worship, I should have felt it my duty to have transmitted a faithful account.[15]

All very encouraging—but this primary evidence needs to be seen in context rather than being accepted at face value. The extracts in fact constitute part of the six-monthly reports which the chaplains of hulks were required to submit to the Superintendent of Convicts. As such, they are likely to contain material which places the work of the chaplains themselves in a very positive light. Using hindsight, it seems scarcely credible to us that such pious, not to say unctuous thoughts, could be consigned to paper and public scrutiny in this way. At best, these letters are simply of their time and naïve in their lack of understanding of the psyche of the criminals with whom they had dealings; at worst they are thinly veiled attempts by the chaplains to justify their own personal roles and jockey for favour and advancement within what can now be seen to be a deeply flawed and largely ineffective punitive system. A few weeks in a hulk were not an encouraging preparation for the hazards of a journey of several months to Australia and the intimidating prospects of what might be awaiting the convicts when they got there.

The hulks themselves stayed in use in declining numbers until 1857, by which time their very existence was widely regarded as a scandal. Once regarded as a temporary expedient, they became holding stations for prisoners awaiting transportation and those who were sentenced to be transported, but who, for whatever reason, could not or did not undertake the voyage. Some prisoners found themselves incarcerated in hulks for years on end, as if their existence had been forgotten by the authorities.

Records of the time list the offences for which prisoners were incarcerated on the hulks. The very broad categories of 'larceny' and 'felony' occur frequently, encompassing such predictable crimes as highway robbery, receiving, embezzlement, burglary and poaching. Lists also feature an extraordinarily diverse range of items which criminals of the day were indicted for stealing. In the case of those imprisoned on the hulk *Dolphin* at Chatham in July 1826, these include tablecloths, whalebone, charcoal, beef, saddles, spurs, gold seals, spyglasses, hop poles, pitch, scissors and an umbrella.[16]

Temporary accommodation for prisoners awaiting transportation to Australia was not only provided by hulks, however. A letter dated December 1785, from Lord Sydney to the Lords of the Admiralty, contains a request for them to make a naval ship available at Portsmouth to house convicts from Newgate prison in London awaiting transportation in the *Fortune*. This convict transport was not yet fitted out. The Lords accepted the request and the naval vessel used was the *Firm*.

A COLONY FOR BOTANY BAY

Despite the continuing use of hulks and other ships, they clearly could not provide a permanent solution. The authorities were thus forced at an early stage to look elsewhere for places to put convicts. Between 1782 and 1784, some attempts were made to use convicts as soldiers at a number of coastal trading posts in West Africa. These were mostly controlled by the Africa Company, a London-based concern whose principal business interest lay with slavery. The intention was that the soldier-convicts would provide protection for the Company's activities. This whole idea seems bizarre and proved a comprehensive failure; fatal diseases carved a swathe through the ranks of the unwilling conscripts, and those who were not immediately struck down deserted, only to succumb to illness later. The scheme caused the Africa Company so many difficult problems that it eventually pleaded successfully with the government to bring it to an end.

Among other destinations considered in 1785 was the island of Lemaine, on the Gambia river in West Africa.[17] This was an extraordinary proposal given that Britain had no territorial rights whatever in this part of the continent. It was intended that only the most hardened and violent criminals would be dispatched to this destination, where they would perform agricultural work in conditions not unlike a modern kibbutz. Considerations, including the likely hostility of the native population, the presence of a host of dangerous creatures (both those already known and others whose presence could only be suspected), a debilitating climate which would discourage convicts from engaging in hard physical labour even under duress, and the existence of a range of diseases inimical to Europeans, fortunately led to the abandonment of this unlikely proposal. The powerful East India Company, meanwhile, made it quite clear that it was not prepared to allow transportation to operate in any of the territories over which it had jurisdiction.

In 1786, after examining a range of other overseas destinations, all of which were rejected, the authorities fixed on the idea of transporting convicts to the even more distant shores of Australia. It was a controversial decision. Even those who argued in favour of transportation to Australia had some misgivings, fearing that the deterrent factor would disappear:

> Transportation answers very imperfectly the purpose of example … Tho' a transported convict may suffer under his sentence, his sufferings are unseen … his Chasm is soon filled up and being as soon forgotten, it strikes no terror into the minds of those for whose correction it was intended to operate.[18]

To some interested parties, on the other hand, transportation offered an ideal solution to fear of crime; there seemed little chance of convicts dispatched to somewhere as remote as Australia ever returning. Supporters of this view pointed to the existence of a 'criminal class' of habitual offenders and recidivists who were beyond redemption, and so an 'out of sight, out of mind' approach was considered the best way of ridding mainstream society of such a perceived nuisance. Prisons and penitentiaries, some argued, no matter how they were designed and whatever their regimes, were simply not an effective way of punishing such people. Others, however, with even less sympathy for those who had been convicted of serious crimes, railed against transportation to Australia because they thought the convicts would be mollycoddled rather than punished in such an exotic destination, and that there would be no useful outcome from whatever work they might or might not do. In 1810, Lord Ellenborough, then the Lord Chief Justice, described transportation 'as a summer's excursion, an easy migration to a happier and better climate.'[19]

Jeremy Bentham, the philosopher and social reformer, also criticized transportation, but from a very different perspective. In his opinion it served no useful purpose. It was costly and inhumane—it meant banishing the felon from the land of his birth and condemning him to a range of horrible possible fates, which might include shipwreck or drowning at sea, maybe starvation, being devoured by wild beasts or killed by savages. Transportation would not deter crime in England because the sentence

A map of Botany Bay in New South Wales made during James Cook's first voyage in 1770. Despite Cook's description of Botany Bay's lush meadows, the First Fleet, arriving in January 1788, found it swampy and sandy, with limited water.

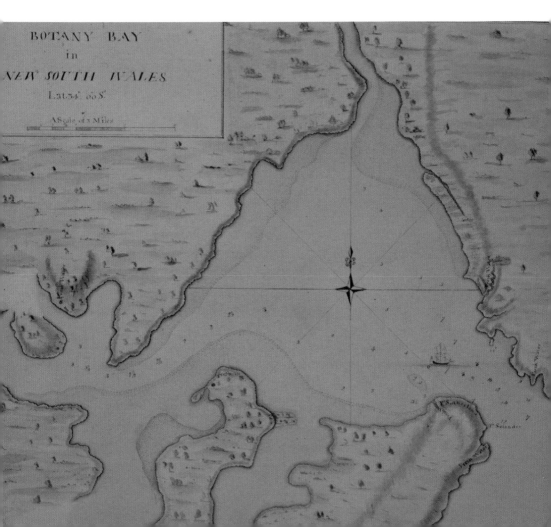

would be served thousands of miles away, and he argued that the whole process involved retribution rather than real punishment. The moral climate of New South Wales would be compromised from the start since the colony was dominated by convicts and they would inevitably stamp their values on its culture. What is more, he believed that transportation would do nothing whatever to tackle the causes of criminality. Bentham, it should be noted, had his own agenda. He was trying to generate support for his 'Panopticon', a penitentiary of a radically novel design. He produced a pamphlet, 'Panopticon versus New South Wales', in 1802. Many of the points he made were taken up and developed by the opponents of transportation for the next 60 years.

Bentham and John Howard, the eminent penal reformer, both favoured a new type of penitentiary in which prisoners would be placed in solitary confinement, given instruction of a practical and religious sort and be required to do useful, productive work. They believed that immorality and irreligion were factors that sustained crime among the lower orders and that therefore attention had to be paid to the spiritual welfare of prisoners. It was hoped that such a regime would inculcate necessary habits of diligence and respect for authority among the inmates. Most reformers of the late eighteenth and early nineteenth centuries emphasized the need for solitary confinement. This, it was thought, would improve prisoners' physical and spiritual welfare while protecting them from the moral contamination that threatened whenever convicts were mixed indiscriminately. On completing their sentences, these prisoners would return to ordinary society embracing religion, rehabilitated and ready to make a useful contribution—or so the theory went.

The attack on the disordered state of the existing prisons and houses of correction, which was another thrust of the penal reformers, was part of a wider effort to control and raise the moral tone of popular culture. It stands alongside attempts to supervise alehouses more effectively, to abolish sports such as cockfighting, pugilism and bull-baiting which attracted potentially riotous crowds, to clamp down on poaching and to attack a general lack of deference among the so-called 'lower orders'. The reformed prison was a weapon in the fight against the irksome criminal tendencies of the masses and another form of control created by the governing classes out of their obsessive fear of the 'brutish' mob.

Relief of intolerable pressure on Britain's prisons was not the only factor behind the choice of Australia as a penal colony. Historians are divided on the primary motive, but there were also political considerations: France and Holland were both developing trading links with the East Indies and China, and the British were in danger of being squeezed out of the region before they had even really established themselves. Both William Pitt and Lord Sydney, Home Secretary and Secretary of State for the Colonies in the mid-1780s, believed that the time was right to establish a strategic base in the Antipodes to pre-empt the activity of rival nation states. From one perspective, a penal colony could prove a cost-effective way to develop a major trading and naval base. The naval presence would protect Britain's commercial interests, present and future, and the Australian colonies could provide resources for Britain's shipyards. Sydney believed that Botany Bay would provide an ideal solution to a dual problem.

He was not the only one keen to use the area, however. Others proposed founding a colony in New South Wales as a new home for Loyalists from the American colonies, who had lost everything in the War of Independence. An enthusiastic advocate for such a use was an American, James Matra, who can best be described as an international chancer, a man quick to spot or create opportunities to advance his own position. He had seen Botany Bay when sailing as a midshipman in the *Endeavour* under Captain Cook and, on the strength of this experience, he put forward the suggestion that there were potentially valuable sources of pine and flax there. In a letter dated 23 August 1783 addressed to the Colonial Secretary, Matra fervently advocated the exploitation of New South Wales: 'Immense tracts of fertile land with only a few primitive natives engaged in little other than fishing. Excellent climate ... it could produce sugar, tea, coffee, silk, cotton, indigo, tobacco and especially timber.'[20]

This proposal did not succeed, but it shows the huge interest in the potential of Botany Bay and the possibility of wider economic advantage that lay behind the government's decision.

It is likely that the convicts neither knew nor cared about government policy. Many of them would have been suffused in understandable misery as they were wrenched away from home, family and friends. Being consigned across the seas must simply have seemed the latest in the series of raw deals that life had dealt them. Nonetheless there were many who must have been relieved to know they had been spared from the grisly ritual of the gallows. After 1770 thousands of people were reprieved by the king's prerogative of mercy and sent to the prison hulks or transported. Large numbers of cases in the Judges Reports on Criminals 1783–1830 testify to the petitions for clemency during this period.

Rueful, resigned or resentful, there was not much that convicts could do while they were at sea. They would have known little or nothing about their destination although rumours, probably inaccurate and alarmist, would have circulated about the man-eating natives and dangerous creatures that awaited them. Some perhaps thought that opportunities to escape might occur once they had landed. A few may have seen transportation as an opportunity to put unhappy events and associations behind them and make a fresh start—and in some cases it was indeed to prove their big break. Yet it was often another story for dependents back at home, left to fend for themselves as best they could. Many had little alternative but to turn to crime or throw themselves on the tender mercies of the Poor Law.

The tragedy was human as well as economic. Only the better-off, or those few who petitioned the authorities successfully, were able to make the passage to Australia themselves to be reunited with convicted relatives. Usually transportation simply meant the end of existing marriages and relationships—as irrevocable and final as death itself.

2

The First Three Fleets

WHEN 16-YEAR OLD James Burley and his friend George Barland stole a coat belonging to the bishop of Peterborough in London in June 1784, little did they know how much it would change their lives. Both were sentenced to seven years' transportation and dispatched on the *Alexander* to New South Wales. Similarly Elizabeth Colley, a servant aged 22 who received stolen goods (one linen gown and a silk cloak worth 13 shillings), was sentenced to 14 years' transportation, leaving on the *Lady Penrhyn*. They were poor people committing petty crimes, and their cases were typical of the hundreds who found themselves sailing on the First Fleet from Portsmouth in May 1787.

The whole process of sending convicts to Botany Bay stems from instructions in a letter ('Heads of a Plan') dated 10 August 1786 and sent to the Lords Commissioners of the Treasury on the authority of Lord Sydney. The official justification for transporting convicts is revealed in the opening paragraph:

> The several Goals [*sic*] and Places for the confinement of Felons in this Kingdom being so crowded a State that the greatest danger is to be apprehended not only from their Escape but from the Infectious Distempers which may hourly be expected to break out.[1]

After reflecting on attempts to find places 'for the reception' of convicts on the southern coast of Africa, the letter goes on to state that it is advisable to 'fix upon Botany Bay situated on the Coast of New South Wales. I am therefore commanded to signify … that you do forthwith take such measures as may be necessary for providing a proper number of vessels for the conveyance of 750 convicts.' (The name 'Australia'—meaning southern land —only came to be used some years later, following the publication of Matthew Flinders' *Voyage to Terra Australis,* 1814.) This momentous decision began a process that transformed the lives of tens of thousands of people. As well as the British and Irish convicts themselves, transportation involved over 800 ships between 1787 and 1868—all with crews, officers, guards and often their families, too.

Botany Bay was in many ways an unlikely choice, but the note of desperation in the description of the gaols indicates the urgency of the problem. The unwelcoming, almost completely unknown coast of New South Wales could hardly have seemed a satisfactory substitute as a convict destination for the expanding economy of the American colonies; distance alone rendered the cost of transportation excessive.

This idea of using Botany Bay had been influenced by accounts given some 16 years earlier 'by the late Captain Cook', as well as 'persons who accompanied him' in the *Endeavour* on his voyage of 1769–71. Among those sailing with him was Joseph Banks, then a young botanist; he later became an eminent and influential figure in many scientific enterprises. When Banks gave evidence to the Beauchamp Committee in 1785, he reiterated his view that the land they had seen on the east coast of Australia (in April 1770) was fertile and largely covered in wood—a potential source of timber for all kinds of building.[2] New South Wales also had the advantage of being difficult to escape from. It was reported to possess a mild climate, fertile soil and plentiful supplies of fish and game birds, and thus was not without economic interest. As one writer pointed out in a letter to Whitehall the following year:

> Besides the removal of a dreadful Banditta from this country, many advantages are likely to be derived from the intended settlement… Some of the timber is reported fit for Naval purposes … but above all, the cultivation of the flax plant seems to be the most considerable object.[3]

James Cook had initially named the bay Stingray Harbour, but this was later changed to Botany Bay because of the many exotic plants that Banks collected there. It seemed that the place would be feasible for farming and cultivation; it also appeared to have no dangerous fauna or hostile inhabitants to speak of. In fact, Aborigines had been living in Australia for about 30,000 years, although it is difficult to know what the population was when the First Fleet arrived. Estimates have suggested 300,000, although the density of local populations varied.

The convicts encountered Aborigines from the outset. They assembled near the beaches as the First Fleet arrived, waving their spears and gesturing 'go away.' But the new arrivals did not leave, and the native presence was addressed with dreadful consequences in the years to come. Relations between Aborigines and convicts started badly and became worse, establishing a pattern of conflict that lasted for many years.

Significantly, Cook's observations on the Aborigine were to prove notably more sympathetic than some of the actions of later settlers.

> From what I have said of the Natives of New Holland, they may appear to some to be the most wretched people upon Earth but in reality they are far more happier than we Europeans, being wholly unacquainted not only with the superfluous but the necessary Conveniences so much sought after in Europe; they are happy in not knowing the use of them. They live in tranquillity which is not disturbed by the inequality of condition. The Earth and Sea of their own accord furnishes them with all things necessary for life.[4]

(New Holland was the name first applied to Australia in 1644 by Dutch explorer Abel Tasman; it remained in usage for nearly 200 years.)

In truth, Botany Bay had little else going for it. Nevertheless, it held an attraction for those in governing circles who were still smarting from the loss of the American colonies and sought an alternative enterprise. Merchants were hopeful that Australia would not only make up for the loss of the American colonies, but would also prove to be a viable long-term investment. As one correspondent from Edinburgh wrote:

> It is much to the credit of those in office that an Empire has been founded in the South which time will render much superior to that which their predecessors have lost in the west.[5]

Sydney's own letter did not overtly say how the colony might benefit the State, but it clearly offered rich resources (particularly the flax, hemp and timber of which British ships were mostly composed in the eighteenth century) and an important strategic position in the South Seas. So how far did the British government really have economic and imperial motives for choosing New South Wales? There is no firm evidence of any great imperial design in those early years, nor were deep-rooted commercial intentions entirely borne out by the limited preparations and resources that were taken by the first ships. In fact, the issue of adequate provisions to sustain the First Fleet and the marines has been subject to question. Nothing suggests an imperial motive at the start of the transportations.

PREPARING THE FIRST FLEET

The decision to establish a convict settlement at Botany Bay was made by Prime Minister William Pitt and the Cabinet, and required George III's approval. The scheme needed close co-operation between the Home

Office who would administer the colony, the Navy who would be responsible for transporting the convicts and the necessary supplies, and the Treasury who would foot the bill. Each of these parties had their own interests to safeguard. The Home Office urgently wanted to reduce the pressure of numbers in its prisons and hulks, while the Treasury was constantly looking to effect economies. The Navy was entering into an uneasy partnership with government departments (senior naval officers were notoriously contemptuous of professional politicians) and with the civilian contractors from whom they hired the convict transports.

The expedition to Botany Bay was to take provisions equal to two years' consumption, surgeons, a minister of religion and—after settlement —women, who, the letter stated, 'are likely to be procured from places in [the Pacific Islands] as companions for the men.' The reference to the Pacific Islands was an expression of hope by officials that the colonists would trade with Polynesia, as well as Savu in the Molucca Islands for food and animals. The decision to send convicts to New South Wales prompted some criticism largely on grounds of cost and efficiency. The *Gentleman's Magazine* of October 1786 raged that it was 'a most extravagant scheme'. Alexander Dalrymple, hydrographer (one who draws or charts maps of the sea) to the East India Company and later the Admiralty, argued that sending convicts to such a temperate climate, where they would have every object of comfort, could only encourage rather than deter felons.[6]

In the months following August 1786, plans to assemble personnel, vessels and supplies went ahead. A series of letters was exchanged between various departmental officials at the Home Office, the Treasury and the Admiralty, requesting money to be spent on wine, victuals and other articles for the troops and the convicts. One letter also stressed that 'marines and convicts should be victualled in the same manner as troops serving in the West Indies ... women to have two thirds of the quantity of provisions.'[7]

A list of surgeon's materials and medicines was among the provisions. These included instruments for amputation, one dozen scalpels, teeth instruments, midwifery instruments, an electrical medical apparatus, two hundred sets

The 'Heads of a Plan' letter from Lord Sydney, 10 August 1786. It gave instructions to the Lords Commissioners of the Treasury from Lord Sydney for the raising of the First Fleet to Botany Bay—effectively the start of the transportation process (CO 201/2).

Heads of a Plan for effectually disposing
of Convicts, and rendering their Transportation
reciprocally beneficial both to themselves and
to the State, by the Establishment of a Colony
in New South Wales, a Country which by
the fertility and Salubrity of the Climate,
connected with the remoteness of its
Situation (from whence it is hardly
possible for Persons to return without
permission) seems peculiarly adapted to
answer the views of Government with
respect to the providing a remedy for the
Evils likely to result by the late alarming
and numerous encrease of Felons in
this Country, and more particularly in
the Metropolis.

It is proposed, That a Ship of War of a
proper Class, with a part of her Guns
mounted, and a sufficient number of Men
on board for her Navigation, and a
Tender of about 200 Tons Burthen,
commanded by discreet Officers, should
be got ready as soon as possible to serve as
an Escort to the Convict Ships and for
other purposes herein after mentioned.

That in addition to their Crews, they
should take on board two Companies
of Marines, to form a Military
Establishment

of hospital bedding, six dozen crooked needles, one dozen best lancets, one dozen tourniquets, two sets of dissecting knives and a set of instruments for trepanning. The provisions seemed insufficient to cover the needs of over a thousand people or the officials were unduly optimistic about the health of those setting out on the voyage.[8]

The Admiralty began the process of raising a fleet by advertising in coffee-houses used by merchants and ship owners. The contractor who made the successful bid for the government tender for the First Fleet was William Richards, who would be paid almost £54,000. He wrote to William Pitt in a confident manner:

> Sir
>
> I read an advertisement in the Public Papers … for a Contract, to carry Convicts to Botany Bay in New South Wales: I being desirous of having the contract if Posible endeavoured to find some means whereby it might ultimately serve my purpose & at the same time hold forth to all Parties such advantages that no difficulty would arise in procuring shipping for it… Having searched the Charts & found the Latitude & Longitude of Botany Bay I was clearly of the opinion that if I could procure Freight for the Shipping from the India Company from China … [I have] hopes of accomplishing it… I have had several conferences with the Navy Board in consequence and have the happiness to think that I understand the Business fully…
>
> Wm. Richards Junr.[9]

The eventual response resulted in the provision of a fleet of 11 ships. The six convict ships were *Alexander* (the largest of the transport ships—carrying 195 male prisoners), *Lady Penrhyn* (which sailed with 101 female convicts), *Charlotte* (which carried 88 male and 20 female convicts), *Scarborough* (sailed in both First and Second Fleets), *Friendship* (carried 76 male and 21 female convicts), *Prince of Wales* (carried only one male convict and 49 female convicts). Three other ships—the *Borrowdale*, *Fishburn* and *Golden Grove*—carried supplies. HMS *Sirius* was the flagship of the First Fleet: built in 1780 as a merchant vessel and a sixth-rate warship bought by the Navy, it was finally lost at Norfolk Island in 1791. HMS *Supply* was the smallest of the fleet. It carried 50 people and led the fleet for most of the voyage. By December, it was decided to send more women on the fleet, but they would need to be clothed adequately, hence the decision to order further supplies for those women due to sail on the *Lady Penrhyn*.[10]

The decision to increase the number of women does not indicate any considered strategy for founding a lasting population in Australia. In fact, the question of how well planned the whole project was—even for the first two years, let alone beyond that—is uncertain. Once convicts, soldiers and other civil staff had reached Botany Bay, the problem for officialdom was to ensure that sufficient resources of clothes, food and animals, as well as a suitable environment for harvests, were available to sustain them. Nor had the convicts on the First Fleet been chosen for their skills and potential for building a colony. Their random selection is borne out by the various ways in which they were described, including 'the most abandoned of scoundrels'.[11]

In January 1787, the plan for transporting convicts to New South Wales was announced to Parliament and the first convicts were embarked at Woolwich on the *Alexander* and the *Lady Penrhyn*. Other convicts were embarked at Plymouth and Portsmouth. The next three months were spent gathering together other prisoners and provisions; this also proved problematic. Illness and fever contributed to the death of 11 convicts, and a shortage of clothing and food exacerbated the situation.

Nine months after Sydney's 'Heads of a Plan' letter, the Fleet was set to sail from Portsmouth. Daniel Defoe described the harbour earlier in the eighteenth century:

> The docks and yards are now like a town by themselves and are a kind of marine corporation, or a government of their own kind within themselves; there being particular large rows of dwellings, within the new works, for all the principal officers of the place. The tradesman likewise have houses here, and many of the labourers are allowed to live in the bounds as they get lodging.[12]

THE FIRST CONVICT VOYAGE

The 11 ships prepared to embark on their historic voyage from Portsmouth in the early hours of Sunday 13 May 1787. For many convicts, some of whom had not ventured far in their own country, let alone travelled beyond it, the time before departure must have been intensely emotional, charged with trepidation, fear and sorrow. Others displayed only indifference. The rich human tapestry included people of diverse character and ages— hardened criminals, drunkards and violent offenders were gathered together with the honest, sober and unfortunate. Some convicts coped

Name	Where Convicted			Date of Conviction	Term of Transportation	On Board What Ship	Casualty
	County	Town	Crime				
Gardner Francis	Middlesex	London	Felony	21 April 1784	7 Years	Scarborough	
Garth Edward	Middlesex	London	Felony	29 Feb 1785	7 Years	Scarborough	
Garland Francis	Devon	Exeter	(Return from Transportation)	24 May 1784	7 Years	Charlotte	
Garth Susannah alias Goath						Friendship	
Gabel Mary	Surry	Southwark	Felony	18 Jan'ry 1784	7 Years	Lady Penrhyn	
Gascoyne Olive	Worcester	Worcester	Burglary	5 March 1785	7 Years	Lady Penrhyn	
Gearing Thomas	Oxford	Oxford	Burglary	8 March 1786	Life	Alexander	Died 2 June 1787 at Sea
Gess George	Gloucester	Gloucester	Horse Stealing	23 March 1785	7 Years	Alexander	
George Ann	Middlesex	London	Felony	11 May 1785	7 Years	Lady Penrhyn	
Glenton Thomas	York	Northallerton	Grand Larceny	5 April 1785	7 Years	Alexander	
Gloster William	Middlesex	London	Felony	29 June 1785	7 Years	Alexander	
Gordon Daniel	Southampton	Winchester	Felony	5 April 1785	7 Years	Alexander	
Goodwin Edward	London	London	Felony	21 April 1784	7 Years	Scarborough	
Goodwin Andrew	Middlesex	London	Felony	7 July 1784	7 Years	Scarborough	
Gould John	Devon	Exeter	Felony	20 March 1784	7 Years	Charlotte	
Goary Charles	Surry	Southwark	Felony	16 Feb 1785	7 Years	Alexander	
Griffiths Samuel alias Bearcrow alias Butcher	Gloucester	Gloucester	Sheep Stealing	24 March 1784	7 Years	Alexander	
Greenwell Nicholas	Middlesex	London	Felony	10 Dec 1784	7 Years	Alexander	Pardoned 10 May 1787
Green John	Berks	Reading	Grand Larceny	11 July 1786	7 Years	Alexander	Died 7 May 1787
Griffiths Thomas	London	London	Felony	15 Sept 1784	7 Years	Scarborough	
Grampese Charles	Devon	Plymouth	Felony	20 Dec 1786	7 Years	Friendship	
Grace James						Friendship	
Green Hannah						Friendship	
Groves Mary	Lincoln	Lincoln	Felony	9 July 1785	7 Years	Prince of Wales	
Green Mary	London	London	Felony	18 April 1787	7 Years	Prince of Wales	
Green Ann	Middlesex	London	Felony	13 Dec 1786	7 Years	Lady Penrhyn	
Greenwood Mary	Middlesex	London	Felony	13 Dec 1786	7 Years	Lady Penrhyn	
Gunter William	Bristol	Bristol	Felony	4 Aug 1785	7 Years	Alexander	

A Home Office document showing details of convicts embarked on the First Fleet in 1787. They sailed on the First Fleet for Botany Bay and Van Diemen's Land (HO 10/7). A comprehensive list of settlers and convicts exist for the years 1787–1859.

less well than others with the transition from the boredom of the prison and hulk to the noise and crowding of the ship. In some cases, the trauma of the move took physical expression in vomiting, hysteria and confusion.

Those sailing on the First Fleet were to be the first European settlers on Australian soil. It was to be a momentous eight-month voyage, which involved twice crossing the choppy seas of the Atlantic, and sailing across the calmer but potentially stormy Indian Ocean before dropping down below the 40th Parallel under the southern coast of Australia. En route the ship stopped at Tenerife, Rio de Janeiro and Cape Town, and finally arriving at Botany Bay between 18 and 20 January 1788. The ships, under the command of Captain Arthur Phillip, carried some 750 convicts, including 192 women; they were guarded by over 190 marines and 19 officers. Records on the 'state of the Garrison and Convicts' for the following month showed the numbers below:

Marines including officers	197
Marines' wives	28
Marines' children	17
Chaplain and wife	2
Surveyor General	1
Servants	2
Men convicts	558
Women convicts	192
Children (of convicts)	13
Numbers victualled	1015
Convicts dead since they were embarked	21
Convict children dead " " "	3
Received His Majesty's Pardon before ship left England	2 [13]

Three weeks after leaving Portsmouth, the fleet reached Santa Cruz in Tenerife. Here the ships replenished their stocks with fresh water, fruit, meat and wine, and the officers and crew had a week to spend on land. While the Governor of the Canaries entertained Captain Phillip and 20 of his officers, the convicts remained on board their ships. One convict, John Power, tried to take advantage of the situation; he attempted to escape, but was recaptured the next day.

A week later, the First Fleet set sail for the eight-week journey to Rio de Janeiro. It was not a pleasant voyage, as crossing the Atlantic at this time of the year entailed stormy seas succeeded by warm weather. The extreme heat of the tropics brought accompanying vermin, rotting food, the stench of unwashed people, sickness and diarrhoea. Six convicts died on the passage from Tenerife; many suffered from low spirits, and thieving and fights occurred which brought floggings. Punishments for female prisoners on the *Lady Penrhyn* included thumbscrews, having iron fetters placed on their wrists or their hair cut off. Despite these problems, some of the officers actually gave the most cause for concern as they argued and drank to excess.

However, Arthur Phillip remained positive and wrote to Lord Sydney from Rio de Janeiro in August that the 'ships under my command are all remarkably healthy.' [14] A report on the condition of the convicts showed the following:

Ships	Fever	Dysentery	Venereal	Scorbutic Ulcers	Convales- cence	Deaths
Charlotte	1	2		6	5	2
Alexander	1	1		9	6	10
Scarborough	1	1		7	4	
Friendship	1	1		4	3	1
Lady Penryhn			2	1	1	1
Prince of Wales			2	2	2	1

In addition, one person on the *Lady Penryhn* was recorded as suffering with cholera.[15]

Rio offered a chance to make repairs and replenish stocks. Once again, officers and crew took in the sights and enjoyed the exotic fruits and foods. The nearest the convicts came to such pleasures was looking from the decks of the ship when they were allowed their daily exercise. One month later, on 5 September 1787, the fleet sailed from Rio de Janeiro and headed for the Cape of Good Hope. Three days before they left Rio, Captain Phillip reported that, 'The convicts have been very plentifully supplied with fresh provisions ... the allowance of meat to the convicts has been twenty ounces every day and they are healthier than when we left England. Only fifteen convicts and one marine's child have died since we sailed from Spithead.' [16]

Five weeks later the fleet arrived in Table Bay, Cape Town. While in port, provisions were loaded and the ships underwent repairs. On 12 November, the Fleet resumed its voyage—the final leg to Botany Bay. In December, the ships experienced sleet and snow, and the convicts must have been particularly cold as all they had to clothe them was their regulation dress and one blanket each.

After eight months and a journey of over 15,000 miles, the whole fleet arrived at Botany Bay by 20 January 1788—a date later celebrated as Australia Day. Among the first cargo of convicts were 10 Jews and at least

11 of African descent. Forty convicts, including four females, died between embarkation and arrival (a marine, a marine's wife and five children also died). On the actual passage itself, 20 male and three female convicts died, as well as five of the convicts' children. Despite these deaths, the numbers were comparatively low for such a journey. However, the sickly state of the convicts who reached Botany Bay may have contributed to the deaths of 10 per cent within the first year of arrival. Arthur Bowes, surgeon of the female ship the *Lady Penryhn*, wrote:

> There was never a more abandoned set of wretches collected in one place at any period than are now to be met with in this ship in particular, and I am credibly informed the comparison holds with regard to all convicts in the fleet.[17]

The voyage of the First Fleet was a success in terms of navigation and the absence of any serious incident such as shipwreck, mutiny or significant loss of life. With the exception of the Second Fleet, the vast majority of the voyages to Australia in the 80 years after 1787 sailed with relatively few deaths on board. However, the experience of thousands of convicts who arrived was to be a combination of hard labour, harsh punishment, the cat-o'-nine-tails, sexual abuse, bullying, deprivation and all the severity of a brutal penal system.

On the ships, convicts were kept below in cramped conditions on the prison deck, in many cases confined behind bars as well as restrained in chains. They were allowed on deck for fresh air and exercise as part of the daily routine, but the benefits could be of short duration. The unfortunates who travelled on the Second Fleet—and some of those on the Third Fleet—were, as we shall see, subject to severe discipline, cruel masters, overcrowding, shortages of food and provisions, dysentery, scurvy and other illnesses.

The decision to transport convicted felons to Australia remains the only occasion in history when convicts were forced to be instruments in creating the society in which they underwent their punishment. An irony not lost on those who criticized the whole concept of transportation was that in England itself it was perfectly acceptable to flog a prisoner or hang him in public, but completely unacceptable to place convicts in chain gangs, performing public works under the control of tyrannical overseers. In the colony of New South Wales, as originally envisaged, such a practice was an integral part of the whole practice of transportation.

CREATING THE COLONY

The lush, fertile land of Botany Bay, described by Cook and Joseph Banks in 1770, was not what Captain Arthur Phillip found on arrival in January 1788. It cannot have been a happy discovery, but the reason, in part, was seasonal. Cook's ship, the *Endeavour*, visited Botany Bay in May, after the rains had fallen; but the First Fleet arrived in January, when it was drier and plants had not been replaced by fresh growth. The soil around Botany Bay proved to be poor for crop growing, and Phillip took the decision to move a few miles further north to a small bay on the southern shore of Port Jackson, where the convict settlement was established. Phillip held a formal flag-raising ceremony on the shore to proclaim the colony of New South Wales, and later named the bay Sydney Cove, in honour of Lord Sydney, the man who had initiated the raising of the First Fleet.

The native Aborigine people lived on local plants and fish, but the settlers were not farmers or fishermen; they relied on the supplies brought with them on the ships. In addition, materials for building and supplies of clothing were limited. By July 1788, all the ships, except the naval vessels

LEFT:
A portrait of Captain Arthur Phillip, commander of the First Fleet's 11 ships in 1787. He founded the British convict settlement in New South Wales and become its first Governor.

RIGHT:
HMS Supply *and HMS* Sirius *by George Raper, 1789. The* Sirius *was the Fist Fleet's flagship, while the* Supply *was its smallest vessel. The latter reached Botany Bay on 20 January 1788, 24 hours ahead of the rest of the fleet.*

Sirius and *Supply* had left and the settlement was isolated. The *Sirius* sailed to Cape Town at the beginning of October with the intention of buying provisions to replenish the shortages.

The *Supply* had sailed to Norfolk Island in February with a small group of convicts and marines to set up another penal colony. The island, three by five miles across and set in the South Pacific Ocean, is about 1,000 miles east of Sydney. It was discovered by Cook and named in honour of the Duchess of Norfolk. In 1856, the island received those who call it home to this day—the Pitcairners, descendants of the Bounty Mutineers. John Call, an advisor to William Pitt, proposed Norfolk Island as a penal colony in 1784. Call thought that the island had the advantage of not being inhabited and consequently saw 'no injury … by possessing it, to the rest of mankind.'[18] Lord Sydney's instructions were to send a small establishment to secure the island. This consisted of a group of 23 convicts, including six females, and a small number of marines. However, this paradise in the South Seas was to become one of the most brutal and notorious of penal colonies.

There was no great hurry in sending another convict fleet until details on the progress of the First Fleet had been received. Governor Phillip's reports from Port Jackson reflected the need for supplies and his desire to take stock of the situation in New South Wales before proposing the dispatch of any more convicts. By October 1788, however, Lord Sydney was waiting for news from Phillips, and was ready to dispatch more prisoners.

A STRUGGLE FOR SURVIVAL

There was now a desperate shortage of food, medicines, clothing, farming implements and resources on Port Jackson. Arthur Phillip sent letters in July and again in October 1788, pleading for more supplies to be sent. By April of 1789, Lord Sydney wrote to the Admiralty:

> There is an immediate occasion for a further supply, together with certain articles of clothing, tools and implements for agriculture, medicines etc. ... His Majesty had given orders that one of his ships of war ... shall forthwith be got ready to carry out the said provisions.[19]

The supply ship was the *Guardian*, which had the unfortunate distinction of being the first vessel to be wrecked on the voyage to Australia. On board the *Guardian* was Henry Cone, aged 24 years, one of 25 male convicts selected for their farming experience. He had been sentenced to death on 28 March 1787 at the Suffolk Assizes for stealing two crown pieces and three shillings, but his death sentence was commuted to transportation for life.[20]

One month and 1,300 miles after leaving Cape Colony on 24 December 1789, the bow of the *Guardian* struck ice. After desperate attempts to save the ship and avoid frequent threats of mutiny, the ship was sadly beached and abandoned.[21] Its loss was a disaster for the settlements at New South Wales and Norfolk Island. Some sheep and a large quantity of flour and salt meat were transferred to other Second Fleet ships and eventually conveyed to the colony, but a vast quantity of other goods, plants and stock had been lost at enormous cost.

Henry Cone was transferred to the convict ship *Neptune* at the Cape and granted a conditional pardon for his role in trying to save the *Guardian*. He lived on Norfolk Island from the late 1790s, where he was described as a landless labourer. In September 1808, he sailed with a woman (Mary Ann) and a child on the *City of Edinburgh* for Van Diemen's

Land (modern Tasmania, about 150 miles from the south-east mainland of Australia), where he was granted 30 acres of land; by 1819, he was recorded as having four children. [22]

THE ARRIVAL OF THE LADY JULIANA

Many female prisoners were waiting in Newgate prison, as well as in county gaols around the country. They sailed from Plymouth on 29 July 1789 on the next convict ship, the *Lady Juliana*. On arrival at Sydney on 3 June 1790, they effectively doubled the number of females in the colony. The number of female convicts on the *Lady Juliana* was between 225 and 240, aged between 11 and 68; their average age, in the mid-twenties, reflected that of many convicts. The voyage was documented, not always accurately, by the steward John Nicol in *The Life and Adventures of John Nicol*, 1822; he referred to the ship as the *Lady Julian*, for example, rather than the *Lady Juliana*. The author fell in love with one of the convicts, Sarah Whitlam, who bore him a son during the 11-month-long voyage, but his seafaring duties forced them apart forever when he had to go back to sea.

The ship had its share of problems on the voyage. In addition to those caused by the women, there was a fire at the Cape caused by a pitch-pot that boiled over, and a near collision with the shore at Port Jackson. In spite of such events, only five women died on the voyage. At least eight children accompanied their mothers, and there were seven births on the passage, the pregnancies necessitating a supply of child bed linen and other appropriate items. On arrival at Port Jackson, 114 women were sent to Norfolk Island, and another 80 joined them later. Over 60 of the women and their families went to Van Diemen's Land after 1805. Many married or lived with men who were on the island, or who arrived in later years. In November 1791, about 100 couples were married on the island by the Rev. Richard Johnson.[23]

THE SCANDAL OF THE SECOND FLEET

The Pitt administration was keen to pursue a cheap solution to the problem of dealing with the prison population. Pitt, defending himself against his critics, made this point clearly to the House of Commons in 1791 when he stated that 'no cheaper mode of disposing of the convicts could

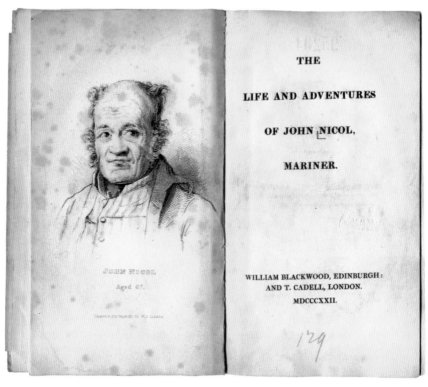

be found.' The Admiralty and the Navy Board, responsible for provisioning and transporting the ships to Australia, put out tenders for private contractors. Although it relieved the departments of having to deal with a mass of administration, the arrangement was the main source of problems associated with the transportation of convicts in the early years. The authorities did respond to some of the worst abuses, but precautions, especially on the ships of the Second Fleet, were less than inadequate. Having committed itself to the system of transportation for an indefinite period, the government needed to strike a balance between justifying the costs and ensuring that the loss of life was kept to an absolute minimum.

The Secretary of State, William Wyndham Grenville, had reflected the desire for a cheaper voyage in a letter to the Treasury in July 1789.

> I am in consequence to desire that your Lordships will be pleased to take the necessary measures for their [convicts] conveyance thither in such manner as may be likely to be attended with the least expense to the public.[24]

William Richards junior, who had been the contractor for the First Fleet, submitted a detailed proposal for the transportation of the Second Fleet to the Treasury in October 1788.[25] However, in the interests of economy, his proposal was rejected in favour of a lower tender submitted by the slave-trading company of Camden, Calvert and King.

ABOVE LEFT:
The wreck of the Guardian *store ship, from a series of pamphlets on 'dreadful shipwrecks' in 1809. The ship hit the submerged part of an iceberg only 11 days after leaving Cape Town in 1789. The brilliant seamanship of its commander, Edward Riou, brought the vessel back to Cape Town, but the crew abandoned the ship.*

BELOW LEFT:
A portrait of John Nicol in the frontispece of his book, published in 1822. It relates the story of the Lady Juliana*'s colourful voyage to Port Jackson from Plymouth in 1789–90. The ship has been immortalized through his lurid account as the 'Floating Brothel'.*

Grenville's concerns had unfortunate consequences, as the decision to employ Camden, Calvert and King was key to the Second Fleet's terrible outcome. The death rate on this voyage was eventually to be ten times higher than on the First Fleet—a consequence of significantly worse conditions and the brutality displayed by many of the crew and officers towards the convicts.

Lady Juliana was followed by the Second Fleet of the *Surprize, Neptune* and the *Scarborough*, under Lieutenant John Shapcote. The fleet arrived at Port Jackson on 26 June 1790, after the most disastrous voyage in the history of transportation to Australia. The statistics were appalling: 256 men and 11 women had died;

three-quarters of the transported convicts were starved, beaten, abused and ill; and many of those who survived the journey were so ill that they could not walk. A temporary hospital of tents awaited them on arrival.

Problems on the voyage arose in part from the expectations that already surrounded convict vessels. The crew on the *Neptune*, alerted to possibilities by fellow seamen, were aggrieved that they could not have the free and easy access to female prisoners that had occurred on the *Lady Juliana*. They sent a written demand to the captain, Donald Trail, arguing that this arrangement had been agreed; he repudiated this. Trail, a 44-year-old Scot from Orkney, took a hard line by flogging any of the crew who attempted to have sexual relations with the females.[26]

Many of the prisoners had spent months, or years, in prison or on the hulks; they would thus have been in a poor state of health by the time they embarked on the convict ship. Although the British Government had regulations for the treatment of prisoners, including access to fresh air, exercise, regular cleaning and fumigating, these were frequently neglected by some of the officers and crew on board the ships of the Second Fleet. This was reflected in the high levels of starvation among the convicts who were chained beneath the decks on this voyage and treated with terrible severity, particularly with the regular use of the cat-o'-nine-tails. Confinement below deck was the main reason that so many died. The death rate was already rising by the time the ships reached the Cape, with 46 deaths on the *Neptune*, 15 on the *Scarborough* and eight on the *Surprize*. Surgeons on the ships complained and demanded fresh supplies.[27] The settlement chaplain, Rev. Richard Johnson, visited the *Surprize* on arrival in New South Wales and described the convicts as a shocking sight:

> A great number of them laying, some half and others nearly quite naked, without bed or bedding, unable to turn or help themselves... The smell was so offensive that I could scarcely bear it.[28]

The *Sydney Cove Chronicle* of 30 June 1790 reported that:

> The landing of those who remained alive despite their misuse upon the recent voyage could not fail to horrify those who watched. As they came on shore, these wretched people were hardly able to move hand or foot. Such as could not carry themselves upon their legs, crawled upon all fours... Some expired in the boats; others as they reached the shore... A sight most outrageous to our eyes were the marks of leg irons upon the convicts, some so deep that one could nigh on see the bones.

Public and official opinion was outraged at the reports and an inquiry and trial at the Old Bailey of those responsible for the brutal conditions followed. In February 1792, papers were presented to the House of Commons requesting a civil or criminal action.[29] The trial commenced on 8 June 1792 and was sensationally reported in the papers. Hopes of justice were disappointed, however, as those accused were acquitted; neither the contractors nor Donald Trail, captain of the *Neptune*, were prosecuted. Ten years later, in 1802, Trail had his half-pay cut because of ill-health and applied to have it restored. In support of his claim he received a personal written testimonial from Lord Nelson: 'I have no difficulty in saying that during the time Mr Trail served with me I considered him as the very best master I had ever met with.'[30]

After the high death rate following the Second Fleet, the Home Office gave an incentive to the shipping companies by paying them for every convict who, on arrival in Australia, was checked and approved by a colonial official. This put the onus on the companies to ensure the welfare of each convict during the voyage.

When war with France broke out shortly afterwards, in 1793, the whole issue of the disastrous Second Fleet was swept away. In fact, the contract for the transportation of the Third Fleet had been agreed with Camden, Calvert and King in November 1790, before the report of the conditions of the Second Fleet was known. The cost of the Second Fleet was £22,370 for the transportation of 1,250 convicts, compared with the cost of £54,000 for the First Fleet. Calvert, Camden and King received more than £45,000 for the transportation of the Third Fleet (over £66,000 for both the Second and Third Fleets) and they continued to make substantial profits from the slave trade. However, the Third Fleet was to be the last contract with the company.

THE THIRD FLEET AND BEYOND

Two convict ships, the *Mary Ann* and the *Gorgon*, sailed for Port Jackson in 1791 in what was a relatively trouble-free voyage. The other ships that made up the Third Fleet were the *Atlantic, William and Ann, Britannia, Matilda, Salamander, Albemarle, Active, Admiral Barrington* and *Queen*. *Queen* sailed from Cork and was the first ship to transport wholly Irish convicts. This ship carried 136 men and 23 women. The fleet arrived in

Ship *Minerva, Sidney Cove, Port Jackson, New South Wales.*

New Holland is supposed to be 2400 miles from E. to W. and 2300 from N. to [South] but the territory of New South Wales extends only from the Latt. 10.39 South to 43.39 South and all the country inland to the Westward as far as the 13[5] of East Longitude from the meridian of Greenwich; that the claim which [England] gland has to this territory, is indisputable, as the whole of the Eastern coast had been untouched by any navigator, till by Captn. Cook, except the most [South] ern point by the Dutch, but a South part called Van Diemen's Land, has been found to be seperated from the main land by a large strait, it will decide any future litigations that may occur between us and the Dutch.

This coast was surveyed about six months since by Mr. Bass, Surge[on] of the Reliance, who discovered a large strait which you enter near point Hicks in the Latt 40. and come out in the same Latitude, running for [some] degrees in a Western direction. This gentleman has since sailed for England, I hope he'll meet the reward his merit so well deserves.

The town of Sidney, the metropolis and Head quarters of N.S.W. is sit[uated] on the face of a rising ground, fronting that beautiful bason of water the Cove, it about one mile in length and half a mile in breadth and is improving daily, [some] of the houses are large commodious and elegant, but in general they are small

Australia between August and October of 1791 with over 2,000 convicts. The *Matilda* set a new record by completing the voyage in 127 days.

Although the abuses and deaths were not as severe as the Second Fleet, they were still extensive. Convicts on the *Queen* and the *Active* had been partially starved as a result of a shortage of rations. As in the case of the Second Fleet, the officers and contractors were subject to an inquiry but escaped punishment. In the face of such flagrant abuses of convicts, it seems an extraordinary miscarriage of justice that no prosecutions were brought against those responsible. However, the transportation system was still in its early stages and the government clearly did not want the scheme to be discredited from the outset. The *Albermarle* and the *Britannia* had experienced outbreaks of scurvy and the 36 deaths on the *Admiral Barrington* had largely been a result of overcrowding. The death toll on the nine ships, plus the *Mary Ann* and the *Gorgon*, were in total 184. The convict George Barrington described the scene when the *Active* arrived in Australia:

> At 10 o'clock the next morning the convicts were all ordered on shore; their appearance was truly deplorable, the generality of them being emaciated by disease, foul air &c. and those who laboured under no bodily disorder, from the scantiness of their allowance were in no better plight.[31]

He went on to record that upon landing the convicts were newly clothed from the king's store and their old clothes were burnt to prevent possible infections from the ship being introduced into the colony.

The Second Fleet was a low point in the process of transportation. After the first three fleets, there followed a succession of ships, mainly travelling independently, for the next 80 years to different destinations in Australia. Given the large numbers of prisoners involved, the number of deaths on most other voyages were in fact remarkably low. During the first 11 years of transportation, death rates had reached a peak of nearly 19 per cent, as a result of which the British Government reviewed the system of transportation in 1801. Significant improvements followed, including a more prominent role for surgeons, who took on more responsibility for the convicts. After 1800, the death rate on the convict ships was less than two per cent, and these low mortality rates have to be considered a

This view of Sydney Cove in 1800 is from the journal kept on board the Minerva *convict ship, as it brought prisoners from Ireland. Houses, a fort and windmills can be seen in the background; a gibbet and native canoe in the foreground.*

success when measured against the scale of operations, the number of prisoners and the complex logistics involved.

Conditions on the ships could be difficult, indeed unbearable at times, especially when crossing the tropics or during stormy seas, but they were in the main an improvement on the conditions that convicts endured on the hulks or in the prisons. Many of the convicts actually received a level of care from the surgeons on the voyage which had not been available to them before. The voyages themselves were separate from the institutionalized physical and mental brutality of the penal system. Such cruelties were more a feature of certain penal colonies in Australia, especially Van Diemen's Land and Norfolk Island. Both became notorious for their harsh treatment of convicts.[32]

The motives behind the early exploration and expansion of Australia were to discover suitable places of punishment and to occupy land before anyone else arrived. Such was the case of Norfolk Island and Van Diemen's Land, which received mainly re-offenders. In later years, it was the feverish quest for gold that pushed exploration westwards. As a result, Australia did not experience the organized push westward that characterized the European settlement of America. There was some exploration to the west of Sydney Cove, which found better land on the Parramatta river, and it was here that a settlement developed called Rose Hill. The United Kingdom claimed the rest of Australia in 1829.

PEOPLING AUSTRALIA

The diverse population grew slowly but steadily from the start. Captain Arthur Phillip had commented that the majority of the convicts were in a better state of health when they left Rio de Janeiro than when they sailed from England. Between 1788 and 1842, some 80,000 convicts were transported to New South Wales, of which 15 per cent were women. Two-thirds of the convicts were English, and a small number were Scottish and Welsh. The Irish made up the remaining one-third.[33] By 1806, the population had grown to 8,593, of which 1,114 were women and children. In addition, there were some 1,000 settlers and landholders, both men and women.[34] The gender imbalance would continue to be a concern for administrators in the years to come. The issue often emerged in government reports, particularly after 1830, when documents reflect increasing anxiety in official circles about the alleged prevalence of homosexuality.

From the beginning of transportation, the government had shown no great interest in sending out free settlers, although incentives were gradually introduced and their numbers increased.[35] The patterns of life established themselves for settlers and convicts alike. Many female convicts of the First Fleet did marry male convicts. Others married some of the crew and officers, particularly after their term of imprisonment had expired. Between January of 1788 and the arrival of other convicts in 1790, there were at least 185 women of childbearing age in New South Wales. By 1792, there were more than 300 children, and births were beginning to outnumber deaths.

The resilience of those who adapted to their new lives successfully must have been matched by remarkable physical stamina. Given the shortage of medical supplies, farming materials, livestock and essential provisions, combined with the uncertainties of an alien landscape thousands of miles away from their homeland, this pioneer convict society was unknowingly contributing to the extraordinary beginnings of a nation. The legacy of these new arrivals, whether they arrived as convict or as settler, was to change the face of the continent.

3

The Trauma of Exile

ROBERT PEEL (1788–1850) was made Home Secretary in Liverpool's government in 1822. Over the next five years, he became responsible for large-scale reform of the legal system, repealing more than 250 old statutes, as well as recommending the setting up of a police force for London. In the same year that he was appointed to this post, a much less significant matter came to his department's attention—a letter, one of thousands received by the Home Office concerning transportation. Written by a Town Clerk from Carlisle, it represented not only an individual plea for mercy on behalf of a destitute woman, but also a sentiment echoed in the voices of hundreds of similar appeals:

> A poor convict woman whose name I do not know has reached London last Tuesday from Carlisle; she is transported for seven years for receiving stolen goods, her second offence; she is a poor fool and has been made the dupe of some artful thief. She has undergone 22 weeks severe confinement and has a child at her breast and two others with her. If His Majesty's pardon could be procured … she may be restored to her husband, who is a very honest working man and another child he has there.[1]

For those involved, their plights were as important, with more immediate impact, than the highest affairs of state. However, they were not generally accorded much attention. The fate of the woman is unknown and the absence of her name makes it almost impossible to follow up further details. The chances are that little, if anything, was done for her or her family. This example is merely one of thousands of cases reflected in letters pleading for mercy, or for free passage to go with a loved one to Australia, that were sent to various Home Secretaries during the first half of the nineteenth century.[2] They were usually written by a relative, or someone petitioning on behalf of a relative, such as a local rector, Board of Guardians, churchwardens, a Town Clerk, or anyone prepared to appeal against some sense of injustice. Even allowing for a critical reading of these letters, the vast majority powerfully evoke individual tragedies and the desperation suffered by many families throughout the country. They also serve as

BLACK-EYED SUE, and SWEET POLL of PLYMOUTH,
Taking leave of their lovers who are going to Botany Bay.

Published 13 June 1792 by Robt. Sayer & Co, Fleet Street, London.

This cartoon of 1792, published by Robert Sayer & Co, offers a satirical depiction of convicts leaving their lovers before embarking for Botany Bay. It would appear from the bottle in her hand that Black-eyed Sue has had recourse to the hard stuff to assuage her grief.

testimony to the experience of exile, and the stark reality of transportation, which tore thousands of people from the heart of their families, communities, traditions and their native land.

The domestic impact of transportation on families and communities was felt in villages and towns throughout the country. Examples of pleas to the Home Office form a large part of this chapter, offering rich insight into the anguish experienced by individuals and families. The letters, when received by the Home Office, were usually passed on to the Home Secretary with a letter attached 'for further consideration'. Most went no further; the majority of the appeals failed, and applicants were denied support to go to Australia with their family or partner. Finding the money to go independently was out of the question, with the result that many families saw their loved ones leave in the near certainty that they would not see them again, or even know whether they were still alive. Whole communities, rural and urban, were touched by this process, its consequences lasting well beyond the period of transportation.

Some cases can be followed up, but the outcome of most, like so many of the frustrating gaps in history, is unknown. Years later, when a convict received a ticket of leave, he or she could make an application for one or more members of their family to join them in Australia. Some did go and were reunited. For many, however, the passage of time brought a change in circumstances which meant they were unable or not prepared to take up the invitation. It would be pleasing to offer a happy ending to the many cases that follow, but sadly this was not common; the reality for most was getting on and surviving as best they could in a harsh environment. So many letters begin 'I am writing in the greatest distress.' Unfortunately, that distress was to continue and had to be endured.

Popular ballads of the time often featured those caught up in the process of transportation, lamenting the grief of separation or fostering the wistful hope of reunion. The following four verses, from a broadsheet written in the early 1840s, evoke a not untypical and poignant mixture of defiance and resignation:

> *The assizes they are over now, the Judge is gone away,*
> *But many aching hearts are left within the town today;*
> *Tho' crime is bad, yet poverty's made many one to be*
> *A transport from his native land and across the raging sea.*
>
> *The rich have no temptation, they have all things in command,*
> *And 'tis for pleasure and for health, they leave their native land;*
> *But a starving wife and family, makes a poor man's heart to break,*
> *And makes him do what brings a blush of shame upon his cheek.*
>
> *Their sentence some deserve to get, and laws were made to be*
> *Preservers of the public peace, and of society;*
> *But great distress and want of work, starvation, and disease,*
> *Makes inmates for the prison-house, and transports for the seas.*
>
> *Would they but pass an act for man to work and earn his bread,*
> *Crime would soon dwindle from the land, and transportation fled;*
> *Would providence direct their hearts to make such laws, and then*
> *Instead of outlawed slaves we might have free and honest men.*[3]

POLITICAL EXILES

Political prisoners amounted to about two per cent of the total number of convicts transported to Australia between 1787 and 1868. Despite the low number of political prisoners, many of these convicts were involved in collective protests. It is not surprising then that they lived in the same village or town, or that their convictions had a traumatic effect on the entire community, as well as the individual families. In 1831, for example, some 'Swing' protesters in the southwest of England had been sentenced to transportation. Reporting the scenes outside Winchester gaol on 8–10 January 1831, *The Times* recorded that every day 'the wives, sisters, mothers, children beset the gates', which the reporter found to be 'truly heartbreaking'. As the prisoners were led away in a cart, the families wept, cried out loud and tried to hold the hands of their loved ones, knowing that they would not see them again. Scenes of sorrowful farewells were a feature for many who had someone close wrenched away; unlike a domestic prison term, transportation was, for the majority, a life sentence. *The Times* of 12 January 1831 recorded that the wives and mothers of men in Salisbury sentenced to transportation emitted a 'dreadful shriek of lamentation' and uttered cries of ' Farewell! I shall never see you more'. Most of these men were not hardened or violent criminals, but rather victims of rural poverty. They were convicted for protesting against the loss of their livelihoods caused by changes in rural work, such as the introduction of new agricultural machinery. They were attempting to defend a traditional way of life, which was threatened by a changing industrial world and an economic system based on profit and self-interest.

The 'Swing' riots of 1830–31 were an agricultural phenomenon. There were over a thousand separate incidences of machine-breaking, arson attacks and other disturbances in counties across the south, the west and the east of England. The riots were the result of a decline in the prices of agricultural produce and labourers' wages, the introduction of threshing machines, enclosures and an influx of cheap Irish labour. As a consequence of the riots, over 2,000 people were arrested, of whom 19 were executed and over 500 transported.[4] In 1831, 132 agricultural labourers and craftsmen from the southwest of England were transported for taking part in the 'Swing' riots. They all sailed on the *Eleanor* from Portsmouth to New South Wales, forced to embark on a new life in a new country without the familiar bonds of family, friends, community and country.[5]

The 'Tolpuddle Martyrs' from Dorset were transported to New South Wales and Van Diemen's Land in March 1834. Their crime, described as unlawful assembly and 'administering unlawful oaths', was in reality attempting to form a trade union in response to low wages and increasing unemployment. The judge, under pressure from the government of the day, explicitly sentenced the men 'not for anything they had done, but as an example to others'. Public pressure resulted in the men being pardoned, although they did not return to England until three years later.

The fate of many 'Swing' protestors was less happily resolved. One of them, Peter Withers from Wiltshire, wrote to his wife, Mary Ann, from on board the convict ship *Porteus*, moored at Spithead, in April 1831:

> My dear wife belive my hart is almost broken to think I must lave you behind. O my dear what shall I do I am all most destracted at the thoughts of parting from you whom I do love so dear ... you may depend upon My keeping Myself from all other women for I shall Never Let No other run into my mind for tis onely you My Dear that can Ease me of my Desire. It is not Laving Old England that grives me it is laving my dear and loving Wife and Children... I hope you will go to the gentlemen for they to pay your Passage over to me when I send for you ... if I can get a comfortable place should you not like to follow your dear Husband who lovs you so dear?[6]

For whatever reason, Mary Ann did not reply, and two years later Peter Withers wrote to his brothers from Van Diemen's Land, asking of her well-being and expressing concern that she may have forgotten him. As the years passed, Peter resigned himself to the loss of Mary Ann and tried to make a new life for himself. It must have been something of a shock for him 11 years later to receive a letter from Mary Ann. She told Peter that she was in great distress and asked to be reconciled with him. However, she could not have known that Peter had married during this period of time. He replied, attempting to explain his situation to her: 'I sent a great many Letters before I took a wife... So we must not think about Coming together again.'

A poster offering a reward for information about the 'Swing' letters, 1830 (HO 52/6). 'Swing' riots were a response to low wages and poor conditions, particularly in the South West and East of England in 1830. Tactics such as rick-burning and cattle-maiming evoked a ferocious response from the authorities.

The agricultural riots had clearly alarmed local authorities, who showed little sympathy towards the rioters. In Hickling, Norfolk, the local curate, churchwardens and the overseers of the poor offered no hope of a return home for

Farrell Whitaker who, with 'several persons [had] engaged in riot' and the destruction of threshing machines. In a letter to the Home Office in 1832, the local dignitaries made their feelings clear, insisting that any return by Whitaker to the parish would lead 'others to acts of felony' and further encourage discontent. Whitaker wrote to his wife, pleading with her to

192

FIFTY
POUNDS
Reward.

Whereas, on Saturday last, Letters signed

"SWING"

Were sent to Mr. Hawkings, and Mr. D. Symes, Farmers of Axmouth, threatening to destroy their premises by FIRE; whosoever will give information leading to the discovery and conviction of the writer,

SHALL RECEIVE A REWARD OF

50 POUNDS

All Communications to be addressed to the *Church Wardens and Overseers of Axmouth.*

N. B. The above Letters passed through the Colyton Post Office, & bear the Axminster post mark.

Dated December the 6th. 1830.

T. Ham, Printer, Bookbinder, and Stationer, Lyme and Axminster.

bring their six children and join him in New South Wales. The authorities were keen to be rid of the family, stating that 'the Parish will pay their express to Portsmouth and will be benefited by the removal of them as the population is very much more numerous than required.'[7] There is no record indicating that the family went to Australia to join Farrell Whitaker.

PLEADING LETTERS

The majority of letters involve wives pleading to be with husbands. However, there are also many others from mothers, fathers, sons and daughters, as well as a few cases of letters from husbands requesting to go with their convicted wives. Some of the letters reveal a surprising level of literacy among the correspondents, although many had to rely on the services of a literate or 'respectable' person to write their appeal for them, as well as giving a supporting character reference. The history of transportation took place prior to the introduction of the Education Act of 1870, which provided education to places that lacked it.

Prior to the convicts leaving their native country, many relatives requested to visit those who were waiting in prison—the last opportunity, for many, of ever seeing one another. Many letters seeking permission to visit were written on behalf of mothers, wives, husbands, sisters and brothers. 'A poor woman by the name of Williams residing at Cheltenham whose two sons are now at Woolwich under sentence of transportation is anxious to be admitted to them before they sail' was typical of many requests.[8] One correspondent, William Berkley, writing on behalf of the mother of a convict, had received an unfavourable response to his first letter. He abandoned the usual polite protocol expected by the Home Office and stated that, 'If you will only just take the trouble to read [my first] communication you will find that I ... merely ask to obtain permission for the mother and sister to see their son and brother.' Unfortunately the letter did no favours for the anxious relatives, as the Home Office took umbrage and replied in a pompous tone, 'The use of language of this kind, in official communications to the Home Office is, I believe, unprecedented.' Predictably, there was no response to the request concerning the mother and sister.[9]

Those who petitioned more diplomatically on behalf of a dependent stressed the sober and industrious character of the person involved. The

Foreign Assistant Secretary to the Bible Society, writing on behalf of the wife of a sentenced convict, stated that '…through the wishes of a wicked person [she] has been involved in a theft and consequently is very much in distress at the idea of being separated from her husband—an honest, sober, hardworking man.' [10]

Whether written by relatives or representatives, the letters poignantly illustrate the misery of separation. However, a determination as well as desperation shines through, and a courage willing to defy the obstacles. James Storman from Boston was sentenced to life and was in prison await-ing his ship at Sheerness in January 1819. His wife of only 12 months, described as a 'poor woman wretchedly distressed', begged to go with him, regardless of what peril she might undergo. The letters reflect a com-bination of emotional and economic desire in women to be with a hus-band—unsurprising, as the alternative for single mothers with children was usually the parish and poverty. Hannah Yardley asked to be with her husband. 'I am in distressed circumstances, having seven children, six of whom live with me … I am anxious to follow my husband and take my children with me.' Thomas Mitchell, described as a man of good charac-ter until he stole a heifer, was sentenced to life at Lincoln in 1835, but was then transported to Van Diemen's Land. His wife of nine years, Charlotte, aged 27, and their twin daughters petitioned to be sent to him. The letter, as with so many, appealed for support: '…a dressmaker [she is] very poor and unable to pay anything towards her own passage.' [11]

For many wives, the transportation of a husband meant destitution as they struggled to bring up children. Dire economic circumstances were particularly evident with Ann Flanagan, who wrote to Home Secretary Lord John Russell in November 1837, regarding her husband, John. Asking that her 'deplorable state' be taken into consideration, she described her particular circumstances since her husband had been transported:

> I have been almost famished for want of food. My husband left me with one child, I have neither father or mother, relatives or friends to give me and my child any assistance whatever … I have nothing to get my bread with … I will do my utmost endeavours to make myself useful in the colony, I am very young, 20 years of age in good health and of sound constitution…[12]

Similarly, another woman, Sarah Smyth from the county of Monaghan in Ireland, petitioned in 1842 to be with her husband, who had sailed on the

Dumfries 14 April 1835

Sir,

I have been transported for life. My poor wife is like to go out of her reason about the thoughts of such a seperation and is anxious to suffer voluntary banishment if she could get leave to go with me, I therefore humbly pray that you will tell me whether she can be permitted, or whether a Petition from the clergyman and others of our parish might be attended with success. This is my first offence and I humbly trust that the innocent will not be made to suffer

An extract from one of thousands of similar moving letters received by the Home Office during the convict years (PC 1/83).

This poignant example, from a prisoner sentenced to transportation for life, begs that his wife be allowed to accompany him.

Calcutta in April 1837. The letter stated that she 'has three children from eight to 13 and no means whatsoever for her or their support except what she earns daily.' Her husband, Hugh, had received a stolen watch for which he pleaded his innocence. He wrote to Sarah on a number of occasions, encouraging her and the children to join him in Australia. The letter stressed Sarah's plight:

> [The] petitioner has no means of an outfit for herself or family… Should your Lordship be kind enough to intervene with the Home Government to have a passage granted for the petitioner and her children [she] and her family would ever pray for your happiness.[13]

Another woman, Elizabeth Mitchell, pleaded as much for her husband's grief of separation as her own. He had served 10 years and was now employed as a baker making a reasonable living. In her appeal she asked the Secretary of State 'to consider how hard it is for a husband to be parted from his wife and children, particularly when he is able to earn a comfortable maintenance for us all. I have five children and nothing to depend on but the Parish Allowance.'[14]

Thomas Newman had been on board the hulk *Justitia* at Woolwich for 12 months, awaiting his seven years' transportation sentence. A petition on behalf of the family asked for a mitigation of the sentence 'as there is the wife and five small children, the eldest under nine years of age, wholly destitute of support with exception of 3/6 per week from the parish …'[15] Desperation is also evident in the letter from the wife of one Benjamin Griffiths, who assured the writer that 'she would be willing to become a slave if she could be with him.' She had also been offered support from the local community: 'If she and her children can go to her husband, they will be conveyed to London onto whatever Port from whence the vessel may sail, by a subscription voluntarily proposed by the inhabitants of this town and neighbourhood.'[16] Parish assistance was often offered to convey a convict's wife and dependants to the nearest port, but was contingent on the government funding the passage to Australia.

Elizabeth Radford from Exeter was the wife of Thomas, who had been sentenced to 14 years for stealing hay to the value of four pence.[17] She, too, had local backing—her petition to be with her husband in Sydney was signed by all the inhabitants of the parish of Sidwell. Others were unable to draw upon the support of friends, such as Rhoda Evans from Gloucester. After her husband Thomas was convicted of sheep-stealing and transported for seven years, Rhoda, aged 23, petitioned on behalf of herself and her two children, Caroline and Dinah. She claimed that she was desirous of accompanying her husband, but lacked any friends to whom she could look for support. Twenty-five-year-old Sarah Smith from Sheffield asked to go to her husband, who had been on Van Diemen's Land for four years. As an orphan, Sarah stated that 'I have no parents or friends to leave behind me, my only desire is to be with him.' However, Mary Cantivell of Kilkenny was in no doubt as to whom she could appeal for her references that might allow her to go to her husband James who, she stated, ' left her in the utmost distress with a large family to support.' Asking for charitable consideration to allow her and her six children to become emigrants, she wrote that 'I can produce credentials from the Gentry and clergy of the county.'[18]

Attitudes in communities varied. In some parishes, there was sympathy and support. In others, the families were considered a burden and had to bear the stigma of being a convict's wife and children. This point was made by those representing Mary O'Hara of Newport, County Mayo, when they wrote of the misery and ruin that Mary and her four sons had suffered since her husband had been exiled for stealing sheep. They added that '…these four little boys have no means of support, no house to shelter themselves and their poor mother has no dependence but that is derived from common charity generally marred by the insults which the children of the convict must receive.'[19]

Jane Eastwood of Manchester made a similar point when she pleaded to be prevented 'from the shame of casting myself and Child upon the Parish for relief … work is not only so scarce but so ill paid.'[20] Jane was more fortunate than others as she was allowed to go to Australia to join her husband. Possessing a ticket of leave was the main criteria for giving permission to a relative to travel to Australia, although the convict still had to prove that he could support a family there. A ticket of leave, which might be granted before the penal sentence expired, enabled convicts to seek employment under a master or look for employment themselves. However, they were obliged to report each month to the local Resident Magistrate and could not leave the allocated district without permission and a pass. The ticket had to be renewed after one year and it could be taken away at any time. In practice, it kept the convict in a state of uncertainty, facing the likelihood of apprehension.

Nancy Ryan, with her three children, joined her husband in 1836, after he had received his ticket of leave and asked Nancy to join him in New South Wales. She travelled with other 'free women and children' on the female convict ship, the *Thomas Harrison*. After disembarking, she moved to the Hyde Park Barracks with her daughters and waited for further arrangements before she could meet her convict husband.[21]

The alternative to receiving a free passage to Australia was to be confronted with a cost for the voyage beyond the means of relatives, who were often largely poor or destitute. The family of Thomas Littlejohn was faced with such a dilemma. Thomas had been sentenced to life in 1830, but was to receive a ticket of leave seven years later. In 1837, Thomas believed that his wife had died and his two children, John and Hannah, had been sent to America. In desperation he asked his master, J.B. Thomas, to write on his behalf, requesting that his children be sent to him in Hobart Town where he worked. As a measure of his support for Thomas Littlejohn, his master made clear in the letter that 'Littlejohn's relatives may well imagine that I should not trouble myself', but added that Thomas had been so well behaved in his service that 'I shall probably hire him when he obtains his ticket of leave.' A particular appeal in the letter was to estimate the cost of sending the children to their father.

To the surprise of Thomas, his wife Ann was still alive and living as a pauper with the two children. The churchwardens of the parish and the overseers of the poor enquired on behalf of Ann as to the cost of travelling to Van Diemen's Land. Having contacted an Australian emigration agent —a Mr Marshall of Birchin Lane, Cornhill, London—they noted that 'the lowest charge he could take them [the family] to the colony for would be £45, a sum by far too high for the parish to advance.' The next resort was to appeal to the Home Office for support in sending the family 'in one of the Government convict ships free of charge.' As with many parishes, the usual justification was offered—that the leaving of the family would be a benefit not only to them, but also to the parishioners and the parish. In addition, there was an acknowledgment of support by the local officials in their commitment to 'provide the family with the requisite clothing and convey them to such place as your Lordship may be pleased to direct.'[22]

After years of waiting, the eventual invitation to join a husband, who was ready to obtain his ticket of leave, offered families the chance of reunion and an opportunity to start a new life—often with the promise of

Registry Number Col. Off. Letter	No. of Application	Convict's Name	Ship in which Transported	Names of Persons included in Permission	Residence	Married		Single		Children			
						Male	Female	Male	Female	Boys 1-14	Boys Under 1	Girls 1-14	Girls Under 1
✓ 758 To pay	447	Sutton Thomas		Sutton Elizᵗʰ Sarah Mary				24				6	3
✓ 333 To pay	448	Tootell Joseph	"Baropa"	Tootell Mary	57 Henry St Manchester			27					
✓ 93 To pay	449	Dunn John		Dunn Mary Elizabeth Marcella				35				11	7
✓ 214 To pay	450	Ferris Louisa		Ferris Louisa								13	
✓ 162 See No 559 recommended for pay	451	O'Neill Arthur		O'Neill Bridgt Ann Simon Catherine Jane Elizᵗʰ Patk	Stonestown			23	44 46 21 16 14	10			
269	452	Neill William	Duke of Richmond (1843)	Neill Mary Margt Samuel Elizᵗʰ Joseph Sarah	Armagh	s s s s s s	18		23 20 16	12		10	
306	453	Grice Thomas	George Seymour (1845)	Grice Hooke Mary A Anna L	Mr J Hooke Ofornsea Hallowell Flintshie	s s			28			9	

Referee written to			Answer returned		Ship		REMARKS
Name	Address	Date	No.	Nature of Reply	No. of E. O.	Name	
Revd J P Cleather Chirton Vicarage near Devizes £15 paid —			5287	Certe returned complete	17	"Ramillies" 8/3/50	N. S. W. all sailed
To pay £7. 10/ —			9429	Certe returned complete			
Revd W J Black Bradford York — To pay £15 —			10526	Certe returned complete	213 No	"Ann Thompson" 20/1/50	(3 Sailed)
Mr John Franklin Police Sergeant S Phillip Station Prahran To pay £3. 15/ D.C. 11/5/50.			10878	Certe returned complete	214 No.	"Ann Thompson" 9/1/50	(Sailed)
Revd J P Gell To pay £48. 15/ D.C. 23/5/50				Certe returned complete O'Neill returned through P.Off.			
Revd Mr Dinney Revd Mr Henry Mr Walker	Armagh	1st June		Letter to Mary Hill returned through Post Office			V D Land
Roger Jones Esq Revd F Ould Willm Harris Esq Willm Piff Esq	P.P. Aspinwall Holloway Liverpool Neaham Liverpool	1st June	13985	Certe returned complete	171 No	"Harry Lorrequer" 21/1/50	Port Phillip S. Wales both sailed

PREVIOUS PAGES: *Part of the Register for Applications for Passages to the Colonies for Convicts' Families, 1848–73 (CO 386/154). Convicts who had gained their ticket of leave could, in principle, invite families to join them in Australia; but relatives were often too ill or too poor, or had rebuilt their lives in the years of absence. Nevertheless, some families were re-united.*

financial advantages unavailable in England. Ann Bamborough of Stafford had waited for her husband to serve his sentence, and was no doubt pleased to hear that he was to obtain his liberty within 18 months because of his good conduct. He wrote and asked her and his 18-year-old son to join him. Ann, like so many who wrote to the Secretary of State, expressed her 'anxious desire' to meet her husband, but acknowledged that, 'being situated in the humblest class of life', she had 'no means whatever of attaining that object.'[23] Mary Campbell from Birmingham, whose husband Richard had been transported for life in 1832, wrote in 1838 that if she was sent to Australia, she could 'earn a much better living than ... in England.' At 30 years of age, Mary was supporting her three children by working as a laundress.

George Stevenson from Belfast, transported for life 'for a trivial offence' in April 1834, was another who wished for his wife to join him in New South Wales. George was employed as a gardener in New Town, two miles from Sydney, and had been praised for his good conduct. A letter by the Rev. E Leslie of County Antrim written three years later, in December 1837, argued that George's wife 'is most anxious to see her husband for whom she entertains unaltered affection.'[24]

'THE GREATEST DISTRESS'

For a man or woman with a family who had been sentenced to transportation, grief at parting must have been compounded by a guilty awareness of the financial suffering caused to loved ones. The convict William Maitland, serving a life sentence for burglary, stated this clearly in his plea for assistance. 'Owing to my misconduct [she] has been reduced to a state of poverty ... and has no Protector or friends to support her.' William had been married for only 12 months and beseeched the Home Secretary to allow his wife to travel to New South Wales 'in any vessel bound with female convicts or settlers.' He added that she would 'act as a servant or in any capacity' and that she had several testimonies to her good conduct from highly respectable families. In acknowledging his shortcomings, he reflected on her innocence and the distress he had caused, for which he was eternally sorry.

> She is 25 years of age, with no earthly prospect in life and must be reduced to the greatest misery… She has no children, her only one having fallen to a victim a short time ago to the cholera. In New South Wales I will be enabled by her joining me to redeem the character I have lost in this country.[25]

Financial privation entailed years of acute hardship and struggle. Some wives kept their heads above water, however; the wife of one convict, in 1815, was in a position to offer her husband financial support. In her letter, she apologized for not writing earlier, 'but it was not in my power', adding that she had all to do looking after their daughters. She offered news of local developments, such as the building of a cotton factory, and then added that she had 'enclosed a one pound note which I hope you will get … Write to me as soon as you receive it … if it is not enough I will send you some more.'[26]

The number of female convicts sent to Australia between 1787 and 1868 was much less than male convicts—less than one-fifth of the total. It is thus not surprising that letters concerning wives desiring to join husbands were much more common than vice versa. Nevertheless, there are instances of husbands wanting to go to their convicted wives. Thomas Black, a 36-year-old labourer from Newcastle, begged to accompany his wife Ann, who had been sentenced to 14 years for buying stolen lead. Ann was set to sail on the *Atwick* for Hobart Town in 1838, and Thomas sought permission and free passage for himself and their son, aged eight. 'Thomas wishes to proceed after his wife… He is able and willing to work and make himself any way useful in working his passage.'

Sarah Armstrong, a convict in Sydney, requested that her two sons, aged 21 and 19, be allowed to join her. Thirty-nine-year-old Robert Blinkhorne asked that he and his four children be permitted to go to his wife Catherine, who was serving a life sentence on Van Diemen's Land. Recognizing the demand for skilled labour in the colony, Robert added in support of his application that he was a healthy man accustomed to navigation, bricklaying and farming. Elizabeth Brooks, a female convict awaiting transportation, pleaded that her children be allowed to go with her as they would be unprotected and she was in a state of distress. Pleading for forgiveness, she promised that she would never stray again if she was restored to society.[27]

Wives and children of convicts, who had to rely on the support of the poor law, suffered financial difficulty as well as social stigma. As far as the parish was concerned, anyone who could be removed from the burden of drawing on poor relief was a benefit. The pressures of increasing population and the numbers of people reliant on poor relief combined to motivate some parish officials to appeal for free passage, especially for female dependants. The Guardians of the Poor were often instrumental in some parishes in lending their voice in support of wives joining their husbands. The Guardians of Southampton were typical in assisting such appeals when they wrote on behalf of a destitute young woman, Louise Culley, and her four-month-old child. Her husband had been sentenced to death, but this was commuted to transportation for life. The Guardians wrote that Louise would 'become an outcast from society if permitted to remain apart from her husband.' The wife and eight children of George Turnbull, a veteran of the battle of Waterloo in 1815, were considered to be a 'burden on the Parish' in 1832. George, it was reported, had been a man of good character until he became a victim of the times—post-war recession and unemployment.[28]

Harsh economic circumstances and the loss of a wage-earner resulted in destitution for many women. A petition signed by the 'respectable inhabitants' of a parish in Ayrshire pleaded for the wife and child of Peter Cailin 'that being natives of Ireland, destitute of the means of subsistence and not having acquired a legal settlement in this Parish or any other in Scotland, they are in destitute circumstances.'[29] Many families remained in destitution.

The impact of transportation ran very deep. Years after a convict had been transported, relatives continued to ask about him or her, wondering whether they were alive or in good health. In 1822, the Rector of Newbury asked about one William Cook, who had left England in April 1814. Cook had 'last wrote in March 1821 and was living at Mr Barkers, Hobart Town, Van Diemen's Land [he is] reported as dead. [His wife and friends] are in great distress and requested me to apply for information.' In the same year, the wife of James Knowles from Bolton asked whether her husband was still alive as 'recently returned convicts talk of him sailing for England.' Likewise a Nottingham town clerk, writing on behalf of a wife, asked whether the convict Thomas Fierney was still alive.[30]

For many of the convicts, separation from loved ones was the most painful part of their punishment. The strength of attachment between couples as reflected in the letters was particularly strong. There are countless expressions of hope that one day they would be together again. For the convict, the pain was compounded by the guilt of knowing a wife and children could be thrown on the mercy of the parish poor law, or become dependent on a ruthless employer. Those left behind were left to experience the varying emotions which would vacillate over the years from hope of a reunion to the dreadful realization that they would never be together

Some of the thousands of letters in the National Archives' Privy Council records (PC 1/67–92) for the years between 1819 and 1844. Many are from relatives pleading with the Home Secretary for permission to go with loved ones to Australia.

again. In an age when communication was often based on rumour and hearsay, or at best a rare correspondence interspersed with long periods of silence, there was the uncertainty of not knowing whether a relative was still alive. Yet some families did manage to keep in contact. The prisoners on the *Eleanor* in 1831 maintained a regular flow of communication, and those who were illiterate relied on scribes.[31]

Although the vast majority of letters are appeals to be with loved ones or requests for information about them, some relatives had other motives for finding out about an absent family member. A letter from W. Berney, magistrate for Norfolk, sought to confirm whether Mark Skeet was still alive 'as his wife, a commoner of very poor character, has married a Boy in the Parish to which she belongs. It is the intention of the overseers to indict her for bigamy.' Financial motives also prompted the wife of William Harrison from Leeds. Someone who had attended his funeral in New South Wales had informed her that William had left £44 and a silver watch to his next of kin. His wife clearly wished to pursue this legacy. Another enquiry from a local magistrate regarding Anne Thorne, the wife of Ralph transported for seven years, asked for confirmation that he was still living because 'his wife has claimed credit on payments on the grounds that her husband is serving time.' Clearly local shops were concerned about how long this charity might extend.[32]

It was unusual, though not unknown, for both a wife and husband to be convicted and transported. In Edinburgh, in 1830, Helen Gould wrote from her prison cell pleading not to be separated from her husband of six years, also awaiting conviction. She begged that 'he and I may be sent abroad to some place as near each other as we may with propriety be sent.' The pain of separation was as great as if one of them was being cast into exile, but the prospect of going to the same country and still finding themselves miles apart was agonizing. Reflecting on the reasons for their downfall, Helen added, 'Your sanction would be received with more sincere pleasure than even my liberation.'[33]

THE LOST BOYS

Parents also expressed acute anxiety to know of their sons. The family of Edward Leigh from Ryde on the Isle of Wight, ignorant of his term of sentence, enquired as to when their son might return; Edward had already been in Australia for 11 years. The mother of John Griffiths from Liverpool had not heard from him for four years and appealed for information that would 'relieve her anxiety'.[34] The parents of a convict by the name of Lightfoot, who had been brought back from Botany Bay and was due to be released in four months, were concerned that he should not fall back into bad ways.

His parents … are anxious that he should be released before the expiration of his time and placed under the protection of some friends who are willing to take charge of him in Portsmouth. They are fearful lest being set at large when his time is up, he may be led astray by some of his companions … into his former evil practices.[35]

Earl and Elizabeth Pettitt asked that their son be returned to his parents in order that he 'redeem that good character he so unfortunately lost', adding that his return 'will save the life of a poor, afflicted, broken-hearted mother.' Elizabeth Pickering from Leeds wrote concerning a son and a son-in-law who had been transported to New South Wales; her son had attained his freedom and asked if his mother could go and settle with him. Elizabeth was keen to join him and enquired as to what the expense would be. Thomas Pickup from Bolton pleaded with the Secretary of State, Lord Sidmouth, to be sent to Australia to see his father. 'My unfortunate father is lying at New South Wales and as I am young and in good health it is my only desire to go to him.'[36]

Sarah Smith, a 'poor mother from Worcester', enquired about the whereabouts of her son Anthony and 'prayed night and day' that she might hear news. William Hoskins of Swansea, aged 16, was sentenced to seven years' transportation for stealing a small quantity of cheese in 1831. Seven years later, on the completion of the sentence, his father was anxious to know of William's whereabouts and asked that his son be returned to him.[37]

The loss of children through transportation was deeply distressing for many parents; their anxiety and uncertainty about their children's health or their prospects of return are familiar themes in correspondence. In 1844, Henry Scannell, aged 13, was waiting in Parkhurst to serve seven years' transportation for stealing a plum cake from a baker's shop in Southampton, together with two other boys. His parents received a letter from Henry saying that he was sorry for the grief he had caused. They wrote to him regularly for two years, but when they did not hear from him, they wrote to Sir James Graham, the Home Secretary, enquiring about Henry. They received no reply and only when they were sent a letter from Portsmouth, revealing that Henry was going to New Zealand, were their suspicions aroused. It transpired that the Governor of the prison had offered Henry his liberty if he would emigrate to New Zealand as the government there 'was in want of hands.' Henry did not even have the time or opportunity to consult his parents before the ship sailed from Portsmouth. The parents' distress was compounded by the fact that they heard nothing further from their son. Henry's father, William, a ropemaker by trade, was described as 'respectable … sober and honest until misfortune attended him at work.' This was a reference to yet another misfortune for the family; their misery was increased when an accident, caused by a machine, crippled William. [38]

The extent of pleading from desperate relatives could reach almost embarrassing proportions. An example occurs in a petition from the 'aged and miserable parents of Daniel Allen', on board the hulk *Retribution* at Woolwich. Begging for the return of their son, the letter's author, writing on behalf of the parents, flew into an exceptional piece of purple prose:

> [If your] Lordship give him a pardon … he and them will ever pray that you and yours may ever flourish like the green or like Aarons which budded and brought forth fruit; praying may the blessings of the Almighty God ever attend you and your posterity, may the Sun of Glory shine round your head, may the Gates of plenty honour and happiness ever be opened to you and yours, may no sorrows distress your days … May the Pillow of Peace kiss your cheek and may the pleasures of imagination attend your dreams and when the light of time makes you tired of earthly joys and Curtains of Death closeth the last sleep of human existence, may the Angel of God attend you…[39]

The searing grief of separation progressed through the stages of sentencing, exile and the lingering hope and despair of whether relations would return. John Bennett of Bath, who had sailed on the *Prince of Orange* in 1822 to Van Diemen's Land, had served his seven-year sentence by 1832. His mother, who was described as having 'been very miserable' since her son had left, had been informed in September 1830 that he had received a Free Certificate (introduced in 1810 and issued to convicts on completion of their sentences), but nothing else was heard of him. John, the only child, had it seems been 'unjustly convicted of stealing a waistcoat from a gardener valued at ten-pence.' Two other boys had actually stolen the waistcoat and 'wrote word of this to Lord Sidmouth.' [40]

William Holland's son had been transported with 'Swing' machine-breakers and William was anxious to know whether the men would have to find their way back to England 'in the best manner they can'. The father, clearly desperate to hear some information concerning his son, pleaded that an answer to his enquiries 'will tend to relieve the painful sus-pense under which we are suffering.'[41]

The records of the first three fleets show that female convicts took infants with them. However, for children considered to be beyond the dependence of the mother, the pain of separation must have been heart-breaking. Esther Wallace, who had a 10-year-old daughter, was under sen-tence of transportation in 1842. The local Minister appealed on Esther's behalf stating that, 'a poor unfortunate parishioner of mine ... is anxious to take [her daughter] along with her.'[42]

An unusual letter demonstrated forgiveness towards a convict from his victim. E.W. Hughes, the curate of East Haddon, wrote on behalf of the wife of the convict Benjamin Johnson, who had been sentenced to trans-portation for breaking into Hughes' home and stealing goods. However, Johnson had attempted to reform himself during his time in Australia and it was reported that his 'conduct has been most exemplary'. Hughes, show-ing his Christian sense of forgiveness and support to someone who had demonstrated redemption, spoke in positive terms about Johnson.[43]

LEAVING ENGLAND

The reality of exile and the leaving of their native land, probably for good, were not lost on many of the convicts. Some relatives came to see their loved ones depart on the day the ship set sail. The brother and sister of the prisoner J.G. Godden were permitted on board the *Norwood* to say their farewells in the presence of the surgeon-superintendent and a warden. The sadness of any farewell was rendered acute by the uncertainty as to whether they would ever meet again, and the accounts of such meetings particularly distressing. The convict John Ward, for example, looked on, as his mother was 'ill able to support herself for grief choaked her utter-ance, and shame kept me silent.'[44]

In 1791, the notorious 'Prince of Pickpockets', George Barrington, was allowed visitors who brought him the 'last necessaries' for the voyage. He described in his journal his reflections on what he believed would be his last sight of England as the convict ship *Active* set sail: 'We ran through the Needles. It was delightful weather ... but alas, it brought a fresh pang to the bosom of one who in all probability was bidding it adieu forever.'[45]

Others displayed a sense of defiance and embraced the idea of being sent to Botany Bay. Such robust views were endorsed by the surgeon-superintendent Dr Bromley, who wrote in 1820 that most of his passengers were 'happy to leave' their home country.[46] There was clearly a gap between some perceptions of what was good for the convict and the reality of punishment. Some observers thought convicts were getting a better deal than they deserved by going to a better climate which offered greater opportunities. The reality for the convict was of spending time on a hulk, surviving the long voyage to Australia and, depending on the penal colony, a life of hard labour and harsh discipline. The anxiety of convicts was expressed by Watkin Tench, who served as a marine on the First Fleet and provided a first-hand account of the voyage. As the ship left the Isle of Wight, he recorded, 'I strolled down among the convicts to observe their sentiments at this junction… The pang of being severed, perhaps forever, from their native land could not be wholly suppressed.'[47]

The unlikelihood of return was expressed in the poignancy of convict ballads, such as 'Bound for Botany Bay':

Farewell to olde England forever,
Farewell to my olde pals as well,
Farewell to the well known Old Bailey,
Where I once used to look such a swell.

The ballad goes on to reflect on a loved one left behind and the possibility of redemption which keeps some portion of hope alive:

There is a girl in Manchester,
A girl I know quite well,
And if I ever get set free,
With her I intend to dwell.

Which means, I mean to marry her,
And no more go astray,
I'll shun all evil company,
Bid adieu to Botany Bay.

Many of the convicts who were transported between 1787 and 1868 did not have the support of families to draw on. Lloyd Robson, in his 1965 analysis of convicts, showed that more than half of those transported were widowed or single, many being mainly young, unmarried men.[48] This in itself was seen as problematic by moral commentators of the time. When Thomas Watson offered his personal views on 'improving the present system of transportation' to Lord John Russell in 1840, he justified sending families, where they existed, to Australia in order to reduce the extent of homosexuality (although never mentioning the word) among convicts.

> The most disproportionate transmission of the sexes to our penal settlements whereby the most revolting Crimes and humble propensities have been nurtured, rendering callous to the opinions of their fellow men... To obviate this outrage of both the Laws of God and Man ... I feel that ... if there was a possibility of a convict having his wife and family with him during a certain portion of his sentence would exercise a moral tendency on his mind and conduce largely to the extermination of those vices and immoralities so persistent in the absence of domestic socialism.

Although Watson was using what he saw as a moral argument against the danger of 'vices and immoralities', he also acknowledged the causes that brought many men to the sentence of transportation: 'In favour of this transmission of wives and families of convicts it must be remembered that a large proportion of crimes are committed from the necessities and privations surrounding men's families which are then goaded by despair.' [49]

Watson, despite his perception, was certainly not 'soft' on the convicts or their circumstances. He suggested, for example, that the Falklands ought to be considered as a site for transportation as they offered 'the impossibility of escape'.

MEMENTOES AND MEMORIES

An attempt to sustain memories came in a variety of forms. As a farewell memento some prisoners produced, or had produced for them, love tokens or 'leaden hearts' to provide a lasting reminder for those they were leaving behind. While incarcerated on the hulks, convicts passed time engraving tokens from defaced copper pennies; the king's head and Britannia were sanded off and replaced with a variety of messages, hopes and fears. Engravers were often among the convicts on the hulks, and many were commissioned by other prisoners to produce a token for their loved ones left behind.

Inscriptions on the tokens asked those remaining behind not to forget the convict. They ranged from a simple message, bearing a name and date of transportation, to elaborate poems and, in some cases, drawings of couples holding hands, a convict in chains or ships. Messages such as

'When you see this think of me, forget me not' or 'A love-token from an unfortunate lover' were not uncommon. Some were a little more poetic, reflecting the heightened emotions of the occasion.

The rose soon drapes and dies
The brier fades away
But my fond heart for you I love
Shall never go astray.

May the rose of England never bud, the thistle of Scotland never grow,
The harp of Ireland never play, till I, poor convict, gain my liberty.[50]

Another form of memento that served various purposes was tattoos of convicts. Not as elaborate as modern tattoos, these were not multi-coloured and created from commercial dyes; they relied on materials that were available to convicts, such as lamp-black or soot. They were decorative, as well as a statement of identity and a reminder of previous lives and loves for those entering a new, alien world. Tattoos were less common among female convicts, and few were as extensively tattooed as men. The women who did wear tattoos had a similar pattern to men—sets of initials, for example, which might be taken to be those of loved ones. One convict, Peter Purdue, who travelled on the *Lincelles* in 1862, had his own initials tattooed on his left arm together with those of someone else—'PP MM'. Other convicts had first names or whole names on their arms. On the *Clyde* in 1862, 23-year-old John Croker had 'Ann Fanny' on his left arm, while Rueben Parker, aged 52, wore the names of two women, Ellen Young and Betty Howden. John Shirkey, aged 31, went one better and bore three names—Catherine Rence and Hepzibah Wilson on his left arm and Elizabeth Quite on his right. Frederick White had the inscription 'This is the heart that can feel for another.' Thomas Evans on the *Norwood* in 1862 wore the single name 'Mary' on his arm, and John Bassett, who sailed on the *Racehorse* in 1865, wore Emma Bassett on his right arm, presumably the name of his wife.[51]

An engraved metal coin produced as a memento by convict Thomas Alsop in 1833. The hauntingly simple inscription reads 'Accept this dear Mother from your Unfortunate son.' Such tokens were often the last message from a transported husband, father or child.

Many convicts had tattoos before conviction, but others had them produced while waiting on the hulk, or during the voyage itself. This may have been in part a response to the boredom of long hours aboard ship, suspended

[*84*]

between the sadness of the past and the uncertainty of the future. On arrival in Australia, however, convicts would add more, as if narrating the new events and emotional happenings in their lives. Other keepsakes included locks of hair, which were kept in paper envelopes or cloth pouches. Letters, tokens, tattoos, locks of hair and other reminders and mementoes formed part of a tradition of attempting to keep memories alive, as well as a way of coping with absence and possibly permanent separation from loved ones.

'DECLINES TO EMIGRATE'

The thousands of letters received by the Home Office from wives and parents—sometimes sons and daughters—pleading to be sent to Australia to join their convicted loved ones make for sorrowful reading. Many reveal great longing and desperation, as well as a readiness to abandon communities and country and reconstruct their lives on the other side of the world, often with virtually no knowledge of what to expect.

The families of most convicts had to endure a devastating pain of separation, echoed time and again in letters and records. Such an experience was not unique to those suffering forced transportation, of course: emigration itself was a traumatic experience for families, whether undertaken voluntarily or imposed by economic circumstances. Convicts sentenced to deportation to Australia could, at least initially, cling to the hope that once they had served their time or received their ticket of leave, then their family might be able to join them. For many convicts, this entailed years of waiting and hoping that the desire to be reunited had not diminished, particularly for the family left behind.

Time, however, did not stand still, and people throughout the country, who had lost someone through transportation, had no alternative but to come to terms with a new life, adapting as best they could. As the years went by, circumstances and people altered in the absence of their husbands, fathers or sons. Years later, when asked to go to Australia to be with those who had been convicted, the decision about whether or not to go had to be taken. Many decided against the journey and the happy reunion did not materialize. In registers of applications for passages to the colonies for convict families, hundreds of comments hint at the natural changes that had occurred for many people. The details of these documents also mask what must have been a heartbreaking realization that some families simply could not go to Australia, and others did not choose to attempt it.[52]

It is difficult to estimate what proportion of families was eventually reunited. A G. L. Shaw states that the granting of free passage to the wives and children (boys had to be under 10) of recommended prisoners in the 1830s involved an average of 200 a year. He adds that only about a quarter of male convicts were married, and that some had no wish to see their wives again. Nonetheless, it still satisfied about one-sixth of the prisoners who had families.[53]

The most typical responses on behalf of families include 'declines to emigrate', 'gone to America', 'unable to emigrate', 'cannot raise money' and 'dead'. There are some positive responses marked, such as 'circular offering free passage' or 'to pay half passage'. Behind these brief comments in the register for applications are hundreds of stories. Samuel Sykes from Cheshire sailed as a convict on the *Maitland* in 1840 and was, nine years later, asking for his daughter to join him. The brief reply was 'daughter declines going'. The family of the convict Thomas McDonnell, who sailed on the *Java* in 1833, had, like many others, taken the decision to emigrate to America. The long passage of 18 years meant that the family of George Montgomery 'could not be traced'. Many wives declined to join their husbands in Australia, for a variety of reasons. One such was Mary Raynor, the wife of James, who was transported in 1834 on the *Houghton*, and Mary Jacobs, wife of Isaac, who left in 1836. Both said they did not want to leave their families. Many convicts had whole families who declined to go, such as the wife and six children of the convict John McKoudie, who was transported on the *Norfolk* in 1837.[54]

It was not uncommon for families, who had reconstructed their lives during the long period of separation, to feel unable to travel to an unknown land. Such a discovery must have been devastating for convicts, left to create a new existence and find redemption on the other side of the world. We may not know the reasons why many declined to go to Australia, but some cases carry hints. Edward Murphy sailed on the *Governor Ready* in 1829, but 20 years later his children had grown up and, not surprisingly, established lives of their own. The reason Edward's family offered for not joining him was 'the children having been married and have got families.' James Sharkett also left England in 1829, this time on the *Larkin*. When, 20 years later, he asked for a free passage for his wife Anne, she said that she 'was too old for the voyage'—a response offered by many other wives. Fifteen years and severe economic circumstances saw sad changes in the lives of John Rock's family. John left on the *Java* in 1833, but by 1849, when he was ready to receive his family, his wife was dead and his children were 'too destitute to obtain an outfit.' Among the families who wanted to go but could not afford a full passage, several looked for support from the local parish.[55]

Despite the volume of refusals, there were also many women and children who were ready and able to join their husbands and fathers. Images of reunion after many years of separation make for some happy endings. John Breen was transported on the *Earl Grey* in 1836; 13 years later, his wife Margaret said her daughter had now married and asked permission for the daughter and her husband to go with her. Many wives did accept the invitation to take the long journey. Mary Delany seized the opportunity 'to go to her husband' Michael, who had been separated from her for 14 years; Daniel O'Brien's wife, by contrast, gave her 'consent to [the] children going alone.'

Such decisions must have necessitated a great deal of self-sacrifice as well as a pragmatic acceptance that the economic opportunities were significantly better in Australia. However, the majority of convicts were not like Magwitch in *Great Expectations*, who made his fortune when his master left him a large sum of money and land. This success was the exception and convicts became part of the working class of Australia. It has been noted that 'colonial Australia was no more a working-man's paradise than Victorian Britain.'[56]

Some historians have argued that many convicts had migrated considerable distances within Britain and from Ireland in their pre-transportation lives. Such flexibility may have eased their adjustment when they were transported to Australia—in contrast to younger prisoners, who might not have moved far outside their local town or village. Statistically, over 35 per cent of all convicts sent to New South Wales had already migrated from their country of origin.[57] However, the trauma of transportation was not a one-way experience, even if this was the case. Many families were irrevocably scarred, personally and financially, by the loss of a son, daughter, husband or wife. The theoretical chance of reconciliation, when the convict had served his sentence or received his ticket of leave, was often denied by changed circumstances and the passage of time. Years away from his or her family meant that, for practical and emotional reasons, it was no longer possible for them to be re-united. Such awareness in hindsight does not diminish the intense pain of separation that affected thousands of convicts and their families, and which speaks so powerfully through their letters and appeals.

4

Who Were the Convicts?

IN AUGUST 1854, after a journey of 79 days, the *Ramillies* arrived in Fremantle, Western Australia. It had a cargo of 277 prisoners bound for the Swan River colony, including five murderers and 12 rapists (one of whom had raped his daughter and another of whom had 'raped and carnally abused a girl under 10 years of age'). There were also five prisoners convicted of bestiality, six charged with malicious wounding, one person found guilty of sodomy and 27 convicted of robbery with violence. Star of the show was one William Hamilton, a bricklayer, who had fired a pistol at Queen Victoria.[1] Such details reflect the significant changes that had taken place over 70 years of transportation; the nature of the convicts' crimes (there were no murderers or rapists on the first voyages), the length of the voyage (now averaging 88 days) and the ultimate destination were all different from those of the First Fleet. Transportation was not a static procedure; it evolved and developed over the 'convict years' (1787–1868) in response to changes and influences within the society that sanctioned it. Industrialization, urbanization and concerns over increases in poverty and crime engaged the energies of moral reformers. Imposing social discipline and morality became their concerns and this was reflected in the momentum for legal reform which had been growing since the eighteenth century.

Tracing the crimes of the prisoners is a useful starting point in understanding the people who travelled on the convict ships. The overwhelming majority in the 80-year period were convicted of theft, but details of their crimes, ages, occupations, attitudes, physical condition and general experiences reveal a great deal of diversity. Over 162,000 people were transported between 1787 and 1868, of which about 70 per cent were English, around 25 per cent Irish, roughly five per cent Scottish and one per cent Welsh; others came from parts of the British empire, including Canada, India, Bermuda, the Cape of Good Hope and Mauritius.

The wealth of documents sheds light on many forgotten voices. Home Office records include prison registers, census returns and correspondence relating to convicts and former convicts in the colonies and those transported in various ships. Colonial Office papers contain correspondence relating to the First Fleet, as well as reports on the conditions of convict prisons and hulks in the United Kingdom and the colonies. There is a rich abundance of letters, written by families to the government concerning their convict relatives, among the Privy Council material. The huge amount of Admiralty records includes hundreds of surgeons' logs recording the medical condition of convicts at sea. Prison Commission and Home Office Prison documents offer information on trials at the Central Criminal Court. Through official lists, contemporary reports and some of their individual voices, we can build up an intriguing, if fragmented, picture of those who made the long and arduous voyages.

As the eastern penal colonies came to an end, the west became the principal destination for British criminals. It began its life as a free colony in 1829, but convict labour began to be supplied to assist the economy in 1850; the first 75 male convicts arrived at Fremantle on the *Scindian* on 1 June, and in total around 9,720 convicts were dispatched there, in 43 ships, between 1850 and 1868. The *Scindian* convicts' crimes, occupations and backgrounds were typical of many on convict ships: the vast majority had been convicted of theft, ranging from robbery with violence to horse-stealing, and a small contingent of rape and manslaughter. Convict occupations were generally very varied, but the largest group consisted of labourers and low-skilled groups such as porters, newsboys, drifters, hawkers, gypsies, sweeps and domestic servants. On the *Scindian*, over 30 per cent were labourers, and the trades of the others included blacksmith, carpenter, mason, baker, painter, saddler, tailor, as well as a clerk and three sailors.[2] The average age there was 30 (higher than the general average convict age of 26); the youngest was 17 and the oldest 58. Those transported on the *Scindian* were drawn from all over Britain, but they reflected the prevalence of urban areas in crime statistics. London was a particular focus of crime; it accounted for some 22 per cent of the total number of convicts transported during the 80-year period.

RURAL CONVICTS

Although far outnumbered by convicts from urban areas, there were also prisoners from rural regions. The difference was also often reflected in their crimes: poaching and stealing animals or agricultural produce, for example, were frequently associated with the countryside. Prisoners from rural areas had often fallen foul of the Game Laws, which made the killing and poaching of game a serious offence. Poachers were often heroes rather than criminals in the eyes of the populace, however, especially between 1750 and the 1830s when tensions in the countryside between landowners (and their representatives) and ordinary people ran high. Hostility to the Game Laws of the time was not confined to any one particular class, and there was often widespread public anger when convicted poachers were transported. The emotional charge also found expression in ballads such as 'Van Dieman's [*sic*] Land', which deals with the fate of three poachers. Four of its verses are as follows:

> *Poor Tom Brown from Nottingham, Jack Williams and poor Joe,*
> *They were three daring poachers the country does well know,*
> *At night they were trepann'd by the keepers hid in sand*
> *Who for fourteen years transported us into Van Dieman's Land.*
>
> *Our cottages that we live in are built of clods and clay,*
> *And rotten straw for bedding, and we dare not say nay,*
> *Our cots we did surround with fire, we slumber when we can,*
> *To drive away wolves and tigers, upon Van Dieman's Land.*
>
> *God bless our wives and families, likewise that happy shore,*
> *That isle of great contentment which we shall see no more,*
> *As for our wretched females see them we seldom can,*
> *There's twenty to one woman upon Van Dieman's Land.*
>
> *So all you gallant poachers, give ear unto my song,*
> *It's a bit of good advice, although it is not long,*
> *Throw by your dog, gun and snares, unto you I speak plain,*
> *For if you knew our hardships you'd never poach again.*[3]

['Trepann'd' in this context means trapped.]

Poverty in the countryside, especially by the 1830s, was exacerbated by a combination of economic depression, decline in work such as domestic industry and the effects of new machinery, an inefficient poor law system and the pull of the towns, which impacted adversely on rural populations. Unsurprisingly, those who committed rural crimes were, as in the cities, often the products of poverty and low wages. Their occupations included farm labourers, farmers, thatchers, blacksmiths, ploughmen, dairymaids and shearers.

There was a high level of rural crime among Irish convicts, and those who were transported directly from Ireland made up about one-quarter of all convicts. Many Irish were victims of a defective land system, which meant the peasant became increasingly dependent on the landlords. White Boy Associations had acted as a trade union to protect the Irish peasantry since the eighteenth century, and were predictably viewed by landowners as a 'disobedience to the law'. Many men were transported for so-called White Boy offences, ranging from disturbances and taking illegal oaths to stealing cattle, sheep and horses. In times of hardship and famine, particularly when potato crops failed, it was no wonder that people resorted to stealing food or money. In better times, such as between 1825 and 1830, when the peasants had the means of

A poacher caught in the act, from Knapp and Baldwin's Newgate Calendar *of 1825. Landowners preserving game were supported by a battery of draconian laws, brutal mantraps and spring guns. They conducted a virtual civil war in rural areas with highly skilled poachers, many of whom were transported on conviction.*

Harrow, while poaching, discovered by the Gamekeeper.

paying rents, it was noted that there was a 'great lull' in agrarian crime in the previously 'disturbed' counties of Limerick and Cork.[4]

On the ship *Robert Small*, which arrived in Fremantle in August 1853 with 300 convicts, one-third were convicted of stealing or killing animals (cattle, pigs, sheep, horses) and three of stealing turnips. Another 286 convicts arrived on the *Phoebe Dunbar*, which also sailed from Ireland in 1853. Forty per cent of the prisoners had been committed for offences relating to stealing or killing animals, while other crimes included stealing turf and potatoes and the theft of a plough.[5]

The availability of transportation led to the amount of executions significantly diminishing as the nineteenth century progressed. Numbers of people sent to Australia increased between 1811 and 1830. Peak years were during the 1830s, when over 43,500 men and 7,700 women were transported to Australia. Three-fifths of the total number transported arrived after 1830.

Before 1840, the destination for most was New South Wales, with more serious offenders directed to the notoriously brutal penal colonies of Van Diemen's Land and Norfolk Island. The last shipment of convicts to arrive on Van Diemen's Land was in 1853, and three years later it changed its name to Tasmania.

POLITICAL PRISONERS

After 1815, Britain's economic recession, combined with population increase, unemployment and crime, produced a climate of low wages and popular unrest. Protests occurred in places such as the fens around Ely, Littleport and at Downham Market in 1816, where rioting led to five executions and the transportation of a number of men and women. In total, some 1,200 people were transported from England, Scotland and Wales as a result of social or political activity. The second largest group after the 'Swing' rioters of 1830 were the 102 Chartists, transported in the wake of the three core years of protest in 1839, 1842 and 1848. The Chartists, the largest working class movement in the nineteenth century, demanded a radical re-alignment of political power, including a secret ballot and an extension of the franchise to all males. In 1839, an armed Chartist uprising took place in Newport, resulting in the death of 22 people. The intention was to seize the town and then march on Monmouth to release Henry

Vincent, a leading Chartist speaker, but the plan failed and three leaders were captured. John Frost, Zephaniah Williams and William Jones were found guilty of treason and sedition and sentenced to be hanged, drawn and quartered. Large-scale protests led to their sentence being commuted to transportation for life. The drama was celebrated in ballads, such as the three verses given here (note that the three men were actually sent to Van Diemen's Land, not New South Wales):

Tens of thousands had petitioned,
Overcome with grief and woe,
Every rank in all conditions,
A free pardon us to gain,
We anxiously each hour expected,
That some messenger to see,
To our dismal cells approaching,
With the sound of liberty.

But oh, alas we was mistaken,
All our hopes has proved in vain.
We for ever now are banished,
Never to return again.
A long farewell our wives and children,
Adieu our friends and neighbours dear,
While in slavery we are pining,
Oft we'll think of Monmouthshire.

We will conclude our mournful ditty,
Which fills our aching hearts with pain
Shed for us a tear of pity—
We never shall return again;
And when we've reached our destination,
O'er the seas through storms and gales,
O may you live at home in comfort,
While we lament in New South Wales.

Chorus
Across the seas, Frost, Jones and Williams,
Through tempests and dreadful gales,
We leave our native land behind us,
To end our days in New South Wales.[6]

Several people connected with the Newport rebellion and Birmingham riots were transported. They included Thomas Aston, aged 16, who arrived in Hobart, Van Diemen's Land, on board the *Asia* in August 1840.

Three others—Jeremiah Howell, aged 39, a Birmingham gunsmith, John Jones, a woodturner from Welshpool, and Francis Roberts, a black-smith—all sailed on the *Mandarin* in June 1840. John Ingram, aged 36, charged with 'drilling the mob in the use of firearms', sailed on the *Maitland* in July 1840. Humphrey Lewis, a 29-year-old boot- and shoe-maker, and Abraham Owen, a 45-year-old weaver, both sailed on the *Woodbridge* to Sydney in February 1840.[7]

The Chartist John Campbell was quick to make his views known about the dreadful state of the prisons, when he was arrested in 1842. Campbell, an engineer, was taken from his shop in Holborn and placed in 'a filthy prison in Westminster not fit for a dog to lie down in.' He was then conveyed to Manchester and, after travelling all night, was locked 'in a dirty, filthy cell swarming with bugs.' This only served to harden Campbell's resolve, as he wrote, 'I am your political opponent [and] … I will continue to do my best to destroy your unjust power.'[8] Unlike many of his colleagues who suffered similar prison conditions, Campbell was spared the sentence of transportation. Industrial unrest continued during the 1840s; strikes in the Staffordshire potteries in 1842 led to the trans-portation of 54 people.[9] Among the first political prisoners to be trans-ported to New South Wales were the 'Scottish Martyrs', charged in the 1790s with distributing radical pamphlets and supporting the French Jacobins. Irish political prisoners followed them. Three-quarters of the 1,067 passengers on the nine ships that arrived in New South Wales after the 1798 Irish rebellion were political convicts. The transportation of Irish political prisoners to New South Wales continued to 1840, and the last convict vessel to arrive in Australia in 1868, *Hougoumont*, carried some 40 Fenians on board, who had been charged with treason. Much has been written about the political prisoners and their legacy to political radical-ism or the cause of republicanism, but they were not typical of the vast bulk of convicts transported to Australia, and accounted for less than two per cent of the total.

A CRIMINAL CLASS?

By modern standards, there is no doubt that many convicts—criminals as well as political activists—did not deserve the sentences they were given nor the punishments they received. The surgeon-superintendent Alick Osborne, for example, who sailed on nine convict voyages, said that most

PEACE, LAW, AND ORDER!!!

"For a Nation to be Free 'tis sufficient that she wills it."

A GREAT PUBLIC

MEETING

WILL TAKE PLACE

ON THE SANDS,

ON WHIT TUESDAY, MAY 21ST, AT FOUR O'CLOCK,

For the purpose of adopting such measures as may be deemed expedient under the present circumstances of the country, for securing, as early as possible, the full enjoyment of the principles of the

PEOPLE'S
CHARTER.

DR. J. TAYLOR,

AND SEVERAL OTHER

Delegates from the Convention

OF THE WORKING CLASSES, AND OTHERS, WILL BE PRESENT.

The PEOPLE are requested to assemble on the SANDS

It is particularly requested that no persons come to the meeting Armed with any offensive weapons of any description whatever, so that no advantage may be taken of them by the authorities. Let the people be firm and determined; let their mien be bold and erect, like men engaged in a holy and righteous cause; at the same time watchful and circumspect; nor allow themselves to be goaded into the slightest breach of the peace, so that their Enemies may not have an opportunity of persecuting them, and *retarding the progress of Liberty.*

It is hoped that the MASTER MANUFACTURERS *will see* THE PROPRIETY OF ALLOWING THEIR WORKPEOPLE TO ATTEND *the* MEETING, so that any UNPLEASANT COLLISION BETWEEN THEM may be *avoided.*

Members of the Radical Association are informed that the QUARTERLY MEETING of that body will take place on Monday evening, the 27th of May, at 8 o'clock, in the Theatre, for the purpose of choosing Office Bearers, &c. when a statement of the accounts will be read, and a report of the progress of the cause in Carlisle and neighbourhood. *Admission to all parts of the house One Penny.*

By Order of the Committee of the
CARLISLE RADICAL ASSOCIATION.

HENRY LOWES, PRINTER, ENGLISH-STREET.

convicts on his ships did not deserve the 'punishment inflicted on them.' However, some were indisputably corrupt, and not the innocent victims that romanticized views present. Their contemporaries described convicts as depraved, vicious, wretched, miserable and innately dishonest. Even the infamous pickpocket George Barrington, himself transported in 1791, described his fellow convicts as being 'scarce a degree above the brute creation, intoxicated with liqueur, and shocking to the ears of those passed with blasphemy.' The sight of convicts en masse drew particular opprobrium. In 1838, a report made for the Secretary of State on the character and description of 39 convicts awaiting transportation in the *Castle of York*, described all, except four, as 'idle, drunken, indifferent and of bad character.' All 35 had previous convictions. The other four, the only ones without previous convictions, were by contrast perceived by the authorities to be 'good, hard-working and sober.'

Two of the convicts, aged 15 and 16, had 'travelled from town to town picking pockets and stealing.' It was said that 'they appear to have been much neglected.'[10] They were typical of thousands who had fallen into an impoverished state because of the dire economic conditions they had found themselves in, as well as those who had been abandoned from an early age and were coping by whatever means they could. Some historians have suggested that between one half and two-thirds of convicts were previous offenders; others have argued that most convicts were first offenders found guilty of petty offences, such as work-related crimes—stealing tools or materials from employers—or receiving stolen goods, and were certainly not part of a criminal class.[11] There were also many hardened criminals who preyed on others. As with the four convicts above of 'good and sober character', many reports comment on those who had been led astray and fallen into bad company.

The notice of a Chartist meeting at Carlisle on 21 May 1839 (HO 40/41). The Chartists were the largest working-class political movement of the 19th century, and their public meetings alarmed the authorities. Many Chartists were transported for their activities.

Fears that the convicts constituted a particular class of habitual criminal caused concern among the free settlers. In *The Fatal Shore,* Robert Hughes noted that a colonial judge of the 1850s believed that 'crime descends, as surely as physical and individual temperament.' A more generous view is endorsed in the accounts of several surgeons, who travelled and cared for convicts during the long voyage to

Australia. These officials often showed a genuine sense of compassion towards the prisoners, with some expressing not only pity, but also hopes of redemption for the convict. William Evans sailed on the *Indispensable* in 1809 and settled in Australia, his wife joining him a year later. He worked as an assistant surgeon in Australia and also served as surgeon-superintendent on 10 further voyages between 1816 and 1836. During one of his voyages, on the *Bencoolan* which sailed from Cork to New South Wales in April 1819, Evans commented:

> Voyages such as ours have been characterized as scenes of gambling, immorality and impropriety of every kind, but it affords me pleasure … to state a different character. Not a single pack of cards or any gambling apparatus was to be found since embarkation and the attention to the prayer books and religious and moral tracts coupled with their uniform decency and propriety of demeanour … leads one to hope that they are sensibly affected and contrite for their past misdemeanours and now mean seriously to relieve their injuries.[12]

Thomas Logan, surgeon-superintendent on the *Albion* in 1828, expressed a similar compassion. At the beginning of the voyage he wrote with some optimism:

> I joined the *Albion*, male convict ship, on 9 May 1828 and never having before the dispositions of a prison ship, I examined those of the *Albion* with much interest. They seemed to be judicious and proved that considerable attention had been bestowed in perfecting this melancholy service.

He also noted the reluctance of some prisoners to wash themselves. 'A certain number of convicts keep themselves clean; others would not bother rather than take the trouble … some are deplorably ragged as well as filthy. So soon as the weather permits they shall be brought to their senses!'

As the ship approached Australia, he recorded that the sight of the coast gave the convicts 'the liveliest satisfaction … fun and frolics arise out of the common hilarity.'[13] Logan commented on the games they played in which the victors won the 'Freedom of Australia'. He recognized the psychological benefits of such activity, as prisoners were distracted from the pain of exile and their assorted illnesses. 'The horde of trifling cases, which used to assail us, has disappeared. They seem to have left off getting sick, or have become indifferent about being cured.' Logan had cared for the men throughout the voyage with concern and humanity. He clearly shared their sense of delight as they approached their destination, relishing their 'animated eagerness to behold their future country' and noting that 'everyone's looks betray a lively interest.'

There were convicts who continued their criminal activities in Australia, although these were not typical of the tens of thousands who found new lives. The convict Ikey Solomons (born *c.*1785) was transported for life in 1810, after conviction as a pickpocket. In 1816 the authorities had ordered the release of another prisoner with the same surname, but made a mistake and released Ikey instead. For reasons that are unclear, he gave himself up and, in October 1816, he was granted a free pardon. It is not known whether this was recognition by the authorities of their own mistake or by way of gratitude for the fact that he had given himself up.

Ikey Solomons then became the mainspring of a criminal business based around his family in the metropolis. Its main activity was the receiving of stolen goods, and Solomons was so successful that he earned the nickname 'Prince of Fences'. In 1827, his premises were raided and £20,000 of stolen goods were recovered. Solomons was arrested and charged with receiving, but he escaped from custody. Although the details of his time as a fugitive are few, it seems likely that he first fled from London to the provinces and possibly spent some time in America. It is definitely known that he sailed from Rio de Janiero in July 1828, in the merchantman *Coronet*, and that its destination was Van Diemen's Land. His intention seems to have been to rejoin his family, most of whom now resided in Australia, after his wife Ann had herself been convicted and sentenced to transportation for receiving.

Solomons was a fugitive, so a return to territory under British sovereignty was risky. He arrived in Van Diemen's Land on 6 October 1828, and opened up a number of businesses which soon proved very successful. The Australian authorities were clearly disconcerted by the arrival in their midst of a man of considerable notoriety, and they were uncertain about how, or even whether, to proceed against him. In London, however, the powers-that-be were determined that he should be brought home to stand trial. Solomons fought a clever, drawn-out and determined fight against what was, in effect, his deportation, but ultimately without success. On 25 January 1830, Solomons was placed on board *Prince Regent,* and six months later he found himself back inside Newgate prison. Charged with a total of eight crimes concerned with burglary and receiving, he was found guilty on two counts and then sentenced to 14 years' transportation. On 2 June 1831 he left England for the last time aboard the convict ship *William Glen Anderson*. It arrived in Hobart on 1 November, but during the voyage Solomons informed the ship's master of plans for a possible mutiny, which may account for the fact that he was given relatively privileged work as a convict when he reached his destination. No happy reconciliation with his family took place, however. Ann had become the mistress of an ex-convict who, having done his time, had made good and become a successful, rich and influential businessman.

Solomons died in 1850, alone and virtually unknown. It was reported that his assets amounted to £70—not exactly an inconsiderable sum by the standards of the time, but not a lot to show for the criminal activity he had masterminded so brilliantly in London, or for his subsequent globe-trotting activities and adventures. It is believed that Solomons was the model for Charles Dickens' immortal character Fagin in *Oliver Twist*.[14]

FEMALE CONVICTS

Although less than one-sixth of the convict population were women, they were condemned as particularly abhorrent. Contempt for their morals was reinforced by popular stories of the *Lady Juliana*, part of the First Fleet which sailed in 1790 and attracted the epithet 'the Floating Brothel' on account of the numerous liaisons between its all-female convict cargo and the officers and men. Perceptions of female convicts were created from illustrations, publications and opinions.

> There was rarely a comment on colonial society, scarcely a passage of evidence to the various Select Committees on Transportation, hardly a tract or a diary or a letter home, that missed the chance to describe the degeneracy, incorrigibility and worthlessness of women convicts in Australia.[15]

In an age which revered and required the virtuous purity of womanhood (the theologian, Wetenhall Wilkes, wrote that 'the least slip in a woman's honour is never to be recovered' and Samuel Johnson stressed the importance of women remaining chaste. 'They who forfeit it should not have any possibility of being restored to good character'), the 'wild and abandoned' convict women were viewed with a mixture of fascination and horror. An official reporting to the Molesworth Committee in 1837 claimed that the female convicts were 'with scarcely an exception, drunken and abandoned prostitutes.'

Despite the stereotype of the 'useless whore', however, only one-fifth of the women were known to have practised prostitution before transportation. The majority came from urban centres and included many domestic servants; convictions largely involved larceny and crimes against property, with less than 40 per cent having previous convictions. The women brought useful skills from generally low-paid employment, ranging from servants and housemaids (the most common) to cooks, seamstresses, milliners, silk weavers, chambermaids, bakers, dressmakers, boot-makers, nurses and jewellers.[16] Most were also young; a large percentage were in the 21–25 age range and thus of childbearing age, able to contribute to a future labour force.[17]

The arrival of young female convicts was an issue for those concerned about the fears of propagating a criminal class. This view certainly was reflected by sections of respectable Australians, but their fears did not materialize as the first generations of native-born Australians proved to be among the most law-abiding citizens. John Bigge, a Royal Commissioner who examined the transportation system during the 1820s and who considered convicts as irredeemably evil, tried to explain this away by suggesting that the children of convicts had a natural aversion to sin, a

An illustration of female prisoners in Newgate prison from Knapp and Baldwin's Newgate Calendar *of 1825. (Most would have come from London and Middlesex, 'hotspots' of soaring urban crime.) They appear degenerate and unruly, a point often made by ship's officers, who transported over 26,000 women to Australia.*

reaction to the vices of their parents. Despite the fact that an inherent criminal class was not produced, the stigma continued. The historian Michael Sturma, in 1983, wrote, 'Ultimately the community's reaction to its convict origins proved of more lasting and profound significance than convictism itself.'[18]

LIFE AND DEATH ON THE HULKS

Even before setting sail, the process of imprisonment and sentencing was a destructive, brutalizing experience. Most convicts were confined in hulks, former merchantmen ships converted into notorious dungeons-at-anchor in the waters of southern England. Hulks were established as a 'temporary expedient' by an Act in 1776 (page 26), intended to provide 'more severe and effectual punishment of atrocious and daring offenders', but they became fixtures for the next 80 years. Convicts dwelt for months —sometimes years—in these decrepit and dangerous places of confinement. One of the more extreme examples of a decaying hulk, which lay in Langstone harbour, was described in a letter complaining about the difficult conditions in which chaplains had to work:

> The old *Fortune* hulk is now in so bad a state that it is judged unsafe to use…
> She is nearly falling to pieces and will undoubtedly go to the bottom at the
> first gale of wind that happens unless she is laid on shore upon the beach.[19]

An image of the hulks in Portsmouth Harbour is depicted in a painting by Daniel Turner (page 104). People are visible on the sandbanks in the foreground, and the skyline of Portsmouth, a prosperous naval town, appears in the distance. A sailing ship advances towards the long line of anchored hulks, hunched on the water with the 'look of slum tenements'; other ships appear in the background. Those ships, still active as sea-faring vessels, look lighter against the dark, brooding hulks. Such an atmosphere is well captured in Dickens' portrait of the hulks and the surrounding Medway marshland in *Great Expectations* (1860):

> We saw the black hulk lying out a little way from the mud of the shore, like a
> wicked Noah's ark. Cribbed and barred and moored by massive rusty chains,
> the prison-ship seemed in my young eyes to be ironed like the prisoners.

James Henry Vaux, a notorious pickpocket and thief, described his experience of incarceration on the hulk *Retribution* prior to transportation to New South Wales in 1801:

> There were confined in this floating dungeon nearly 600 men, most of them
> double ironed; and the reader may conceive the horrible effects arising from
> the continual rattling of chains, the filth and vermin naturally produced by
> such a crowd of miserable inhabitants, the oaths and execrations constantly
> heard amongst them… On arriving on board, we were all immediately
> stripped and washed in two large tubs of water, then, after putting on each a
> suit of coarse slop clothing, we were ironed and sent below; our own clothes
> being taken from us … I soon met many of my old Botany Bay acquaintances,
> who were all eager to offer me their friendship and services, that is, with a
> view to rob me of what little I had; for in this place there is no other motive or
> subject for ingenuity. All former friendships are dissolved, and a man here
> will rob his best benefactor, or even messmate, of an article worth one half-
> penny.[20]

Vaux went on to compile a book interpreting the language of the criminal
underworld. The glossary of the book was dedicated to the magistrate,
Thomas Skottowe, whom it sought to assist in understanding the convicts
brought before him. Guards and officers on both the hulks and the convict ships were exposed to the cant language of the criminal underworld
that was used by many of the convicts—a language they took with them to
Australia. Some terms such as 'bolt' for someone who escapes, 'fence',
meaning a receiver of stolen goods, 'jemmy' for a crow-bar, 'lush' for liquor,
'cove' meaning fellow or chap and 'shiroo' for a party or celebration,
remained in use for a long time. Some guards were accustomed to the cant,
but for one officer in the marines, Watkin Tench, the 'flash language' was
unacceptable. As early as the First Fleet, it had made an impact. Tench
thought it an 'unnatural jargon' that needed to be abolished if reform was
to be achieved, believing that the criminal cant was 'more associated with
depravity, and continuance in vice, than is generally supposed.' In fact
Tench's concerns were answered through circumstances. As more and
more free people came to settle in New South Wales, the cant language
naturally diminished because of its associations with its criminal past.
Nor did the emancipated convicts or the children of convicts wish to perpetuate the language.[21]

There were occasions when some convicts awaiting transportation
managed to escape from the hulk. When Thomas Bradbury escaped from
the *Wye* at Woolwich, an advertisement for his recapture appeared in the
Police Gazette in May 1849. Unfortunately for those who captured him, no

Prison Hulks in Portsmouth Harbour *by Daniel Turner, late eighteenth century. The dignity of the mid-distance ship contrasts with the sinister line of dark hulks, moored and decaying on the sand. The Hulks were gloomy inside as well as out, as landward portholes were covered to reduce the possibility of escape by convicts*.

reward was specified. Feeling that their efforts should be rewarded, the Chief Constable of Newark, Thomas Wallerton, wrote to the Secretary of State on behalf of his officers that some payment should be given—after all, Bradbury had already cost nineteen shillings in maintenance. After deliberation on what would constitute an appropriate reward, a reply was dispatched a month later stating that there was no particular set payment for recapture, but that 'under the circumstances I would submit that twenty shillings should be placed in the Chief Constable's hands for the purpose of rewarding the officers engaged in capturing the prisoner to be paid together with the nineteen shillings and charged to the Hulk Establishment.' [22]

EMBARKATION

The journey from hulk or prison to embarkation port was one of public spectacle, as convicts either walked or travelled via carts. In England, the usual places were Portsmouth, Plymouth or the Thames ports of Woolwich and Deptford, while Dublin or Cork provided the points of departure in Ireland. The pickpocket George Barrington noted in his journal that 'it was with unspeakable satisfaction that I received a summons to be ready early next morning for my embarkation.' He said his farewells and assembled with the others at 4.45am to be escorted by the city guards from his prison to Blackfriars Bridge. The early morning walk was witnessed by some spectators, and Barrington remarked on the ignominy of being mingled with felons of all descriptions. Even for the renowned thief, this was a 'punishment more severe than the sentence of my country that I had so much wronged.'[23]

The convicts who arrived at port in the winter or in the rain were a particularly bedraggled and miserable sight. The surgeon-superintendent of the *Roslin Castle* in 1830 described the pitiable condition of the women who had 'travelled of 150 miles on the outside of coaches in very inclement weather.'[24] These women had been heavily ironed during their journey to the ship and subsequently were 'afflicted with chilblains, and one woman had both her feet partially frost-bitten.' Henry Bennett wrote in 1819 of the convicts' journey, observing 'several children, all heavily fettered, ragged and sickly' and women who were 'brought up ironed together on the tops of coaches ... exposed to the inclemency of the weather.' Echoing Barrington's experience of the sense of public shame, Bennett commented that the prisoners had to endure 'the gaze and the taunts and mockeries of the cruel, thus exciting

An illustration of convicts embarking at Chatham in Kent, by Robert Cruikshank-Egan, 1828. More orderly and formal than Rowlandson's depiction, the process has become a spectacle for the wealthy visitors.

... the shame and indignation of all those who feel what punishment ought to be.'[25]

Convicts would arrive at embarkation ports straight from the gaols or hulks, often in varying physical conditions. The *Mount Stewart Elphinstone*, for example, left for Australia on 16 May 1849, carrying 163 convicts. The human cargo included 69 from Pentonville, 33 from Millbank, 24 from Wakefield and 21 from the hulks at Woolwich; others were embarked at Spithead and Portland. Significantly, the surgeon-superintendent commented that the men from the hulks seemed to be in a more robust and healthy state than those culled from the prisons. In another interesting insight, he also mentions that many of the convicts who did not attend the school on board were employed as tailors. A large quantity of clothing material had been sent from Millbank prison for making up into suits during the voyage.[26]

Clothing, unsurprisingly, was standardized. Convicts wore regulation jackets, waistcoats of blue cloth, duck trousers (a durable, closely woven heavy cotton or linen fabric), coarse linen shirts, yarn stockings and woollen caps. Surgeon-superintendent Andrew Henderson, serving on the *Aurora*, reported in 1835 that convicts had been picked up from the hulks *Justitia* and *Ganymede* dressed in duck overalls and some in duck trousers. Other convicts wearing cloth knee breeches were taken from the *Fortitude* at Chatham. Henderson complained about the clothes:

> After so many years experience in transporting convicts ... has there not been sufficient [evidence] since to make up our minds in what misfortune convicts ought to be dressed... In the year 1832, I recommended cloth trousers and have not seen a single good reason since to change my mind.[27]

The clothes soon wore out, and convicts were outfitted again by the time they reached Australia. Women were also issued with a regulation dress, although it proved equally inadequate: women's clothing on the First Fleet fell to pieces within weeks of the voyage. By the 1820s, women were outfitted before leaving the prisons or were allowed to take clothing they possessed with them. When they disembarked in Australia, they received a brown serge jacket and petticoat, two linen shifts, a pair of worsted stockings, a linen cap, neck handkerchief and a pair of shoes. The reformer Elizabeth Fry raised public awareness of female convicts' plight and, by the 1840s, parcels were given to women before they left—these included a hessian apron, cotton cap, white jacket and a checked apron.[28]

Convicts boarded the ship in chains. They were then ordered into the hold where battens were fixed for the hammocks which were hung 'seventeen inches apart. Barrington, commenting on his feelings, wrote of 'the want of fresh air' which 'rendered [the] situation truly deplorable.'[29] Conditions in the prison quarters on the ship were cramped, dark, damp and lacking in ventilation. The latter was made much worse during the passage through the tropics when the heat became unbearable. George Fairfowl, the surgeon-superintendent on the *Hive* between 1833 and 1834, allowed the convicts to sleep on the deck in shifts of four hours, 60 men at a time, when the temperature reached 100°F. In storms and heavy seas, the water would sweep through the quarters which kept the bedding constantly wet. In addition to this were the awful, putrid smells of wet and rotting timbers combined with the packed bodies of the prisoners.[30] In such circumstances, the description of those who sailed on the *Lady Penrhyn* as 'never a more abandoned set of wretches collected in one place at any period than are now to be met with in this ship' seems fully justified.

It was not uncommon for the prisoners to have waited months on the hulks before they embarked onto the convict ship. Many were so keen to get away from the hulks that they often concealed details of their medical condition—despite the fact that they were expected to receive a certificate from a doctor before boarding. Andrew Henderson, the surgeon-superintendent of the *Lord William Bentinck* in 1832, refused to accept 23 convicts because of their poor state of health.[31] Surgeons and surgeon-superintendents commented on the poor state of health of some of the convicts and it was left to other prisoners to inform the surgeon about one of their fellow prisoners—often after the convict had died through illness.

Psychological and physical trauma were acknowledged to be a feature of embarkation, irrespective of age or gender. Commenting on the adjustment prisoners had to make in transferring from Pentonville prison to convict ship, surgeon-superintendent John Stephen of the *Sir George Seymour* wrote in 1845:

> The sudden change from seclusion to the bustle and noise of a crowded ship produced a number of cases of convulsion, attended in some instances with nausea and vomiting, in others simulating hysteria and in all being of almost anomalous character. The recumbent position, fresh air, mild stimulants etc were found to be beneficial in all cases and after three days the convulsions disappeared.[32]

'A SEA OF TROUBLES'

The First Fleet was eight months at sea in transporting convicts to New South Wales and stops were made en route at Tenerife, Rio de Janeiro and Cape Town, although only officers and crew were allowed ashore. From 1818, at least half the voyages went direct although, as a result of the bad state of Thames water, later ships often called at Tenerife for fresh water supplies. The voyage usually went via Spain and the Cape, but some surgeons complained that direct voyages increased sickness among convicts and argued that ships should stop at one port en route at least.[33] The first direct voyage had been achieved in 1802, when the *Coromandel* arrived in 121 days. From 1850, the usual destination was Western Australia and the average voyage had been reduced to 88 days.

The ships which carried the convicts were in the main seaworthy. Out of more than 160,000 convicts, only 519 lost their lives because of shipwreck. However, by the mid-1830s, some of the ships were looking rundown, and the growth in emigration to America and Australia saw increased demand for ships between 1835 and the mid-1850s. In order to meet the demand, many of the ships available for convict transportation were those that had been built before 1820. They were still capable of sailing, but conditions on the older vessels were not appropriate for use as convict ships. They often had poor ventilation, and were dark and stench-ridden. The combination of the decrepit state of many of these ships, desertion among the crews and a deteriorating standard of officers provided all the ingredients for shipboard rebellion and a rise in shipping disasters. Joseph Hume, MP for Middlesex and later Kilkenny and Montrose and himself the son of a shipmaster, expressed serious concern over the state of shipping and the incompetence of officers in 1835. Hume wrote to Lord John Russell demanding an inquiry:

> There has been some great neglect on the part of the Government … in the hiring of ships for the carrying of convicts or on the fitness of persons to navigate them, which has led to the loss within a short time, of three ships and 528 convicts. It has been rumoured that the ship last wrecked was a worn-out West Indiaman and that the *George III* was an old ship and the Amphitrite was 21 years of age… The Broker who provides them does not exercise that circumspection, nor the Transport Board take the trouble which they ought to do… I have been requested by many of my constituents to have a public meeting on this subject.[34]

The *Amphitrite* to which Hume refers was the first convict ship to be lost on the passage to Australia. It went ashore, blown by a strong gale against the French coast in 1833, with great loss of life from its cargo of 136 people, including 102 female prisoners and 12 of their children. Tragically, many could have been saved had the owner and master, John Hunter, not rejected the help of a pilot-boat which could have helped the *Amphitrite* ashore; he underestimated the danger facing the ship and feared that the female prisoners might escape once on land. Thousands of people watching from the beach could only look on and listen to the desperate cries of those on board. The rising tide took its toll and the *Amphitrite* was smashed within minutes. The only survivors from the disaster were three seamen who swam to shore.

Another casualty, the *George III*, was within reach of the coast of Van Diemen's Land in 1834, when she hit a rock. On this occasion the lifeboat was launched and managed to rescue some of the luckless people on board. The *George III* carried 308 people, of whom 220 were male convicts. In total, 133 people were drowned, with 127 of them being prisoners incarcerated below deck. Despite their cries to be let out, the guards, according to the

An engraving of the wrecked Amphitrite by Rouargue in France Maritime, 1833. The ship, carrying female convicts bound for New South Wales, ran aground on Boulogne sands and of the 133 on board, all but three were drowned.

remaining convict survivors, fired at those in the prison to deter any thoughts of escaping.

Other ill-fated voyages of transportation included that of the *Hive*, which ran aground in 1835 just off the New South Wales coast, causing the death of the boatswain, and the *Neva*, also in 1835. The *Neva*, which carried 150 female convicts and 55 children, hit a reef during bad weather in Bass Strait, resulting in the loss of 228 people. The *Waterloo* ran ashore in the Cape in 1842 and 103 convicts were drowned.

In 1801, the authorities had decided to send out convict ships regularly twice a year, in May and September. However, the Napoleonic Wars made this impracticable and even after the war the decision to send ships in favourable seasons was not implemented. For the next 20 years, sailing was determined by the concern to empty prisoners from the overcrowded hulks and gaols onto ships, irrespective of the time of year. In 1836, the government announced, rather belatedly, that it had decided against sending ships out in the middle of winter when convicts were more liable to succumb to disease on the voyage, their resistance lowered by the cold.

Discipline was a perennial problem on convict vessels. Prostitution proved difficult to eradicate and a challenge to shipboard authority; liaisons frequently existed between female convicts and the crew, and there were also relationships between male convicts and crew members. In the early voyages it was considered unnecessary to separate men and women. In 1786, Sir Charles Middleton, Comptroller of the Navy, saw no problem as 'it is done continually in all the African cargoes that are carried to the West Indies.'[35] However, the practice of separate convict ships for men and women did become the norm, often arousing problematic expectations among the crew.

Complaints about the conduct of female convicts were reported on a number of voyages. Even on the First Fleet in 1787, some of the prostitution could not be prevented and it was found to be extremely difficult to keep the women and the seamen apart. Similar incidents happened on the *Friendship* in the same year, prompting Lieutenant Ralph Clark to describe the women on board as 'these damned troublesome whores'.[36] On the *Friendship* in 1817, the surgeon-superintendent Peter Cosgreave noted that women on the *Lady Penryhn* proved difficult to control, and reported that prostitution had begun before the ship had left England and had continued throughout the voyage. Many convict women contested authority in a variety of ways, and prostitution was one such method which male crews were only too happy to exploit. It was claimed three years later that prostitution on the *Janus* had prevailed in a great degree and the officers had not made due exertions to prevent it. The temptation to avoid irritating the crew must have been considerable, as they were notoriously difficult; Robert Espie, surgeon-superintendent on the *Lord Sidmouth* in 1823, wrote of his 'great joy at having got rid of so troublesome a crew.'[37]

The voyage of the infamous *Lady Juliana* has been well documented.[38] John Nicol, the steward who wrote a colourful, vague and inaccurate account of the voyage, claimed that 'when we were fairly out at sea every man on board took a wife from among the convicts.'[39] Such activity tainted many other voyages. On the *Brothers* in 1824, the surgeon-superintendent John Hall, described as a 'zealous, meddlesome ... individual', found himself confronting similar problems. He became unpopular and drew the wrath of some of the convicts and crew down on his head when he attempted to suppress prostitution. Hall was assaulted by six women who, he declared, 'conspired to murder me.' This attack, Hall claimed, had been provoked by the chief mate, James Thompson Meach, who had offered the women a bottle of rum to carry out the deed. Hall was a strange character, however; when he sailed as surgeon-superintendent on the *Agamemnon* in 1820, he wrote the whole journal in Latin. It was no surprise that he was subsequently considered to be unsuitable for service in that role.

The stereotyping of female convicts as wild, drunken, sexual commodities might make for colourful reading, but it did not reflect the majority of women who were transported to Australia. Governors, ship's surgeons, magistrates, and other officials kept convict mistresses and fathered children by them, but it is too simple to categorize all convict women—even those who offered resistance and hostility[40]—as unruly, immoral whores. Nevertheless, the acknowledged problems on female convict ships brought recognition of the need for suitably qualified matrons to accompany the prisoners. In 1845, the inspectors of Millbank prison argued for

...a suitable matron to go in each female convict vessel ... to take charge of the materials and see that the arrangements made for giving constant occupation to the prisoners are properly carried out. A matron would be of incalculable service in providing discipline, in supervising the school class and in maintaining a higher moral tone amongst the women generally.

Over a year later, it was recommended that a gratuity of £30 (approx. £2,000 today) be given for every matron accompanying a female convict ship, and that 'she should be paid at the rate of forty pounds (approx. £2,700) in the two months she is employed.'[41]

THE CONVICT CLASSROOMS

The 'school classes' which matrons were requested to organize may seem a surprising feature of convict life. However, a form of rudimentary education was given to prisoners both in the hulks and at sea, and many were to benefit from instruction received during the voyage.[42] Eighteen-year-old convict Thomas Berry, for example, reported that 'I can read a chapter out of the testament and write my own name.' Assessments of literacy levels—the ability to both read and write—among convicts vary, but the largest group was mainly low-skilled labourers and other workmen, supplemented by skilled artisans such as cabinet-makers, plumbers, bricklayers, carpenters and weavers, whose practical knowledge would prove useful in the colonies and who had some level of education. It has been suggested that about half the English male convicts could read and write, but the proportion was lower among the Irish. Scottish convicts, although far fewer in number, were best educated, with 65 per cent able both to read and write. From the Reformation, by law there was to be a school and a schoolmaster in every parish in Scotland, paid for from the local rates, and the children of the poor were to be supported by the local community of ratepayers. Scotland's goal of a basic education for all males was certainly different from the English distrust of the educated masses. Literacy levels for female convicts in England and Ireland were consistently lower than those of males.[43]

Although there are examples of convicted clergy, policemen, surgeons and professional people, they were in a small minority. They included one Stephen Stout, a land agent and surveyor aged 29, who had been sentenced to 14 years at the Old Bailey in April 1856 for the forgery of a Bill of Exchange for £25. Stout, married with one child, sailed on the 756-ton *Lord Raglan* in 1858 to the Swan River colony in Western Australia. (Despite his name, Stout was one of only 25 out of 270 convicts described as 'slight'; the rest were 'stout' or 'middling stout'.[44]) Another convict on that voyage was 42-year-old engraver Edward Chater, from Warwick, who had been sentenced to transportation for life for forging bank notes. They shared the voyage with 60 convicts sentenced for violent crimes—including seven rapists and a murderer. Other less violent crimes included poaching, desertion and various types of theft.

Stout was an educated man, who had been taught at a Sunday and day school in France, and was considered by the ship's surgeon-superintendent to be a good scholar. He put his learning to use in March 1858, when he gave a lecture 'which was well received' to the prisoners, supported by illustrations, on an expected eclipse of the sun. In addition to this lecture, he attempted to enlighten the convicts further by giving another lecture on employment in Australia. Stout remained active and edited a weekly convict newspaper called *Life Boat*. Within a year of arriving in Fremantle, he was given a ticket of leave, indicative of his good behaviour. Whether he ever came back to England is uncertain. If so, he must have returned to Australia, as he died in Perth Hospital aged 57, in 1886.

Surgeon-superintendents' logs for some of the voyages to Western Australia after 1850 document the education and educational progress of the convicts. Records for the *Lord Raglan* show that 98 out of 268 convicts had been partially educated during the voyage. There were nine other prisoners between the ages of 18 and 31 on the *Lord Raglan* who, like Stout, were considered to be 'good scholars', as well as unfortunates who missed out on their schooling sessions, such as Phil McLaughlen, recorded as being 'sick all the time.' On the *Sir George Seymour* in 1845, the surgeon-superintendent John Stephen wrote that 'the men had made pleasing progress, labouring with great diligence to benefit and improve themselves.' A number of the more intelligent convicts were selected and encouraged to give lectures after divine service. The diverse subjects included the advantages of education, the use and abuse of music, English history, the origin of names, astronomy, poetry, architecture and the circulation of the blood. As on the *Lord Raglan*, convicts of the *Sir George Seymour* produced a weekly newspaper which was done, according to Stephen, in a 'very highly, credible manner. In fact, every possible means were used to excite and keep up a healthy, vigorous tone of mind amongst the convicts, and with the most pleasing results.'[45]

An interesting chart from the *Sir George Seymour* illustrates the convicts' achievements in literacy and numeracy. It confirms that they clearly benefited from the basic education.[46]

ON EMBARKATION		ON DEBARKATION	
Reading:		*Reading:*	
Read well	144	Read well	182
——tolerably	51	——tolerably	114
——imperfectly	132	——imperfectly	48
——scarcely at all	18	——scarcely at all	—
		Dead	1
TOTAL	345		345
Writing:		*Writing:*	
Write well	31	Write well	38
——tolerably	41	——tolerably	79
——imperfectly	227	——imperfectly	214
——scarcely at all	28	——scarcely at all	8
——none at all	18	——none at all	5
		Dead	1
TOTAL	345		345
Arithmetic:		*Arithmetic:*	
Can do the higher rules	53	Can do the higher rules	104
——to proportion	33	——to proportion	82
——all the compound rules	10	——all the compound rules	64
——all the simple rules	121	——all the simple rules	64
——to multiplication	8	——to multiplication	18
——to addition	52	——to addition	11
——scarcely none at all	68	——scarcely none at all	1
		Died on passage	1
TOTAL	345		345

The improvements on board are quite striking, and the achievements of some convicts, once they arrived in Australia, are quite remarkable. A prisoner with a particular flair for writing was Henry Savery, author of Australia's first novel, *Quintus Servinton* (*The Bitter Bread of Banishment*) in 1830. This is a loosely autobiographical story of a wayward fifth son, like Savery himself. Born in 1791 in Somerset, Savery arrived in Hobart in 1825, having been sentenced to transportation for forgery. He became the subject of an inquiry following a story in a London newspaper, which claimed that he had gained employment with the *Hobart Gazette*. Official concern was aroused that a man who had been originally sentenced to death should be working 'as editor of the official gazette.' Correspondence took place between London and Hobart, the first letter demanding that Savery 'should be removed from his present position which appears to be worthier than any convict of education have had.' The response from Hobart was cautious, stating that we 'cannot comment on the accuracy of a London newspaper report, but will remove Savery if the story is proven to be correct.' Further questions were asked concerning the granting of a certificate to Savery, allowing him to bring his wife and child to Hobart. Arrangements had subsequently been made to bring Savery's family from England in April 1826 on the *Medway*, but for some unknown reason they were unable to leave and Savery waited in vain. A letter from the Colonial Secretary's Office stated that Savery had made arrangements through an agent 'for their conveyance, and they are now daily expected.' There is no indication that his family ever arrived, however; Savery's wife allegedly had an affair with a magistrate on the boat out and then returned to England.

Savery was released from servitude in 1832, but re-offended, again committing fraud. He died in Port Arthur in 1842 and was buried in an unmarked grave on Dead Island, Van Diemen's Land. The selection and naming of the island as a burial ground is described in a religious pamphlet written by Rev. John Allen Manton and published in 1845. It said that the only indication of graves reserved for convicts were to be mounds of earth on the southern or lower half of the Island.[47]

MOVEMENTS TOWARDS REFORM

Although convicts were denied commemoration in death, attitudes were changing in the nineteenth century. Despite having over 200 capital offences on the statute books, the number of executions did decline after 1815, as transportation increased. Death sentences were often commuted, and a large number of convicts had initially been given the death penalty, then reprieved. This was particularly true regarding crimes of property, and by the mid-nineteenth century murder was held to be the only capital crime. The length of transportation sentences, ranging from seven years to life, also shifted as the century progressed, with 10-year sentences becoming more common after 1840. Across the 'convict years' as a whole, over half of the convicts were given seven-year sentences, about one-quarter were given life and the rest terms of 14 years.

More informed debates were assisted by the keeping of national statistics on crime and punishment, which began in 1805. The need for punishment as a deterrent and retribution was still acknowledged, and transportation was still accepted as the best answer to dealing with crime —certainly before the building of more prisons after 1840. Some continued to believe that transportation was a soft option, however. James Stephen wrote in 1831 of 'the strong opinion in England, especially at the Home Office, that convicts … have too easy a time in the Australian colonies.'[48]

Reformers, on the other hand, campaigned against the system of transportation on grounds of its brutality, as well as its inefficiency and failure to resolve the criminal problem. Changes in public opinion in Britain, partly influenced by the anti-slavery campaign, increasingly saw objections to transportation. The emergence of a police force after 1829, a series of graduated punishments according to the different crimes committed and the building of prisons such as Pentonville and Parkhurst (Millbank had been built in 1816) contributed to its eventual decline. The Select Committee on Transportation in 1837 (the Molesworth Committee) inquired into the 'system of transportation, its efficacy as a punishment, its influence on the moral state of society in the penal colonies, and how far it is susceptible of improvement' and was to contribute to the ending of transportation to New South Wales by 1841. By this time the majority of the colonists and free settlers in New South Wales were opposed to transportation. They resented the stigma associated with the convict system and the use of New South Wales as a remote 'dumping ground' for Britain's undesirable citizens. The colonization of the western shore, however, was only just beginning.

Child Convicts

A POWERFUL IMAGE of the Victorian age is that of the Dickensian street child, the ragged, urban scavenger, almost feral from birth. These savage, un-childlike existences in the cities that sustained an empire are vividly described in some of their own stories, and confirmed by hard facts. Children sailed on the First Fleet, such as 13-year-old Elizabeth Hayward, a clog-maker who had stolen a linen dress and a silk bonnet. A month after arrival in February 1788, she received 30 lashes for insolence. James Grace, who stole some clothing, was 11 at his trial in 1784, and John Hudson, a chimney sweep, was only nine when he was convicted in 1783. The young boy received 50 lashes in 1791 for being out of his hut after 9.00 pm.[1]

Thousands of young criminals went through the courts in the nineteenth century, to be sentenced to varying forms of confinement and punishment. Large numbers were placed on the hulk *Euryalus*, specially designed to accommodate children, during the 1820s and 1830s. Similarly large numbers of young offenders, including many from the *Euryalus*, were also transported to New South Wales—many were sent to the boys' penal colony at Point Puer on Van Diemen's Land. Over 200 were brought in one single journey by the convict ship *Elphinstone* in 1842. The statistics beg the question why these children, aged between 10 and 16, found themselves on the hulks, the convict ships and in a penal colony on Van Diemen's Land.

The growth of child crime largely corresponds to the increasing industrialization and urbanization of nineteenth-century Britain. As towns and cities rapidly expanded, poverty and vagrancy came in their wake. Crime was redefined for this new urban society, and new measures to deal with it introduced, such as the establishment of the Metropolitan Police in 1829. The authorities sought to contain the significant numbers of unemployed or semi-destitute juveniles, some of them homeless, who lived, and sometimes slept, on the streets of Britain's largest cities. Although some children pleaded poverty, it was more usual for children to be in some form of employment. The question of age in relation to punishment had varied from the sixteenth century, but it was not until the nineteenth century that age and criminal responsibility were defined by statute.[2] Even this was not always clear and a close connection was often made between the offender and the number of previous convictions. The majority of offenders in such cases were boys, and they were treated severely. Home Office criminal records for Middlesex, for example, reveal that over 90 per cent of juveniles transported between 1791 and 1849 were male. Young girls who were transported tended to be slightly older than the boys, but they were a source of particular concern as the potential 'progenitors of the future of criminals.'[3] As such, many young female offenders were 'protected' through placements in institutions, such as the Philanthropic Society, the Refuge for the Destitute and the Bridewell House of Correction.

Attempts to control the spiralling increase in young offenders from the early nineteenth century saw a series of new initiatives. One was the 1816 Report of the Committee for Investigating the Alarming Increases of Juvenile Crime in the Metropolis, which sparked off a parliamentary debate about young criminals. The report recognized that the young offender 'becomes the victim of circumstances over which he has no control' and acknowledged that boy criminals were often 'penniless, without friends, character or employment' and were reduced to scraping out a meagre subsistence in light of their 'depredations'. It concluded that the causes of such a descent into crime were 'the improper conduct of parents, want of education, want of suitable employment, violation of the Sabbath and habits of gambling in the public-streets; the severity of the criminal code, defective state of the police and the existing system of prison discipline.'

Some measures to improve the judicial system were introduced. The Juvenile Offenders Act of 1847 made it possible for offenders under the age of 14 (shortly afterwards raised to 16) to be tried summarily before two magistrates; this made the process of trial quicker and removed it from the exposure of the higher courts. A series of Reformatory and Industrial School Acts followed between 1854 and 1857, which replaced prison with juvenile institutions. After the 1816 report's criticism of laws which served to 'punish rather than restrain', attempts to reform children were mainly provided through religious and moral training, basic literacy and training for a trade. These became the mainstay of the provision for young convicts on the transportation voyage and at the penal settlement in Van Diemen's Land. Boys sentenced to transportation were predominantly re-offenders with three, four and sometimes eight or nine previous convictions. Re-offending rates among children were high for a variety of reasons—principally unemployment, poverty and the corrosive effect of 'bad influences'. This point was aptly made by William Cook, a 15-year-old thief awaiting transportation in 1836, who observed that 'I would not trust a thief… If they get a place it would be to run away after a month or so with anything they could get hold of.'[4]

Many boys said that their descent into crime was the consequence of 'bad influences'. Such peer pressure and the role of gangs was noted in the report in 1816 on juvenile delinquency. It observed that a 'system was in action, by which these unfortunate Lads were organized into gangs; that they resorted regularly to houses, where they planned their enterprises, and afterwards divided the produce of their plunder.'[5] In 1836, Edward Langan, aged 14, from Salford, was sentenced to seven years' transportation. He admitted that he had run away from home many times—not from fear, but through being 'led off by other boys who had money.' John Edwards, aged 15, acknowledged that he had run away from home because he was induced to 'do so by other boys.' (His father allegedly punished him for running away by fastening him to the bedpost and flogging him with a rope.) Another young convict, John Sheriton, aged 17, was sentenced to seven years' transportation for housebreaking. He described the boredom of street children's lives, spending his spare time 'walking the streets and in beer shops', and acknowledged the pivotal role of 'accomplices' in drawing children into crime[6]—a world from which it was virtually impossible to escape.

A competitive status existed among the boys, which persisted as part of a gang culture on the hulk and could be intimidating for any new boys.[7] A young convict, called Hickman, said that 'young thieves brag to each other of the amount they have stolen—they never think of punishment when at liberty.' The lure of ill-gotten gains to children without security or hope for the future was immense. As one boy observed, 'I have been three years on the town stealing anything I can lay my hands upon… I generally robbed in company … and also with Robinson who is now on board this Hulk… I never have worked since I began thieving.'[8]

The 1840s witnessed a particularly high degree of criminal activity,

A list of convicts embarked on the Elphinstone *for Van Diemen's Land, 1842* (PC 1/2717). *It includes details of age, literacy, crime of which convicted and general behaviour.*

especially larceny, with housebreaking and pickpocketing becoming the most prevalent. Children were closely associated with this form of crime, typified by Fagan's gang in *Oliver Twist*; the vast majority of juvenile offenders under 16 were convicted of larceny[9]. Many 'ragged children' entered into crime at an early age, and quickly acquired an impressive array of

No.	NAME.	Age.	Crime.	Conv: Where:
3997	Henry Bolam.	15	Steal.ᵈ a piece of velveteen	Worcester.
4020	James Campbell	14	Theft.	Glasgow.
4124	Henry Johnston.	15	Larceny & prev. Conv:	Cent. Cr.ˡ Ct.
4127	Frederick Schweder.	15	Larceny.	Cent. Crˡ Ctˡ
4128	Richard Taylor.	15	Larceny by a Servᵗ	Cent. Crˡ Ctˡ
4166	Thoˢ Garrett	14	Larceny by a Servᵗ	Cent. Crˡ Ctˡ
4167	George Hambley	16	Larceny	C: C: C:
4185	John Killesley.	15	Stealing a Coat.	Kingston on Thames
4191	Job Parkinson	13	Larceny.	Grantham
4217	William Shaw	16	Larceny.	Cent Crˡ Ctˡ
4218	Richard Pinnuck	15	Hᵒ. breakᵍ & Larceny	C: C: Ctˡ
4220	Henry Hope.	14	Larceny	C: C: Ctˡ
4221	Josʰ Mood.	16	Larceny & amt conv:	C: C: Ctˡ
4222	James Jerrome.	13	Larceny.	C: C: Ctˡ
4223	Joseph Williamson	14	Larceny frᵐ person	C: C: Ctˡ
4224	Thomas Harper	13	Larceny & amt. conv.	C: C: Ctˡ
4225	William Jones.	14	Larceny	C: C: Ctˡ
4226	Nathan Hant	15	Steal.ᵈ a Watch & jewels Conv.	Pontefract

previous convictions. Fifteen-year-old Thomas Bennet from Salford had six previous offences, while James Mall (13) from Knutsford had 13 past convictions; he had been in Bridewell on eight occasions. George McDonald (12), whose mother had already been transported, had eight convictions. Between the period 1797 to 1847, the percentage of juveniles—those under 16 years old— transported from Middlesex constituted nearly 14 per cent of the total, compared to 70 per cent within the age range 17–35.[10]

n.	Sentence:	Mar-ried or Single.	Read or Write.	Trade.	Gaoler's Report.	Character on board the Hulk.
1839.	7 yrs	"	R.	"	Convicted & twice Whipp'd a Common thief	Good
1840.	7 "	"	R.	"	Often Convicted. Bad character	In.
1841.	10 "	"	h.	"	Before Convicted	D°
1841	7 "	"	B.	"	2 Mo.d 42 Weeks H.s C.o	Good.
1841	7 "	"	B.	"	Not Known.	D°
1841.	7 "	"	B.	"	D°	D°
1841	7 "	"	B.	"	D°	Indiff.
1841.	7 "	"	h.	"	In prison before.	Good
1841.	7 "	"	h.	"	Bad charact connexnt poor but honest.	D°
1841.	7 "	"	B.	"	3 Months H. C.o	In.
∩∩∩	10 "	"	h.	"	Not Known	Good.
1841.	7 "	"	B.	"	D°	In.
∩∩∩	7 "	"	B.	"	Before Convicted	h.
∩∩∩	7 "	"	B.	"	Not Known.	In.
∩∩∩	10 "	"	B.	"	1 M.o H.s C.o	In.
∩∩∩	7 "	"	B.	"	Before Conv.d H. C.o often.	Bad.
∩∩∩	7 "	"	B.	"	Bridewell 21 days.	Bad.
∩∩∩	7 "	"	N.	"	Character very bad 11 times in prison.	Indif.

THE CHILDREN OF THE HULKS

After 1825, many habitual young criminals awaited transportation on the *Euryalus*, an adapted hulk berthed at Chatham dockyard in Kent. In an earlier incarnation as Nelson's old courier ship, the *Euryalus* had been a 36-gun frigate which had kept watch on the enemy fleet at Cadiz prior to Trafalgar, and then accompanied the fleet into the battle itself. The log of the *Victory* recorded that 'the Ships around us [are] very much crippled, several of our Ships pursuing the Enemy to Leeward, Saw Vice Admiral Collingwood's Flag flying onboard HMS *Euryalus* and some of our Ships taking Possession of the Prizes.' A map drawn by Jonas Toby, the purser on HMS *Euryalus*, shows the position of the British fleet at the battle of Trafalgar at noon on 21 October 1805. The *Euryalus* is positioned to the left of the *Victory*.[11]

By 1815, there were five hulks in total—the *Justitia* moored at Woolwich, *Retribution* at Sheerness, *Portland* at Langstone Harbour near Portsmouth and *Captivity* and *Laurel*, both moored in Portsmouth Harbour. In July 1815, John Henry Capper was appointed to take charge of the prison hulks—a post he would hold for 32 years. For many years, boys between 10 and 16, and some younger, had been imprisoned on the hulks and shared the same cells as adult men. After 1815, the situation was only marginally improved when prisoners were divided into separate cells below decks with a corridor between allowing a warder to patrol. This only reduced the numbers that shared cells, but it still allowed men and boys to share cells. In 1823, Capper was ordered to separate the boys from the adults and in his report of January 1824, he recorded that 320 boys had been confined to the *Bellerophon*; for the next two years it served as a boys' prison. The *Bellerophon*'s distinguished history included action in the battles of the Nile (1798) and Trafalgar (1805) and at the site of Napoleon's surrender in 1815, but its last days were served as an inglorious hulk prison ship.[12]

In 1826, the *Bellerophon* was considered to lack adequate space and was no longer appropriate to confine boys. Subsequently 350 convict boys were transferred to the *Euryalus*. The chaplain assigned to the *Euryalus* was Thomas Price. His expectations cannot have been high, as he was told that the boy convicts' depravity was so great 'that every attempt to moralize them would only terminate in disappointment.'

Price initially expressed concern over their physical welfare which he commented on in his first report for the *Euryalus*. Such observations were not what the Home Office wanted to hear, however, and in response John Capper, who was always happy to please his masters, stated in 1827 that the boys on the *Euryalus* had committed 'outrages on the persons of some of the Officers.' Capper did concede, however, that the ship in which the boys were confined was too small, but he then went on to justify the cramped conditions as 'a measure which is requisite for keeping them in a proper state of discipline.'[13]

Price, undeterred by Capper, persisted in his criticisms by saying that the boys on the *Euryalus* needed to be governed by competent persons. However, he had clearly made too many demands as far as Capper was concerned and was soon to be replaced by Rev. H.J. Dawes. The loss of Price was a blow; he has been described as probably the strongest chaplain to be assigned to the English hulks.[14] His successor was to prove more in keeping with Home Office requirements, a point made by Capper when he praised Dawes in his report to the Home Office in 1828. The compliant Dawes reciprocated Capper's compliments and provided the reports that Capper wanted to see, featuring comments

Boy prisoners attending chapel in the mid-nineteenth century (ZPER 34/8 p.125). Sermons were seen as an important opportunity to inculcate higher moral standards into the captive audience, and were part of the reform programme on the convict vessels.

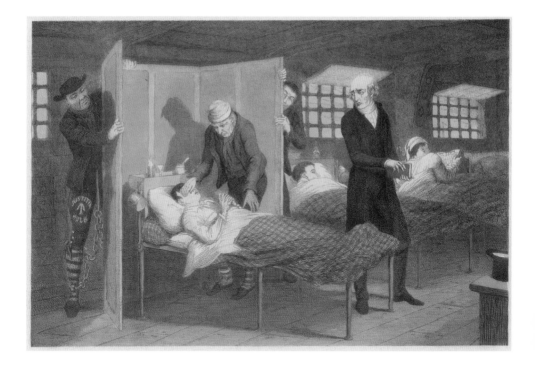

This illustration, attributed to George Cruikshank, shows the death of a boy prisoner on the hulk Justitia. *Weak and sickly boys were particularly vulnerable on the hulks, not only to attacks from older and stronger convicts but also to diseases such as typhus, which flourished there.*

about the excellent discipline on board the *Euryalus*. The discipline was harsh and usually involved a thrashing with the cane.

The boys who found themselves on the *Euryalus* could expect a very strict routine. They rarely, if ever, went ashore. Waking at 5.00 am was followed by washing, inspection of their beds and then morning prayers. Breakfast followed, consisting of a small piece of cheese and brown bread, after which the boys washed parts of the ship before setting to work, such as sewing cut patterns of cloth and making crude jackets and pants for the use of prisoners on all the hulks. Dinner at noon was meagre, usually boiled beef or oatmeal gruel—there was never enough to eat. In the afternoon the boys went on deck for 'air and exercise', but were not allowed to speak to each other. They then returned to work again. Capper reported that about one-third of the boys were excused from work for three hours on weekday afternoons to have academic instruction. Supper was taken around 5.30 pm, followed by evening prayers and then bed. This routine, established on the hulks, would be repeated almost daily on the voyage to Australia.

The 1835 House of Lords Select Committee on Gaols and Prisons was critical of the limited attempts at reform on board the *Euryalus*. One witness who had experienced life on this hulk was to tell the chairman of the committee, the Duke of Richmond, that if a child of his had been sentenced to go to the hulks, 'I would rather see him dead at my feet than see him sent to that place.'[15]

LIFE ON THE STREETS

The experience of many of the boys awaiting transportation was familiar. One, J. Holmes, aged 13, from Stepney, had been sentenced to seven years' transportation. He had four previous convictions and a drunkard father, who punished him for going astray. In his attempts to keep his son at home, the father had stripped his son and tied him to the bedpost. Other boys came to the rescue, however, by bringing the young lad clothes to put on. He then escaped with them and disappeared into the city. The rest of Holmes' story is straight out of Dickens:

> Two of the boys took me to a house in Stepney, kept by a Jew and he agreed to board and house me for 2/6d a week provided I brought and sold to him all I might steal. He has about 13 boys in the house on the same terms and there are four housebreakers living in the same house, they are all grown men... A coat is hung in the kitchen and boys practise how to pick the pockets.[16]

The practice of keeping criminal retainers went far beyond the preserve of this Fagin-like character. One reformer who reported on the problems of juvenile crime in 1822, wrote:

> I have known a Boy of fifteen having a dozen Retainers in his Service, seven or eight years of age (the younger they are the more suitable to their purpose) whom he subsidised and trained to plunder receiving the proceeds of their labour.[17]

The same writer went on to recommend that child criminals should be kept on prison ships, well away from the perils and temptations of the city. Certainly the lures thrown out to younger street children, starving and destitute, were almost impossible to resist. Holmes himself was not optimistic about their chances of 'going straight'. 'They cannot reform if left in London, because they would be enticed away again.'

Alcohol, particularly in cities, played a significant role in the home backgrounds of many of the boys. J. Anderson, aged 15 and recorded as a

George Cruikshank's drawing of street urchins practising their skills in London, from Dickens' novel Oliver Twist. *'Artful Dodgers' they might have been, but many were caught, convicted and transported to Australia. For some, transportation was a chance for a new life.*

'Whitechapel thief', claimed that his mother was a drunkard, and many other children described their parents as being 'heavy drinkers'. In 1837, one 14-year-old boy recalled in a report how he had been begging and thieving for five years, and had been sent to prison on four occasions. He said that his mother, a clog-maker, drank very heavily, especially since his father had run away. While such conditions of poverty and overcrowding existed, transportation could never provide an effective deterrent: the conditions that bred crime were simply not addressed.[18]

Young as many of the boys were, some lied about their age to the authorities, believing that reducing the figure might get them lighter sentences. H. Jones from Bethnal Green was 12, but said that he was 10 'in hopes of exciting compassion at his trial.'[19] Until the 1850s, boys of eight were regularly sent to prison, with the result that they were often 'old lags' by the time they were 12. Not surprisingly, London, a hotbed of adult vice, was a potent breeding ground for thousands of young criminals. About one-third of London's population lived in Stepney, Poplar, Bethnal Green, Bermondsey and Southwark, enduring the oppressive squalor described in Owen Chadwick's *Report on the Sanitary Conditions of the Labouring Classes*, published in 1842. He wrote of drains overflowing into streets, stagnant pools of filth and garbage, cellar dwellings with inches of water and walls oozing untold horrors, mounds of putrefying animal and human wastes, poorly constructed and repeatedly subdivided houses, small spaces housing too many people, poorly ventilated rooms and an overpowering stench everywhere. His description bears a clear similarity to Dickens' portrayal of Jacob's Island in *Oliver Twist*:

> ... rooms so small, so filthy, so confined that the air would seem too tainted even for the dirt and squalor which they shelter; wooden chambers thrusting themselves out above the mud and threatening to fall into it ... every repulsive lineament of poverty, every loathsome indication of filth, rot, and garbage—all these ornament the banks of Folly Ditch.[20]

In such conditions crime, especially theft, was rampant. The police believed that some 20,000 children were being trained in thieving.

By December 1838, Parkhurst prison on the Isle of Wight had opened its doors to 102 boys and within the next few years boys, who would have normally found themselves on the *Euryalus* awaiting transportation, were now being sent to Parkhurst. The first governor was Captain Woolcombe, who ran the establishment very much on military lines in the treatment of the young men in his care. As for the *Euryalus*, its days came to an end in 1843 when it was sentenced to the breaker's yard.

TRANSPORTING CHILD CONVICTS

Children, as shown above, had been transported since the days of the First Fleet. After 1834, many of those serving time on the *Euryalus* left this hulk for one of the ships sailing to Point Puer, a boys' penal colony on Van Diemen's Land. One such ship was the 425-ton *Elphinstone*. This ship sailed from England to Hobart in March 1842 with a cargo of 220 convict boys, aged between 10 and 16, and 10 adults. Under the command of Captain Thomas Franklin, this was the third time that the Bristol-built ship had sailed to Hobart. Dr William Jones, a medical graduate of Glasgow University who eventually made four voyages, was making his first as a surgeon-superintendent in 1826. He was a fair but strict man, who made it clear to crew, officers and convicts what was expected of them on the voyage. After embarking the young convicts at Sheerness, he advised the crew and officers that under no account were they to strike any of the boys and that the wardsmen were to be responsible for any mis-conduct that might occur. However, James was also aware that many of the boys were previous offenders; already experienced in crime, they were likely to present problems. He thus made it clear what they could expect:

> I have to make a return to the Lieutenant Governor on our arrival at Van Diemen's Land of the good and the bad boys so you know what you are all to expect, severe punishment awaits you that behave ill during the voyage and I shall be most rigid in any punishments on board likewise, Bread and Water, solitary confinement is my mode and the cat of Nine Tails.[21]

As part of his discipline, Jones drew up the rules and regulations to be observed. These included complete silence at the ringing of the bell, at which time 'not a whisper' was to be allowed. With an eye to both fairness and the prevention of bullying, he stated that stealing food, gambling and any 'boy accusing another falsely' would receive severe punishment. Rules concerning cleanliness were strictly enforced. Jones stated that 'every boy will be clean in his person and clothing', and any designs on shirking were discouraged by a warning that 'any boy pretending to be ill will be punished.'

A plan of the west coast of Port Arthur, Van Diemen's Land, 1846 (MPG 1/710) Surrounded by water and a large shark population, prisoners were virtually sealed off from the rest of the world. Point Puer, which closed in 1849, was the site of the juvenile penal colony.

The daily routine on the *Elphinstone* followed a similar pattern to that of other voyages. The lashing up of beds and hammocks at 5.30 am was followed at 6.00 by the boys washing

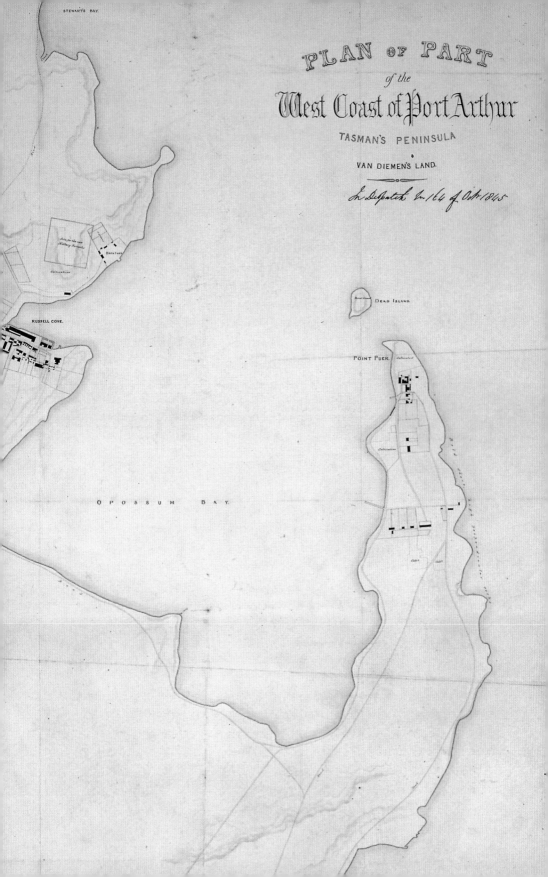

PLAN OF PART

of the

West Coast of Port Arthur

TASMAN'S PENINSULA

VAN DIEMEN'S LAND.

In Despatch No 164 of Oct 1845

STEWART'S BAY.

Site for the new Military Barracks

Barracks

Cultivation

RUSSELL COVE.

DEAD ISLAND.

POINT PUER.   *Cultivation*

Cultivation

O P O S S U M   B A Y.

Cult.   *Cult.*

themselves on the deck. Breakfast was at 8.00, followed by the washing of utensils and the inspection of prisons. At 9.30 prisoners would assemble for prayers, and at 10.00 they had lessons, under the supervision of a religious instructor. Some of the surgeon-superintendents' logs for the later period serve as useful illustrations of how much education the convicts received. Each boy was listed and the state of his literacy (reading and writing) noted; so was progress, highlighting those who benefited from some schooling during the voyage.

Before lunch, the boys on the *Elphinstone* received their ration of lime-juice to prevent scurvy (page 182). Medical inspection was part of a regular routine and the surgeon checked the convicts once a week. Dr Jones reported on serious skin problems among one-quarter of the boys, resulting from inadequate diet and hygiene—clear indications of the impoverished conditions in which the boys had been living before their arrival on the ship. The afternoon included further schooling, and all beds and hammocks were let down at 4.00 pm. Supper was taken at 4.30, followed by prayers and then bed. The boys were given a haircut at least once a week, and on Sundays they had to attend divine service at 10.30 am, when all the prisoners were required to 'assemble in a clean and orderly manner for the worship of Almighty God.'

NATURE OR NURTURE?

Over 90 per cent of the boys on the *Elphinstone* had previous convictions, and many were described as having a 'bad character'. Boys such as 15-year-old Samuel Holmes from Salford, who had been convicted of stealing but had 'never been in prison before', were the exception. More typical is 10-year-old James Brown, convicted four times before. Together with his fellow conspirators Hugh McKinnon (11), William Brown (12), Hugh Fisher (16) and Daniel McKechnie (16), all from Glasgow, he was found guilty of housebreaking and sentenced to seven years' transportation. For William Brown, aged only 12, it was his eighth conviction. Also well experienced in crime were Andrew Kelly (11) from Durham, who had been in prison four times, James Stevens (12) with nine convictions, George McDonald (12) who had eight, James Mullony (12), who had been in custody no fewer than 12 times and James Chorlton, with nine previous convictions for theft.

John Moore (14) had fallen 'into bad company', but more severe judgements were made on others. James Wall from Knutsford and Thomas Dunn from Liverpool, both 13 years of age, had eight previous convictions each; Dunn was described as 'artful' and 'stubborn'.[22] Although only 15, Henry Bolam had been whipped as a 'common thief', while John Marshall (14) had already established himself as a 'Birmingham thief'—he was sentenced to seven years' transportation for stealing some pigeons. Henry McConnoll (13), with four spells in prison behind him, was sentenced for stealing 50 pounds of lead and described as 'bad in every respect'. Yet most of these boys had little hope of achieving much else, given the impoverished conditions in which they found themselves. Henry Turner, a 12-year-old lad from Bristol, was, like so many others, simply trying to survive. Turner, described as 'orderly' on both the hulk and the voyage, was recorded as being 'deserted by his parents' and sentenced to seven years for stealing a pair of shoes.

The voyage took 109 days in all. On 28 July 1842, the *Elphinstone* arrived at Sullivan's Cove in Hobart, renamed from the aboriginal name Niberlooner in 1804. Here the adult convicts and 17 boys left the ship for a different penal colony. The rest of the boys on the *Elphinstone* arrived at Port Arthur nearly two weeks later. We are not sure whether the boys rejoiced at the sight of their new country as the convicts on the *Albion* had done. For some of them, transportation must have held fear and dread, while for others it could be no worse than staying in their own impoverished, criminal environment. The latter view was resolutely expressed before the journey by some of the boys while awaiting transportation on the *Euryalus*: 'Most everyone is glad to be out of the country' and I would rather 'go abroad ... than go back to my bad companions.'[23]

POINT PUER AND ITS LEGACY

Young convicts on the First Fleet had no special treatment, but in later years the authorities experimented with various forms of training. In 1803, apprenticeships were introduced, although the system was not a great success. In 1820, another attempt at training young offenders was tried at Carters Barracks at Sydney. This was wound down by 1835, however, and it seemed as if attempts at reforming juveniles were doomed to failure. Their numbers continued to increase. Between 1842 and 1861,

1. What is your name, age, and the offence for which you are in prison?

John Edwards 15 Years of Age for taking a Drawer containing Money out of a Shop

2. Are you single, married, or a widower? Have you children—how many?

Single

3. What has been your calling, or occupation?

I have been two Years in the employ of a Copper Plate Printer & 6 Months in a Druggist Shop

4. Are your Parents living? If not, what was your age when they or either of them died?

Both living

5. If either Father or Mother be dead, has the survivor married again? If so, how long ago?

Both living

6. Are you illegitimate? or a foundling?

not Illegitimate

7. Where were you brought up? At the house of your Parents or at that of any other relation or friend? or in the workhouse, or in the streets, being left without care and controul?

At the House of my Parents

8. Of what calling were your Parents? Did they, or either of them, continue long in any service?

My Father an Auctioneer and appraizer in business for himself

9. Of what character was your Father? Was he honest, industrious, and sober?

Honest Industrious and Sober

10. Of what character was your Mother? Was she honest, virtuous, industrious, and sober?

My Mother left my Father about two Years ago and lives with another Man

11. Did your Parents regularly attend a place of worship, and require you to accompany them?

My Father regularly attended a Place of Worship and required me to accompany him

12. What care was taken of you by your Parents? Did you ever run away from them? What induced you to do so? Were you punished for doing so; and in what way?

Great care was taken of me by my Parents I have run away from them Induced to do so by other Boys I have been punished for doing so by my Father by fastening me to the Bed Post and flogging me with a Rope

13. Did the occupation of either of your Parents necessarily take them much from home?

My Fathers business took him from home in the day time My Mother never from home

14. Did you attend any school? If so, for how long, and at what description of school; whether Dame School, National School, British and Foreign School, Sunday School, Church School, or Dissenting School?

I went to School for about 10 Years for which Schooling my Father paid for

15. Were you taught to read and write?

Both

nearly 1,500 juvenile offenders from the Isle of Wight's Parkhurst prison were transported to the Australian and New Zealand colonies. The Swan River colony in Western Australia alone received 234 male juvenile convicts in the seven years between 1842 and 1849. In the colony, the boys were pardoned on two conditions—that they were apprenticed to local employers and that they did not return to the country in which they were convicted during the term of their sentence. In 1834, convict boys were sent to a purpose-built British institution for convicted male juveniles at Point Puer on Van Diemen's Land, where it operated until 1849. Some 13,000 boys were transported there before 1850.

Point Puer was the only juvenile penal station outside Britain in the British empire. It sought, in the words of Governor Arthur, to rehabilitate 'little depraved felons'.[24] Not surprisingly, the thoughts of escaping were appealing for some boys, and within weeks of arriving Richard Walton, Thomas Dunn, Sam Gartsich, John Carson and George Dawson were reported as having absconded.

The small peninsula of Point Puer is situated across Carnarvon Bay from the Port Arthur penal station, and remains of the settlement still exist today. Facilities at the settlement consisted of a wooden barracks, which served as dormitory, mess room, chapel and schoolhouse. Adjacent to the barracks stood a large building which housed the workshops. It was here that the boys worked at trades including nail-making, metalwork, cobbling, bookbinding and carpentry. Nearby was a cookhouse, bakehouse, store and sick room.

Over 2,000 boys passed through Point Puer during its 15-year existence. In 1842, when the boys on the *Elphinstone* arrived, the penal settlement achieved its greatest annual intake, admitting some 800 boys. Point Puer had a strict, disciplinarian regime, with corporal punishment as a central feature. Convict boys were given an elementary education which consisted of religious instruction and basic literary skills; training for a trade was available to some of them. They wore mainly self-made, rather uncomfortable clothes, such as tanned sheep-skins, coarse woollen grey caps and boots (without socks). Point Puer eventually closed down in 1849, at a time when transportation was decreasing.

A series of questions and responses for one John Edwards, imprisoned in 1836–8 for stealing money from a shop (HO 73/2). Edwards' answers show the family backgrounds and social conditions that led many boys to early delinquency.

The crimes of the vast majority of its inmates involved petty theft. Thomas Shepherd from Liverpool and Charles Cox from Birmingham, both aged 14, had stolen some cheese, while Michael Mullcairns (15) had preferred bacon. George Nicholls (16) from Bristol, John Gorman (14) and John Gibbons (14) had all stolen shoes, and John Cook (16), a pair of stockings. Robert Fulton from Ayr, aged 12, was the exception; he had received a sentence of 15 years for rape. The previous criminal history of eight per cent of the boys was recorded as 'not known'.[25] One of these was 15-year-old Richard Pinnuck, but we do know details of his background, crime, voyage and arrival. His story is a fascinating example of how a boy convict became caught up in some of the shifts of nineteenth-century history. In later life it also reveals intriguing links with one of his fellow convicts, James Porter, showing the inter-relationships of ex-convict settlers as they sought to create a future in a new, evolving world.

Born in Enfield, near London, to William and Elizabeth, Richard was one of 16 children born into the Pinnuck family between 1823 and 1847. He was tried at the Old Bailey in May 1841 for housebreaking and stealing three shillings and sixpence from a till and sentenced to 10 years' imprisonment. Only 4 feet 10 inches in height, he was freckled, with sandy hair. Like many of his companions on the voyage, Pinnuck had been waiting on the *Euryalus* prior to setting sail.[26]

Pinnuck served 20 months at Point Puer, after which he was released for the first stage of his probation. In 1845, he was given six days' solitary confinement for being absent from his work gang. He gained his ticket of leave in October 1847, five years after arriving on Van Diemen's Land, and less than two years later he was given a conditional pardon. At the age of 23, Pinnuck decided to leave Van Diemen's Land and go to San Francisco on the ship the *John Bull*, although he returned over a year later. Within a month of his return he married Amelia Langley, the daughter of two convicts, David Langley and Phillis Skinner, who had arrived in the 1830s. David and Phillis had married in 1836 in Hobart and Amelia was born a year later. Amelia was 13 when she married Richard Pinnuck.

What happened then to Pinnuck is uncertain. It appears that he left Van Diemen's Land around the time of the birth of his second daughter, Elizabeth. He may have gone in search of gold in Victoria (the southern part of New South Wales, made into a separate colony in August 1851), as so many others did. Certainly he is listed as a 'Gold Digger' on Elizabeth's birth certificate in 1855. Such an occupation is not surprising at the time of the 'Gold Rush', when there was a huge exodus to Victoria in search of gold; in just two years, the State's population grew from 77,000 to 540,000. Thousands of prospectors teemed inland towards rough-and-ready encampments in the bush—a mixture of immigrants, 'old lags' and escapees from Van Diemen's Land. Victoria produced over one-third of the world's gold output in the 1850s, and by early 1852, central Victoria appeared to be one vast, rich gold field. The 'Gold Rush' served to stimulate the region's economy through the decade, and the first railway and telegraph lines were among the responses to this growth. The discovery of gold also accelerated the abolition of convict transportation in eastern Australia, as the demand for ships increased enormously and the whole process ceased to be cost-effective (page 255).

An interesting connection now emerges between Amelia and James Porter, another of the other convict boys who sailed on the *Elphinstone*. Porter, aged 13 when he sailed from England, was at 4 feet 8 inches even shorter than Pinnuck. (The growth spurt of convict boys for this period occurred between the ages of 13 and 15, reaching full maturity at 20. Those born in rural areas tended to be taller than those in cities, particularly in London, but evidence shows that the average height of convicts was not short by British standards.[27]) Porter, with three previous convictions, had been sentenced at Lancaster to seven years' transportation for stealing.[28] At Point Puer he served two years' probation and, like many other boys, did not escape some punishment. He was committed to gaol for 48 hours for being absent without leave, and was also sentenced to hard labour for disturbing the public peace in Hobart. Despite this, his ticket of leave was approved in September 1848 and he eventually left Hobart. Porter, like Pinnuck, was probably attracted by the gold discoveries in Victoria. It is here that he formed a relationship with Amelia, Pinnuck's wife—or widow—although it is likely that they had already met in Hobart. In January 1859, James and Amelia had a child, Adelaide Porter, who lived until 1940. Two more children followed, James in 1863 and Alice in 1869, although both died young—James, aged five, as a result of an amputation, and Alice at barely 13 months old. This period must have been traumatic for Amelia, as James Porter also died in 1868 from the effects of an amputation.

Amelia Pinnuck remarried in 1871, in Victoria, to William Watson from

Liverpool. She was declared on the marriage certificate to have been a widow since July 1861. It may be that Pinnuck was dead or presumed dead, although the death of a Richard Pinnuck was recorded at Heidelburg Hospital, Victoria, in 1894. It may have been another Richard Pinnuck, although this would be a strange coincidence given that the parents on the death certificate are named as William and Elizabeth Pinnuck. If this was 'our' Richard Pinnuck, he actually outlived Amelia by four years as she died in April 1890—possibly making Amelia bigamous. Pinnuck's life was certainly eventful, and he participated in some of the key historical moments in the nineteenth century.

Those who appeared before courts and were then imprisoned were generally better documented than most working-class people of the period. An abundance of records exist that give the names of convicts who were transported in ships. They also show the date of their convictions and sailings, ages, length of sentences and the colonies to which they were sent. Records also tell us where convicts settled in Australia. They reveal details of pardons and general musters, of the land and cattle acquired by many former convicts, as well as details from the voyages provided by sur-geon-superintendents.[29] Such records are the more direct sources, but many others exist which give further information.

The varied sources offer historians and genealogists a rich seam for reconstructing lives. There are inevitably many lacunae and unanswered questions; when Pinnuck and Porter became free agents, their lives become less visible and we can only speculate about the intriguing gaps. Yet it is worth emphasizing that those transported were not simply hopeless vic-tims. The tens of thousands of people who were sent to Australia began new lives and created fascinating stories. In the cases of Richard Pinnuck and James Porter, their voyages on the *Elphinstone* and all that followed left, as with so many others, a long and enduring legacy. Historical events cast long shadows; political decisions really do change the world. The direct descendants of Richard Pinnuck, the sandy-haired teenager from Enfield, continued to thrive, and still live today in Western Australia.

CHAPTER

6

Keeping Order

AT 5 FEET 10 INCHES tall, 33-year-old William Wilson was among the tallest of the convicts on the *Clyde*, which sailed from Portland in England to Fremantle, Western Australia, in 1863. Described as very stout, with a scar on his face and the tattoo of an anchor on his hand, the ex-master mariner from Liverpool had been sentenced to 20 years for manslaughter. During the voyage Wilson was insolent to the religious instructor, refused to see the surgeon-superintendent and was accompanied by guards armed with revolvers into the prison. He was placed in irons inside the ship's 'black box', and put on bread and water. The box was used specifically for confining disorderly prisoners, but it was so small that only one person could fit into it. Surgeon-superintendents commented on the oppressive conditions in the box during the hot and humid weather in the tropics, where prisoners could endure no more than four hours in it. The cold weather on leaving England could also render it extremely uncomfortable. On the *Lord Raglan* in 1858, the surgeon-superintendent recorded that one John Anderson was 'sent on deck and confined in the box, but in consequence of the coldness of the evening, he was placed in leg irons and sent below.'[1]

Thomas Tomlinson, aged 29 and from Manchester, had been sentenced to seven years' transportation for larceny; he also sailed on the *Clyde*. Tomlinson's insolence took the form of refusing to go to bed and complaining of cold and hunger. The surgeon-superintendent William Crawford reported that 'this man has had extra rations of barley and tea in consequence of having lost some of his teeth. He is in my opinion a ruffian and a prisoner who would endeavour to get up great disaffection on the ship.' For his misconduct, the red-headed Tomlinson was placed in irons and put in the black box for three days; he was allowed only one hour of exercise per day. Another candidate for the box was 20-year-old Timothy Jones, who called the duty warden a 'sodom'. While he was being placed in the irons Jones threatened the officer, saying he would 'do for him when he got out.' He was also gagged and handcuffed as a result of his behaviour.[2]

Such incidents were not uncommon. Rather, they were typical of the many punishments inflicted during a voyage for misdemeanours such as insolence to authority and petty stealing. There were also more serious as well as unusual offences. These carried different punishments, which varied from whipping, solitary confinement, shaving of convict heads (a punishment reserved mainly for female convicts), being placed in irons in the black box for a number of days, and being put on bread and water. In 1832, John Clifton died of exhaustion after being ordered to walk with a bed on his back for two hours—a punishment for expressing his wish that the ship, the *John*, would catch fire.[3] For prisoners involved in attempted mutiny, execution was the most serious penalty, although many received a severe flogging.

A list of offences, all of which carried punishments, was entered in the log and placed on the wall in the prison deck.[4] These included gambling, stealing, being on deck without permission and absence from musters, prayers, school or inspection. Fighting, the use of bad language, disobedience and insolence towards wardens and petty officers was a hazard that the crew regularly faced. The need for cleanliness was particularly stressed

Convicts were immersed in a brine bath after a flogging to prevent infection. They received a rough and ready scrubbing with salt water by a fellow prisoner, as shown in this illustration from The Martyrs of Tolpuddle, *1934.*

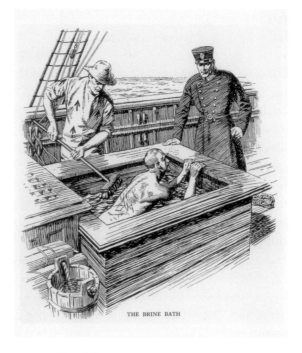

THE BRINE BATH

and punishment could be expected for being unclean, washing clothes on the person, making a mess aboard the decks and towing clothes overboard—this was a common offence as prisoners sought to dry out their clothes. Not surprisingly, the fear of fire on wooden ships was acute, with correspondingly strict rules concerning striking a light in prison, smoking and giving false alarms of a fire.

RULES AND REGULATIONS

The code of conduct to be observed by each prisoner was drafted by the appointed surgeon-superintendent of each ship. These followed a common pattern, with a few minor variations to accommodate particular circumstances. William Crawford, for example, was surgeon-superintendent of the *Vineira*, which left England in September 1865.[5] He drew up a list of 15 key points for convicts and crew to observe. Respectful and appropriate behaviour to officers was required, as was becoming conduct during services and morning prayers. Cursing was forbidden at all times, as was shouting, selling or exchanging items or clothes. Prisoners were not allowed to hold conversation with the guard or ship's company, or to talk to them through the bars below. Severe punishment was threatened for any prisoner found with cutting, sawing or boiling instruments.

A structure of 'mess captains' was often imposed, whereby some of the convicts were authorized to monitor others. These 'middle managers' were responsible for good order and cleanliness in their messes, and for ensuring individual convicts washed and changed their clothes regularly. They were expected to ration out the food and 'tally their pieces of meat and deliver them to the cooks.' Bedding, depending on the weather, was taken on deck every morning and then neatly rolled up by 6 am. Each 'mess captain' was expected to report any impropriety to the surgeon and 'everything they may witness affecting the discipline of the ship.'

Among the rules Crawford outlined was a reminder of his own obligation to make the men aware of how on-board conduct would influence their future prosperity and happiness. Surgeon-superintendents reported on individual convicts' conduct to the governor of the colony on arrival, and miscreants were severely punished.

A system of informers was encouraged and Crawford was typical of many other officers in seeking out or encouraging them. Evidence from

This delightfully legible journal entry outlines the daily routine aboard the Norwood, *bound for Fremantle, Western Australia, in 1867* (MT 32/ 12). *A strict and regular routine was considered important for discipline on all convict ships.*

many surgeon-superintendents' logs show that there was always a supply of people ready to inform in the hopes of some reward. However, such actions always ran the risk of discovery by the other convicts, with ensuing retaliation.

Despite the conditions on the ship, the treatment was less harsh than many convicts experienced on arrival at one of the penal settlements.

Punishment also started for most convicts well before the voyage. After receiving sentence, they were initially subjected to the harsh regime of a prison or a hulk, with an everyday routine regulated and ordered in sometimes brutal fashion. Some convicts, such as John Henderson in 1791 and Donald Turner in 1792, were given additional punishment prior to their transportation; both were sentenced 'to be whipped through Glasgow' and then to be 'transported beyond the seas for 14 years.'[6]

Convicts embarking on their voyage were kept in leg-irons, and they remained shackled for long parts of the journey on early voyages. Ironed to each other, their only exercise consisted of shuffling around the deck. Later voyages relaxed this practice, however, reserving leg-irons for habitual offenders. An enduring punishment existed in their cramped quarters and the consequences of living in such conditions. The combination of darkness, damp, poor ventilation and a stinking atmosphere gave rise to a variety of shipboard diseases (page 173).

The rules of conduct, and the consequences of disobeying them, were communicated to convicts on boarding the ship, and they were left in no doubt of what they could expect if they transgressed. John Hampton, the surgeon-superintendent on the *Sir George Seymour*, noted:

> From the first day of embarkation, persevering and very successful efforts were made to establish order and method amongst the prisoners. To prevent the possibility of mistakes or disputes, the written regulations and daily routine entered in the commencement of my journal were not only hung in conspicuous parts of the prison, but often read and explained to the convicts, and in a short time were so thoroughly understood and acted upon, that there was no confusion whatever on board, every man knowing exactly what he was required to do.[7]

Daily Routine.

5.15 a.m. — Cooks (3) Admitted on deck. _____

5.30 „ „ — Or as soon as daylight to be ready to get up

6.0 „ „ — To commence washing persons — by divisions

7.0 „ „ — Water and biscuit to be issued.

7.30 „ „ — Upper deck Crew to wash decks and Water Closets.

8.0 „ „ — Breakfast _____

8.45 „ — Surgeon Superintendent will see the Sick,

—, —, — Prison deck to be cleaned — one man from each

—, —, — mess in rotation cleaning his own mess, bottom

—, —, — boards up. _____

9.30 „ — Prison deck inspected and then prayers.

10.0 „ — Half on deck — remainder at school.

11.30 „ — Schools to break up. Lime Juice issued.

Noon — Dinner. _____

1.30 p.m. — Wine to be issued, when allowed.

2.30 „ — School for those on deck in the forenoon.

3.45 „ — School to break up, messmen to muster on deck

—, —, — to receive salt meat for next day.

5.0 „ — Supper _____

5.30 „ — Down all beds and hammocks & to be made up

—, —, — for the night & the Surgeon Superin.⁰ will see any sick.

6.0 „ — Or at dusk — all below.

8.0 „ — Evening prayers. _____

9.0 „ — Rounds. _____

Wednesday & Thursday } — Washing days for those on deck in the forenoon.

Saturday — School suspended, Library books changed.

Tuesdays & Saturdays } — all to be shaved. _____

Sundays — Divine Service at 10.30 a.m. & 7.0 p.m.

FROM MISDEMEANOURS TO MUTINIES

Recurring misdemeanours and trivial offences characterized the issue of discipline on convict ships. Their predominance is reflected in the many lists of crimes and punishments produced in the logs, such as that of the *Corona*, which sailed in 1866. Built in Dundee in 1865, this 1,199-ton ship left Portland on 16 October, bound for Fremantle. With a cargo of 304 convicts, this voyage was the 35th out of 37 shipments to Western Australia. Incidents encountered on board during the 67 days of the voyage included 'bad conduct', using foul language, striking a fellow prisoner, gambling, disobeying orders, smoking between decks, destroying towels and drying clothes on the rigging. Theft was common and often involved stealing food from other prisoners or provisions from the ship. The punishments meted out for these offences largely consisted of solitary confinement, which ranged between one and four days, and a diet of bread and water. Serving confinement in hot and humid weather must have been unbearable.

The most serious crime on any ship was mutiny. The actual attempt was rare during the 80-year period of transportation, but threats and rumours of mutiny occurred on many convict ships. Such disquiet often resulted from the combination of overreaction by the crew, boasting by convicts and the intelligence—accurate or exaggerated—offered by informers. Rumours and the talk of rebellion were rife, although such murmuring seldom developed into anything serious. Nonetheless, officers and crew were alert to the danger and there were cases when they overreacted—sometimes with good cause, sometimes with little justification. Officers on many convict ships spoke and wrote of possible uprisings, not surprisingly given the nature of some of the prisoners and their potential to make trouble. Discipline was harsh, and anyone suspected of insurrection was dealt with severely.

On the *Albermarle* in 1791, a group of prisoners attacked the guards and seized their arms. The master, George Bowen, grabbed a blunderbuss and fired at the prisoners, who quickly fled. Two of the mutineers, William Siney and Owen Lyons, were hanged and the other convicts involved were flogged. One prisoner was executed on the *Sugar Cane,* which made the passage from Cork to Port Jackson in 1793. Others were flogged after a prisoner informed the master of a potential uprising. A prisoner told the master of another planned mutiny on the voyage of the *Barnwell,* which sailed from Portsmouth in November 1797. George Bond of the New South Wales Corps was named as a ringleader. He was placed in irons and several of the soldiers and many of the convicts were flogged. On reaching Sydney, Bond was asked to resign his commission although John Cameron, the ship's master, did not support this decision. Cameron clearly felt that Bond should not be allowed to get away with his actions and pressed the governor to bring justice to bear. The consequence of this was that a Vice-Admiralty Court was gathered for the first time in the colony's history. Bond was charged with attempting to use arms and force on the high seas with the intention of causing a mutiny. However, the evidence against Bond proved to be weak and he was acquitted.

During the voyage of the *Marquis Cornwallis* in 1795, both prisoners and guards conspired to take the ship. A month into the voyage, some of the prisoners told the master of the plot, explaining that Sergeant Ellis of the guard was the ringleader. Apparently Ellis had been inciting the guards by assuring them that the convicts were better off than the crew. He and the co-conspirators were arrested and the convicts flogged, while Ellis was confined, placed in irons and thumb-screwed. This was not the end, however, as some of the other prisoners decided to go on the offensive and attack the crew. The officers responded to the volatile situation by opening fire on the convicts, which quickly subdued them. Ironically, maybe intentionally, the only person to die as a result of the indiscriminate shooting was Ellis himself.

Prisoners could expect harsh punishment if they took part in any plot to seize the ship. The *Anne* was three days' sail from Rio de Janeiro in 1801, when the crew acted swiftly to put down an insurrection by overpowering the mutineers. One of the convicts on the *Anne*, Marcus Sheehy, was singled out as a ringleader and was formally executed on the ship. An unsuccessful mutiny on the *Hercules* in 1801 culminated in the deaths of 13 convicts, which made it the bloodiest event on a convict ship.[8]

It was in 1797 that the only successful mutiny during the entire period of transportation to Australia took place. The *Lady Shore* carried 66 female convicts and one male, Major Semple Lisle, who established a reputation for himself not only as a thief, but also by writing an account of the mutiny shortly after.[9] The voyage of the *Lady Shore* was plagued with difficulties even before the ship left England. Warning bells must have rung when a dubious and unreliable bunch of men in the guard arrived on the ship at Portsmouth, under the command of Ensign William Minchin. The men included six from the Savoy military prison, as well as Irish and French deserters, some of whom could not speak English and had been pressed into service.

The master, James Willcocks, was to have a taste of what was to come when some of the soldiers disobeyed orders at Portsmouth, requiring the calling of Lieutenant-Colonel Francis Grose. Grose held an inquiry into the incident before the *Lady Shore* sailed, concluding that the ship would never reach its intended destination. Despite his warning, no action was taken, and within four days of reaching Rio de Janeiro some of the sailors began the mutiny to the cry of 'Vive la Republique!' In the fracas that followed, the sailors attacked some of the officers, bayoneting Willcocks and killing the chief mate. Willcocks, who was badly wounded and saw that the situation was now hopeless, called on his men to give up the ship in order to avoid further bloodshed. The order was met by the cheering of the mutineers, but it proved to be the master's last command as he died three days later.

The enterprising Semple Lisle acted as interpreter between the French-speaking mutineers and the officers. The mutineers agreed that a number of persons would be allowed to leave when the ship reached Rio, including Semple Lisle, although the rebels would retain the unwilling services of the surgeon, carpenter and boatswain. Some days later, on a wet and stormy night, a lifeboat was lowered containing 29 men, women and children, and stocked with provisions. One of those lowered into the longboat was John Black, purser on the *Lady Shore* as well as an excellent navigator. His skills proved a great asset when he directed the lifeboat and managed to reach St Pedro on the coast of Brazil. His father, the Reverend John Black, wrote *A Narrative of the Mutiny on Board the Ship Lady Shore* shortly after the incident.

The downfall of the mutineers on the *Lady Shore* came 12 days later, when they were taken as prisoners of war by the Spanish. The female convicts were distributed as domestic servants to prosperous Spanish women. The *Lady Shore* was seized as a Spanish prize and then dismantled and sold. Semple Lisle left Brazil and made his way to Barbary, eventually giving himself up a year later. He returned to England, where he was sentenced to transportation some years later, although this time he served his sentence in Australia.

They consisted for the most part of men who by repeated acts of misconduct in their Hulks had forfeited every claim to indulgence, had formed a resolution to take whatever Ship they should be put out in, had actually attempted to possess themselves of the Ocean & concerted measures to repeat their attempt — It will be admitted that the desponding naturally arising from disappointments in those repeated mutinies added to a quick transition from a tropical, to a high Southern latitude, is calculated to produce the effects so generally prevailing — But not quite satisfied with [own] opinion on the Subject, I suggested to His Excellency Governor Brisbane the propriety of a search into the circumstances of this condition on board — my attention to & care of their comforts during their passage as well as the development of a cause that

might

The surgeon-superintendent of the Ocean *describes a case of attempted mutiny in his journal in 1823 (ADM 101/57/9). In addition to completing medical returns, these men were expected to document unusual and untoward cases involving disciplinary measures.*

Some masters and surgeon-superintendents on the convict ships clearly became nervous at the prospect of conveying those whom they deemed to be dangerous people on a voyage lasting several weeks. This climate of fear fostered overreaction to perceived threats of mutiny, leading on occasion to bloodshed. Such an event occurred on the *Chapman* in 1817 and the *Ocean* in 1823. Mutiny on the *Chapman* seemed evident from the outset, when the master John Drake became alarmed at the sight of nearly 200 'dangerous' convicts embarking at Cork. His fears were to be fully justified. Attempts to pick locks or break into other decks were common occurrences on the convict ships, and when an informer on the *Chapman* told the master of such an incident, an inspection of the prisoners took place. News of the prisoners attempting to escape and seize the ship caused a nervous crew to panic and to fire indiscriminately into a crowd of convicts. The voyage was rife with rumours of mutiny and harsh reprisals in the form of floggings; extensive sessions in irons were also frequently resorted to. By the time the ship reached Port Jackson in

Sydney, the guards had killed 14 convicts and many others were suffering from wounds and malnutrition.

Six years after the *Chapman*'s ill-starred voyage, an informer on the *Ocean* revealed a plot to seize the ship. The surgeon-superintendent James McTernan, who was making the first of 10 voyages, revealed suspicions from the outset. He described the convicts as men of infamous character who had declared an intention to take the ship:

> They consisted for the most part of men who by repeated acts of misconduct in their Hulks had forfeited every claim to indulgence ... [They] had performed a resolution to take whatsoever ship that should be first at hand and to possess themselves of the *Ocean*.

Many informers, seeking to ingratiate themselves with the officers, were unreliable sources and their evidence could not always be believed. Such was the case on the *Ocean*. However, McTernan remained vigilant and eventually placed those whom he considered to be the five ringleaders in irons. It was not unusual to employ convicts as guards, and McTernan selected 12 'good' convicts to guard the prison at night. He wrote to Governor Brisbane asking that an inquiry be made into the circumstances for the 'future good and satisfaction to me.' Although the threat on the *Ocean* amounted to little more than rumour and skirmish, its officers certainly believed that a serious uprising was likely.[10]

Also in 1823, the convict vessel *Isabella* was believed to be threatened with a 'dangerous mutiny'. However, this proved to be more to do with the vivid exaggerations of the informer than with any real threat. A similar set of events occurred on the *Mangles* in the following year, when suspicions were aroused by convicts whispering in groups, bragging and generally inciting the crew. Despite officers' fears of imminent rebellion, the voyage passed off with little incident. The cases of the *Ocean*, the *Isabella* and the *Mangles* were repeated on many voyages. They reflect the tensions and mutual suspicion between crew and convicts typical of so many convict ships during this period.[11]

Officers were understandably quick to act on information they received regarding plots. In 1825, George Fairfowl, an experienced surgeon-superintendent of nine voyages, reported he had been informed that over 40 prisoners were planning to murder the officers and seize the *Royal Charlotte*. Fairfowl secured the ringleaders in irons and put them on bread and water, which served to diffuse any potential problems and make for a

relatively peaceful passage to Port Jackson. Daniel McNamara, the surgeon-superintendent on the *John Barry* in 1821, handcuffed five men suspected of plotting a rising, but he could not stop a drunken guard
shooting indiscriminately at the prisoners and seriously wounding two of
them. A more serious attempt at mutiny occurred in 1841 on the *Somersetshire*. The ship was en route to Hobart when a plot by both convicts and
some of the guard to take over the ship was disclosed. It was decided to
pull in at Table Bay in the Cape. Here, an enquiry was held, which led to
the death sentence being passed on Private John Agnew and terms of
transportation given to other members of the guard involved.[12] The
Somersetshire continued its voyage to Hobart, while the accused guards
were left to face the judgement and punishment:

> The Court Martial assembled on board for the trial of three soldiers of the
> Guard for mutinous conspiracy… His Excellency Sir George Thomas Napier
> came on board and promulgated the following sentences approved of the
> court that Private John Agnew 99th Regiment be shot and private Walter
> Chisholm and John Kelly be transported as felons for life.[13]

In 1866, on the *Corona*, seven convicts—George Eagan, John Barker,
Hugh McGrisken, Carl Verner, Mark Barnett, Henry Hughes and
Michael Giblin—attempted to cut through the prison deck. Although
their motives were unclear, their efforts proved fruitless, and the men were
caught. Eagan and Barker received 24 lashes and McGrisken 18. Verner,
Barnett, Hughes and Giblin were placed in leg-irons. In fact, prisoners
cutting, or attempting to cut, through the deck of a ship was not uncommon. The reasons could have been the planning of a mutiny, attempting to
escape or simply trying to steal provisions.[14]

William Smith, the surgeon–superintendent on the *Merchantman* in
1864, wrote a long and detailed report concerning several convicts who
had tried to cut through the deck into the hold. Suspicions were aroused
when items went missing and a search was carried out among the prisoners. Rope, candles and a makeshift saw were discovered and cheese, tea
and sugar found among the prisoners' swag, as well as preserves in bottles
and jars. One of the convicts involved was Charles Kemble, a 29-year-old
who had been sentenced to 15 years for larceny. Described as 'cunning
and suspicious', he confessed to cutting through the deck and was even
prepared to take all the blame for what happened. Kemble said that he
could not subsist on the ship's rations, and for good measure he also

Punishment List.

Punishment Awarded	Date	Register	Name	Crime	Punishment Awarded		Date
	1866						1866
1 day Solt.ʳ Conf.ᵗ with Bread & Water	Sept. 8	9311	Eagan George	Cutting through the	24 Lashes	To be placed in Hand and Leg Irons	Nov. 26
3 days d.ᵒ d.ᵒ	" 8	275	Barker John	Prison Deck, beneath	24 Lashes		"
3 days do do	" 10	456	McGuiskin Hugh	their Mess.	18 Lashes		
3 days do do and Irons	" 19	432	Verner Carl	Vide Journal		To be placed in Leg Irons	
7 days Solt. Conf. with Bread & Water	" 28	431	Barnett Mark	.			
1 day do do	" 29	470	Hughes Henry				
Caned on Hand ay Sol. Conf. and Irons	Oct. 2	390	Giblin Michael				
ne night Sol. Conf.	" 3						
One day Sol. Conf.	" 7	411	Lang Thomas	Washing Clothes between decks	One day Solt.ʳ Confin.ᵗ		Nov. 27ᵗʰ
ne night Solit. Conf.	" 8	5090	Flack Charles	Being on deck against rules	One day do do		" 28ᵗʰ
ne night d.ᵒ	" 8	9409	Cunningham Jno	Using foul & threatening language to Capt. of Chatham divisⁿ	Two days do do in Hand & Leg Irons		Dec 5ᵗʰ
Two days d.ᵒ	" 9						
ne day d.ᵒ	" 14	3068	Pitts Richard	Having a file in his possession	Two days Solit. Conf.ᵗ		" 7ᵗʰ
ne day d.ᵒ	" 17	292	Brown William	Having Shoemakers' Tools in his possession	One day do do		" 11ᵗʰ
One day Sol. Conf	" 19	452	McDonald M.	Abusive language to Aplland. Bowring	One day do do		" 16ᵗʰ
Caned on hand	" 20	4442	Thomas John	Towing his clothes out of Port Hole, contrary to orders	One day do do		" 19ᵗʰ
2 days Sol. Conf. and and Leg Irons	" 20						
2 days Solt. Conf.ᵗ	" 23	7790	Dinsdale William	Hanging his clothes on the rigging	One day do do		" 19ᵗʰ
1 day do	Nov. 2						
2 days do	" 3						
1 day do	" 3						
1 day do	" 9						
3 days do Hand & Leg Irons	" 15						
3 days d.ᵒ d.ᵒ d.ᵒ	" "						
3 days Sol. Conf.ᵗ	" 17						
3 days d.ᵒ d.ᵒ Hand & Leg Irons	" 17						

blamed his behaviour on the cruel treatment he had received at Millbank prison. Clearly the idea of gaining access to additional provisions was a motivation for the men's actions, but Kemble also acknowledged that he had designs on escaping. How far he expected to get can only be guessed at, but many convicts on the voyages during the period of transportation did jump overboard—the lucky ones were retrieved later. Despite their denials, the conclusion was reached that the men on the *Merchantman* had attempted to take the ship. They were placed in leg-irons and solitary confinement for a number of days. In his report, Smith stressed the need for greater vigilance in guarding arms, rifles and bayonets to prevent prisoners trying to seize them.

There was never a shortage of convicts prepared to inform on their fellow prisoners for potential mutinous threats or trivial cases of theft. As early as the First Fleet in 1787, a convict informed the master of the *Scarborough* that a mutiny was being planned. His response was to arrest the suspected ringleaders and give each of them 24 lashes. The infamous convict George Barrington, who sailed on the *Active* as part of the Third Fleet in 1791, informed the captain of impending trouble. He wrote:

> I was immediately joined by the captain and the rest of the officers, who, in a few minutes, drove [the mutineers] into the hold, and two of the ringleaders were instantly hung at the yard-arm.[15]

LEFT: *The punishment list of the* Corona *in 1866 shows the variety of crimes and punishments meted out to offending convicts during the voyage* (MT 32/11).

RIGHT: *A portrait of the notorious pickpocket and Irish adventurer George Barrington by Sir William Beechey c.1785. Barrington was sentenced to seven years' transportation in 1790; he later became a superintendent of convicts in New South Wales and is credited with writing* A Voyage to Botany Bay *(1801).*

Barrington, pleased with his success, recorded that the captain 'paid me many handsome compliments ... and assured me that when we arrived at the Cape, he should on part of the owners think it his duty to reward the service ... I had rendered them.'

For the informer who was found out by other convicts, life would be deeply unpleasant, not to say dangerous. Some degree of protection was offered, but this could not always be guaranteed. One informer, 34-year-old Richard Billet from Lincoln, had been sentenced to transportation for life for stealing a mare. In 1815, he was awaiting transportation, but lived in fear of his life. A report on prisoners considered 'unfit to be sent to New South Wales' stated that Billett:

> begs to go on another ship for fear of being injured by his fellow prisoners for having given information so as to prevent an escape whilst in gaol.[16]

THE STRAINS IN THE SYSTEM

It was inevitable that some convicts would go overboard during the long voyage—whether with the intention of escaping, for bathing or by accident. On the *Merchantman* in 1864, Donald Hossack and William Davis dived overboard to bathe, for which they received two days' solitary confinement in irons. Some convicts were induced by the heat to dive in the sea or conversely to bask in the sun. On the *Lord Raglan* in 1858, one convict, James Raitton, 'continually exposed himself to the sun' despite warnings of the consequences to his health. His motives are uncertain: it may have been an attempt to give his weary body some relief from the cramped, squalid conditions, or an overwhelming sense of liberation that defied caution. It may even have been the effects of the sun clouding his judgement. For whatever reason, Raitton unfortunately did not heed the warnings; he subsequently died as a result of exposure and his body was 'committed to the deep'.

An ill-fated escape attempt was made by William Staples in 1844, when the convict ship *Agincourt* disembarked at the Cape of Good Hope for one week. Here Staples was 'believed to have slipped aside after answering his evening muster and to have concealed himself somewhere on deck.' Thinking himself to be safe by nightfall, he attempted to swim to shore—but was later found drowned. Two other convicts, Thomas Ford and John Ryan, both jumped overboard from the *Racehorse* in 1865.

However, Ryan had taken on more than he had bargained for and had to have a life buoy thrown to him.[17] Both men were retrieved and received 14 days on bread and water.

During the voyage, convicts were obliged to live in close confinement for long periods and sexual relations between some of the prisoners were inevitable. Sodomy was a capital offence until 1861, the last execution taking place in 1835. It was also considered a 'monstrous sin against nature' and an unnatural act against God—yet it was pervasive on convict vessels. The prisoner George Lee reported from the hulk *Portland,* in 1803, that the 'horrible crime of sodomy rages so shamefully throughout that the Surgeon and myself have been more than once threatened with assassination for straining to stop it.'[18] One officer wrote that 'sodomy is a regular thing on ships that go on long cruises.'[19] Despite protests from various quarters, homosexuality received little mention in official reports before 1830. Reformers, in their attempts to abolish transportation after 1830, protested loudly that this whole system of punishment depraved the convicts and threatened their moral welfare. Homosexuality was an established part of prison culture, but few prosecutions were brought considering the number of incidents on the voyages or in the penal settlements in Australia.

Benjamin Clarkson, a convict on the *Lord Raglan* in 1858, was removed from his berth to a hammock close to the sentry after he was caught for 'allowing liberties in his berth from older men'. The 27-year-old housebreaker William Thompson embarked on the *Merchantman* in 1864 to serve his 20-year sentence, but was put on shore at Portland to return to prison for committing an 'unnatural offence'. Before he disembarked he received 36 lashes.[20]

More attention has been given to sexual relations between men and women on convict ships than relations between men. Despite the image of sexual licence and 'floating brothels', punishment was meted out on most ships to any member of the crew or officer discovered having a sexual relationship with a female convict. This could reach the highest level. In 1838, the *John Renwick* sailed to New South Wales with 173 women and girls on board. Shortly after its arrival at Sydney, a court of inquiry was instituted to investigate 'the conduct of the master ... regarding alleged intimacy with one of the convicts.' The inquiry stated that Andrew Smith, the surgeon-superintendent on the ship, had reported that 'some women had been troublesome [but] nothing extraordinary happened on the voyage.' Smith was pressed to be a little clearer about the troublesome women, as he had made no report of any 'improper intercourse between any of them and the officers or crew.' Despite Smith's initial reluctance to offer details on this matter, it transpired during the inquiry that a prohibited relationship had developed during the voyage. This was 'between the master Mr John Byron and a female convict named Mary Hartwell, and there was reason to suppose that similar intercourse had occurred between some of the officers of the ship and other female convicts.'[21]

Relations between Smith and Byron had in fact been a problem since the outset of the voyage. The inquiry claimed that Byron had offered Mary Hartwell 'privileged indulgences', such as food. Such favours must have caused resentment in the other convicts, some of whom provided information against Byron and Hartwell to the inquiry. Although the report went through the motions of bringing the issue to light and reprimanding some of those concerned, it concluded that there was conflicting or insufficient evidence to bring any charges. Surgeon-superintendent Smith paid a price for being economical with the truth. Governor George Gibbs stated in a letter to London that:

> Mr Smith performed his duties on board the *John Renwick* zealously and properly, but I cannot certify that he conducted himself satisfactorily in every respect, in as much as he failed to report to me misconduct on the part of the Master and a female Prisoner named Hartwell which were within his knowledge.

This affair had affected the fee due to Smith for his duties. Two years later he was a little more forthcoming with details of what happened between Byron and Hartwell on the *John Renwick*. He wrote a letter to the Colonial Secretary, the Marquess of Normanby, describing how he found Mary Hartwell in Byron's cabin, '...secreted immediately after the other prisoners were locked away for the night ... I found the prisoner Hartwell secreted in a locker underneath his bed and [became] satisfied that criminal intercourse had taken place.'

Smith's motives for divulging this become a little clearer in the final paragraph of the letter: 'Having a wife and family totally dependent on my exertions ... I trust your Lordship will be pleased to direct that I may receive the remaining £45 of any withheld gratuity.'[22]

Keeping order on the convict ships applied not only to the prisoners—

on many voyages the crew proved more problematic. The examples of the *Marquis Cornwallis*, *Lady Shore* and the *Somersetshire* showed how both crew and prisoners were willing on occasions to conspire in mutiny. However, there were also many other instances where officers and guards initiated the trouble. Their offences, like those of the convicts, were often trivial, but they were a frequent occurrence on many voyages. Those on the *Merchantman*, which arrived in Fremantle in 1863, were typical examples of crew indiscipline. Drunkenness, insolence and leaving their post whilst on duty were among the most regular. Donald McAlister, William Dunlop and John Roberts were punished for being 'irregular on guard' and leaving their post. Enoch Pinder and Patrick Meehan were disciplined for using 'filthy and abusive language'; Clarke McCulloch was given two days in the cell for being drunk while on duty and William McDonald's liquor allowance was stopped for seven days for being drunk. McDonald was travelling with his wife and three children, as were John Roberts and Patrick Bagley; the last, who was drunk, using abusive language and fighting, had had the misfortune to lose his two-year-old child during the voyage.

Another convict, James Slavin, also experienced the death of his child, this time an infant of 12 months. When Slavin resorted to threatening language, he was put in solitary confinement for two days and had his liquor allowance stopped. John Hamilton, who travelled with his wife Tabitha and their two children, proved to be a regular offender. On two occasions he was insolent and used threatening language to a major, but he was also disciplined for ringing the ship's bell when not on duty. His punishment, as with most, was the stopping of liquor. There were also instances of intervention with disciplinary action in cases of domestic problems. William Atkinson, aged 42, was given seven days' stoppage of his liquor allowance for beating his wife.

Reports of arguments between officers and crew provided regular comments in reports. On the *Norwood* in 1867, the surgeon-superintendent W.M. Saunders wrote of 'frequent squabbles during the voyage between the wardens and the Sergeant Major on account of the differences in their provisions... Also convict guard Michael Fitzpatrick reported for theft which he denied.' Fitzpatrick went on to threaten the Captain by saying 'I will have you punished when we arrive at Fremantle.' Fitzpatrick was described as a 'troublesome character throughout the voyage' and, not surprisingly, he was locked up for seven days. The *Norwood* had been plagued with problems with the crew from the outset. They stole provisions, such as wine, pork and biscuits; they drank and were insubordinate. The surgeon-superintendent resorted to direct action and wrote:

> As the crew cannot be trusted I deem it necessary to have a sentry over the hatch at night and have given directions to the Sergeant Major to be placed there between 8.00 pm and 6.00 pm for the remainder of the voyage.[23]

Rebellious tendencies in the crew who manned the convict ships were in part understandable, given the appalling living and working conditions they had to endure. The problems became particularly acute during the 1820s and 1830s, compounded by the poor state of some ships and the poor quality of the officers.

THE ROAD TO REDEMPTION

It was hoped that the past crimes of the convicts, as well as any committed on the voyage, might be redeemed by moral instruction. The importance of sending chaplains on the convict ships to Australia was recognized by the authorities from the beginning:

> As for the increase in the number of convicts sent to New South Wales ... one person will not be able to attend in a proper manner to the Performance of the religious duties of the colony. His majesty has judged it expedient that an additional clergyman should proceed hither.[24]

Implicit in the disciplinary code was the attempt to instil a sense of morality in the convict. Improved minds, it was predicted, would provide the first steps in becoming a reformed person. Such redemption would entail a long road to conversion, which could only be travelled by a combination of reflection and retribution. Andrew Miller, the surgeon-superintendent on the *Anson* in 1844, wrote:

> The regulations for discipline were scrupulously carried out, accompanied by admonitions based upon the principles of religion and morality that the minds of the convicts might be directed to better things.[25]

Colin Browning had been surgeon-superintendent on eight voyages between 1831 and 1849. When he addressed the convicts, he spoke of their 'apostasy and depravity; their ignorance and utter helplessness'. He flattered himself that, thanks to his administration, the prisoners were in abiding and immediate contact with the gospel of Christ. He warned them against the company of 'wicked men' and the 'importance of the observation of the Seventh Commandment ... on the awful sanctions, the duties, obligations and privileges of the marriage covenant.' Browning's parting speech before debarkation was to ask the men, 'Have you felt the enormity of your guilt? Have you been humbled to the very dust under a just apprehension of your crimes?'[26] One can only guess at how this admonition was received by many of the convicts who had been found guilty of little more than minor offences.

Sundays in particular were dedicated to prayers and preaching in order that the convicts would be instructed in '...what they owed to their maker and to society that by a reformation of their conduct they might show they were fit to be restored to freedom when the laws of an official legislature admitted it.'

For the convict, firm lessons in religious morality backed up by harsh punishments were the roadmaps to redemption. Surgeon-superintendent Andrew Miller acknowledged that 'the measures for discipline were directed by the able views of Captain Coghlan, and armed with his authority, I was enabled to perform an arduous service.'[27] Such were the many and varied burdens that fell upon those such as Miller. Interestingly, Miller commented on the use of hammocks, which were supplied instead of beds after 1840. He considered them more appropriate for both 'health and morality.'

A more optimistic and enlightened attitude came from the surgeon-superintendent of the *Sir George Seymour*, who wrote that 'Sunday schools were evidently valuable in consequence of the attendance being altogether voluntary. 198 of the [345] prisoners attended these schools with great diligence, and, there is every reason to believe, much profit.'

Such was his faith in the reforming tendencies of the convicts that he noted how 'prison doors were opened every morning at daylight, never again locked until sunset; and the whole 345 men, except at school hours, allowed to be on deck at the same time, although the guard consisted of 30 soldiers only.'[28]

The success of *Sir George Seymour*'s voyage was reflected in the only punishment inflicted—putting five men in solitary confinement for short periods. Nonetheless, for some prisoners the exposure to moral guidance continued when they arrived at their various destinations. Convicts who worked on road gangs in Van Diemen's Land were provided with the following books as sources of ever-present inspiration: [29]

Christian Remembrance
Considerations for Young Men
Missionary Records
Christ Set Forth
Repentance Explained
Spiritual Perfection
Adam's Private Thoughts
Fulfilling of the Scriptures
Religion and the Eternal Life
Godwin's Christ Set Forth
Fuller's Gospel Worthy
Essays to do Good
Sincere Convert
Weak Grace Victorious
Precious Remedies
Scripture Portions for the Afflicted
Jesus Showing Mercy
A Treatise on Afflictions
Persuasions of Early Piety

Ships carried copies of the New Testament, while books of Common Prayer and two Psalters were to be provided for every prisoner and a Bible for every 16 convicts. An essential requirement was that 'the minds of the people on board convict ships [are] as constantly and usefully employed as possible.' Crucial to this was a church service which had to provide 'a Sermon, or some well selected parts from the religious tracts which are supplied to you.' Instructions made it clear that it was important to 'promote a religious and moral disposition in the Convicts.'[30] Many convicts went through the motions of a religious service and received religious and moral instruction on the voyage. There were also those who enjoyed communal singing whatever the reason, and it did provide an opportunity for them to express themselves.

However, the chaplain often became the subject of abuse. Thomas Buckley from Salford, aged 24 and a convict on the *Clyde* in 1863, was put on bread and water and placed in irons for being 'impertinent to the religious instructor.' Thomas Tomlinson, travelling on the same ship, 'boasted that he had no reliance on a God and [denied] any responsibility or allegiance to a Divine being.'[31]

There were those in authority who remained optimistic that reform would lead to self-discipline and eventual redemption. Chaplain Henry Donne wrote:

> I have great pleasure in telling your Lordship that on Sunday I administered the Sacrament to twelve convicts on board the *Captivity* and last Sunday to fifteen on board the *Portland*. Their behaviour was devout, solemn and impressive—and indeed the conduct of all the convicts during the divine service exceeds my most sanguine expectations. I believe many of them will be brought to habits of reflection.[32]

It might have been that Donne's optimism was a response to a recent augmentation in his salary, which he acknowledged with gushing thanks in his letter, accompanied by promises to work hard. Thomas Reid, a surgeon-superintendent on the *Morley* in 1820 and a prison reformer who was influenced by Elizabeth Fry, also believed in the possibility of reform through moral improvement. His evidence was based on the convicts on his first ship, the *Neptune*, which had sailed in 1818. Out of 170 convicts, only nine had re-offended in nearly three years.[33]

Religious instruction, however, did not prevent prisoners from gambling for any items of value, particularly for tobacco. Gambling was in fact regarded as a 'prevailing vice', and the surgeon-superintendent Peter Cunningham, travelling on the *Grenada* in 1821, wrote that it required great exertion to stamp it out:

> Dice, cards, pitch and toss, and various other speculations soon becoming general, unless checked... I have known a country simpleton go three whole days without food, having gambled away all his rations... Until gambling is stopped, thieving will always be carried on.[34]

Friction could also reach beyond convict and religious instructor; on occasions there was tension between surgeon-superintendent and chaplain. In 1819, a chaplain on the *Hibernia* complained that he had been obstructed by the surgeon-superintendent, Charles Carter, from visiting sick prisoners. Carter had also mocked the chaplain's plans for the moral improvement of the convicts and took no action when 'Bibles and Prayer Books were destroyed to make Cards' for gambling.[35]

Training in religious discipline on the voyage would be continued for many during their period of penal settlement. Being in church, irrespective of whether they wanted to be there or not, kept them from mischief. On the other hand, the rigid, compulsory attendance at a religious service, it has been suggested, turned the convicts' view of the church from one of indifference to one of hatred and opposition. As a result, the church failed to win over the majority of convict settlers.[36]

LIGHTENING THE LOAD

On a long voyage lasting many weeks, bearing a cargo of prisoners with the potential to create problems, it was important to keep the convicts occupied by a strict daily routine of work and education. As a result, many convicts did benefit from the basic instruction in literacy and numeracy that was provided on the voyage (page 112).[37] Even so, the long journey to Australia was generally marked by boredom, punctuated by efforts to supply convicts with some form of activity.

When well away from land, the prisoners' irons were usually removed and, if conditions allowed, they mustered on deck for fresh air and exercise. Whenever possible they were set, under close supervision, to doing menial tasks, such as holystoning the decks, swabbing, scrubbing and laundering. Alternatively, they whiled away the time fashioning scrimshaw models and carvings out of bones extracted from salt beef, which formed a major part of their diet and which frequently hardened to an almost rock-like consistency.[38] Despite the best efforts of a regular routine of chores and schooling, however, there were long periods of idleness on board.

John Martin, along with six other 'Young Irelanders', was sentenced to 10 years transportation to Van Diemen's Land for treason. He had written an editorial in his newspaper, *The Irish Felon*, encouraging the Irish to retain their arms against the demands of the British government, who had demanded that the people give up all weapons.

Martin kept a diary which gives unique insight on the monotonous daily routine of the voyage. It also illustrates the discipline on the ship, and highlights moments that brought some diversion from the boredom. As the *Mount Stuart Elphinstone* left Cork in June 1849, Martin lamented on leaving Ireland: 'Poor Ireland!... Will thy misery be still thy national characteristic when next I come in sight of these dear headlands? Am I ever to return to my country?' His comments throughout are mainly about the weather, his health (which remained good) and general observations of life on board the ship. This is punctuated by his description of his hours of 'reading and looking out upon the waves or ... upon the various human crowd of sailors, soldiers, convicts upon board.'

Martin was an educated man who wrote of wanting to learn German and also history in order 'to make myself acquainted with some of the thousand subjects of which I am shamefully ignorant.' He described his living quarters as being 'comfortable', but the smells were 'not nice.' To alleviate this, he had obtained a 'jar of Chloride of Lime (Solution) … provided from Cork against the stink.'[39]

Martin thought favourably of those in charge. He described the surgeon-superintendent George Todd Moxey as an amiable but a 'dry formal old chap [who] never meddles with us.' Moxey was serving his fourth and last voyage on a convict ship. Martin described how every day Moxey had some ceremonious occupations with his convicts. 'He gets a big tub containing a mixture of lime-juice water & sugar placed upon the quarter deck, and to it all the convicts are passed in succession and dosed with a large tin measure of the liquid. Some of them seem to like it well enough: but some make wry faces and attempt to shirk the duty.' Martin thought the officers were 'quite civil'. He had plenty of time to look out upon the ocean and he recorded watching 'the beautiful clear dark blue water below the sides of the ship', as well as encounters with other ships on the vast ocean. At night he appreciated the 'millions of stars in the clear blue or bluish-white sky… The Pole star is got very low now. And we see many brilliant constellations not visible in Ireland.'

The dullness of the daily routine on one occasion was broken by the excitement of seeing a huge turtle which 'the whole 350 human tenants of the ship came to view.'[40] The diary also chronicles sightings of other marine life, such as flying fish, porpoises and sharks. In addition to the creatures of the sea, bird life was also in abundance. 'Great numbers of Cape Pigeons & Cape Hens following the ship. Saw an albatross for the first time, a bird seemingly about the size of a goose with great expanse of wing. Cape hens are jet black & seem as large as poultry. Soldiers fishing for the birds all day with bait & hook.'

Reports on the weather dominate his journal in which he wrote, 'weather very warm. Sun terrible upon the head… Heat very great … glare off the sea very oppressive to the eyes… We are to have tremendous torrents of rain pouring down with such violence that our little window must be closed and hatchery above our door also … how are we to breathe below? Most piercing frosty air … my breathing was a good deal affected

... I sat on my bed clothed in my warmest garments & with my horse-rug wrapped round my shoulders.'

The death of a convict on the voyage was a cause for solemnity and Martin noted that the man 'was buried in the sea fashion today at 11 o'clock.' The body was sewn up in a blanket and wrapped in a Union Jack. It was laid on a board supported on casks beside the water gangway until the time of burial. 'The Chaplain ... read the Episcopalian burial service... Then at the proper time the body was let slip down by ropes attached to the outer ends of the board on which it lay. A heavy stone was attached to it & it sunk immediately. I had seen the Shark's fin at the ship's side an hour or two previously... The poor convict seemed to have no friend on board to grieve for him.'[41]

Over half way into the voyage, Martin records that for the first time since leaving Ireland, he opened the package of daguerreotypes (an early photographic process with the image made on a light-sensitive silver-coated metallic plate) and 'contemplated the countenances of my dear kind friends & relatives. Oh! What would I not give for a likeness of my mother! And for one of my poor Jane!'[42]

With regard to discipline, Martin offers more comment on the punishment given to sailors than the convicts. One sailor, who was arrested for shouting and using threatening behaviour, was 'handcuffed, and taken up to the Poop ... where he was compelled to sit down, while fetters also were in preparation for him... We are told he is to be kept a prisoner till the ship reaches Sidney & then tried for insubordination.' Another example involved a sailor who had been ordered to go up the masts and grease some part of the machinery, which he refused to do. An officer then tried to force the sailor to do it by placing a grease pot in his hands. A skirmish followed whereby the officer was too strong and reduced the sailor into submission. Martin records that 'after a severe flogging he [the sailor] took the grease pot and ascended the mast.'

The most frightening parts of the voyage were those when the ship encountered storms. At one point the ship:

> ...rocked abominably, more than ever we had experienced. About 8 o'c, she was laying her sides alternately upon the water, down to the very hammock nettings. Such abominable sensations as the rocking produced! For noises there was the continual creaking & groaning of the strained timbers, the rolling clashing rattling & thumping of every moveable upon deck & in the

cabins, except such as were firmly lashed... What a mess! I was sitting on my bed, holding on by hands & feet, and thanking my stars that I had two legs & thighs & hands & arms... We heard that the poor convicts in the prison thought the ship was going to the bottom & many of them fell on their knees in the water to pray for mercy, while others cursed & some kept on playing dominoes.

On arrival in Australia, Martin wrote of the very beautiful land and the pleasant weather. The ship arrived at Moreton Bay before departing to Van Diemen's Land. Martin was clearly aware of the resentment towards 'the sending of convicts ... in all the settlements of Australia. Even at Moreton Bay (to which place this human cargo is consigned) the colonists protest against receiving any more.' In 1858, John Martin returned to Ireland and became active in Irish national politics. After 1868, he became an MP for County Meath and helped found the 'Home Government Association of Ireland', which advocated Home Rule.

An illustration of the ducking and shaving ceremony –the traditional ritual of crossing the Equator—from An account of a voyage to New South Wales *by George Barrington, 1810. The induction of those making their first crossing provided light relief from shipboard routine.*

The unfortunate combination of boredom, idleness and close proximity provided the basis for petty crimes, arguments, fights and speculation of revolt and insubordination. Complaints

Ceremony of Ducking & Shaving.
Published May 1810 by M. Jones.

from surgeon-superintendents about 'foul conversation' and filthiness were frequent events on many of the voyages. The tedium of unfolding days was punctuated by daily routines and fluctuations in weather, which ranged from stifling heat in the tropics to rain, cold, rolling seas and ice in winter. Such variation contributed to the unpleasant damp and powerful stench. Added to the physical discomforts were the frequent complaints of illness from those on board, especially about constipation, diarrhoea, haemorrhoids and sea-sickness (pages 174–9).

Nevertheless, convicts found ways to entertain themselves by gambling, arguing, fighting, dancing and even fishing over the side of the ship using makeshift lines. Almost any variation from the normal fare was welcomed, and types of fish that would not normally feature on even the most adventurous gastronome's menu were eagerly hauled on board and despatched, before being made the subject of negotiation with the cooks. The huge turtle that fascinated the crew and convicts on the *Mount Stuart Elphinstone* finished up in the cooking pot. They also trapped birds, which they would skin, eat or sell. Even albatrosses were sometimes caught, as John Martin's diary testifies. These large birds put up a good fight and could inflict frightful wounds on their assailants. They were not destined for the cooking pot, however, because, skinned and later stuffed, they could fetch a good price ashore. Not surprisingly, the seasoned and superstitious mariners who composed the crew deplored this activity. They believed that albatrosses embodied the souls of dead sailors.

The convicts attempted to extract what little pleasure was possible from their ordeal. On some ships they had sing-songs, often featuring ballads of a powerful poignancy. 'Farewell to Your Judges and Juries', for example, reads as a dialogue between a convict, who has been transported for seven years, and Polly, his loved one, back at home. It ends in this fashion:

> *How hard is the place of confinement*
> *That keeps me from my heart's delight.*
> *Cold chains and cold irons surround me,*
> *And a plank for a pillow at night.*
>
> *How often I wish that the eagle*
> *Would lend me her wing, I would fly,*
> *Then I'd fly to the arms of my Polly,*
> *And in her soft bosom I'd lie.*[43]

Dances were held on some ships, and prisoners occasionally staged plays or mock trials. Cheers went up and games were held when the coast of Australia was sighted, and celebrations took place whenever a vessel crossed the equator. In 1791, George Barrington expressed a sense of excitement as everyone prepared for Neptune to board the ship and initiate those who had not previously crossed the Equatorial line. The 'ceremony of shaving and ducking was punctually observed ... and then half a dozen grotesque figures entered the ship. The principal personages were Neptune and Amphitrite, attended by their nymphs and mermaids, personated by the oldest seaman in the ship.' The maritime theatre was sustained by receiving a double toll from the captain, consisting of half a gallon of liquor and two pounds of sugar. This carnivalesque ceremony continued and as the day closed, dancing and songs were performed. 'Everyone forgot their temporary mortifications and joined in the evening's conviviality.'[44] In 1826, Lieutenant William Coke wrote to his father from the *Regalia* on the appearance of Neptune:

> He was a sulky Old Fellow and covered his new sons over with tar from head
> to foot... He and his Constables drank three gallons of my Whiskey and
> made my head ache terribly by obliging me to drink raw spirits with him.[45]

Most voyages passed without major incident, despite a spate of minor misdemeanours. Punishments were meted out according to the surgeons' codes, but these paled into insignificance compared with the brutality that awaited many convicts in the penal colonies. Such features were the reality of convict voyages to Australia between 1787 and 1868, and rumours of mutinies were rife, but they were seldom translated into action. There was only one 'successful' mutiny, that of the *Lady Shore*, in the history of transportation—a remarkable statistic for ships transporting unwilling passengers in difficult conditions.

The reason is summed up by the maritime historian N.A.M. Rodger, who has observed that discipline owed almost everything to the collective understanding of seamen. When a ship was at sea, most knew that orders had to be obeyed for the safety of all. Acceptance of authority was not a matter of unquestioning obedience, but of intelligent co-operation in survival: 'The prospect of drowning concentrates a man's mind wonderfully.'[46] The upholding of law, order and discipline was thus maintained on most ships, even in difficult conditions.

Daily Sick Book of the
"Barrosa"
Male Convict Ship, between the 13th day of August 1841 and 22nd Jany 1842

Date	Thermometer	Men's names	Age	Quality	Disease or Hurt	When put off the Sick List	How disposed of
1841 Augt 13th	68°	Benjamin Luff	20	Soldier	Catarrhus	Augt 16th	Duty
20th	64°	Joseph Platt	40	Convict	Opthalmia	" 26th	Cured
"	"	James Amy	21	do.	Scrofula	Sept. 23d	do
21st	62°	John Seawood	18	Soldier	Rheumatismus	Augt 27th	do
23d	64°	Richard Harrison	24	Convict	Catarrhus	" 30th	"
"	"	William Hampshire	32	do	Ulcus	October 10th	"
"	"	Enoch Thacker	20	"	Catarrhus	Augt 30th	"
25th	55°	William Johnson	23	"	Colica	" "	"
"	"	John Lane	22	"	Catarrhus	" "	"
26th	64°	Henry Smith	23	"	Catarrhus	" "	"
"	"	Ralph Reckless	23	"	Catarrhus	" "	"
"	"	James Haslam	25	"	Phlegmon	Sept. 5th	"
"	"	Samuel Chambers	19	"	Bronchitis	" 27th	"
"	"	William H. Keave	20	Soldier	Hernia Humoral	" 4th	"
Sept 2d	57°	Thomas Sams	21	Seaman	Gonorrhea	" 20th	"
"	"	Thomas Crockelbank	19	Seaman	Gonorrhea	" 20th	"
"	"	John Leary	20	Convict	Fractura	" 22nd	"
3d	59°	Joseph Toothill	19	do	Herpes preputialis	" 12th	"
6	"	Henry Barrett	18	do	Hemorrhoidis	" 12th	"
"	"	John Pinder	28	"	Nodus	" 12th	"
"	"	Charles Briggs	28	"	Syphilis	" 30th	"
7th	55°	John Shardlow	22	"	Dyspepsia	" 12th	"
"	"	Henry Winrow	18	"	Catarrhus	" 12th	"
"	"	William Williams	28	"	Sycosis Menti	" 26th	"
"	"	Benjamin Claridge	28	"	Dyspepsia	" 12th	"
9th	62°	Alexander Fitzcharles	19	"	Catarrhus	" 12th	"
"	"	William Murray	27	"	Catarrhus	" 12th	"

7

Staying Alive on the Convict Ships

THE COMMONLY held view has been that the convict ships were a living hell, not least because of the use of contractors to transport the prisoners overseas. 'Nearly all the evils associated with the actual conveyance of the convicts had their origin in the contract system. It was responsible for incalculable human misery, suffering and loss of life.'[1] Certainly, no one should underestimate the trauma experienced by convicts sentenced to terms of seven or 14 years on the far side of the world, abruptly wrenched away from family and familiar surroundings and dispatched in crowded ships to hazards and challenges beyond the imagination. A dispassionate look at transportation, however, shows that conditions did improve over the 'convict years' of 1787–1868 and that most of the prisoners stood up to the experience remarkably well. The real evil lay quite simply in the concept of transportation to Australia itself, favoured by successive generations of politicians and inflicted by judges and magistrates accordingly.

Transportation across the seas could be, and often was, a perilous activity. It endangered the health and lives of those who engaged in it, be they mariners, free passengers, guards or prisoners. The Royal Navy's rule of thumb calculation during the Napoleonic Wars was that one sailor in 30 would die of disease or accident and one in six would be receiving medical attention at any particular time. In contrast, the death rate for civilian males on land aged between 20 and 40 was only one in 80. Even in ships carrying free emigrants to the United States in the mid-nineteenth century, one in 30 died. This is perhaps not surprising as conditions on the emigrant ships were usually even more cramped than those on the convict transports.

CONTROLLING THE CONVICT FLEET

The First Fleet was entirely organized, fitted out and provisioned by the commissioners of the Royal Navy, although the vessels used were chartered from private ship-owners who contracted for the job. The naval

authorities worked closely with the Home
Office, who were responsible for the prisoners
and the running of the convict colony, and the
Treasury, who footed the bill and kept a keen eye
on expenditure or, as the modern euphemism
would have it, 'value for money'.

The experience of the First Fleet clearly convinced the Admiralty that they had no desire for
direct involvement with the everyday mechanics
and minutiae of transportation. It was devolved
to the Navy Board, where it quickly became evident that it was easier and more economical to
offer the job to contractors. Tenders were submitted at prices enabling the
contractors to make a profit, while the government relieved itself of a complex operation that it had no wish to undertake. For this reason, guidelines
were drawn up for the contractors conveying convicts from Britain to
Australia from 1787; they were to become increasingly rigorous.

What kinds of regulation were specified for the convict ships in the
early years of transportation to Australia? The Commissioners of the Navy,
known as the Navy Board (which was a subsidiary of the Admiralty),
supervised the tendering arrangements and the formulation of the contracts. Their officials inspected the suitability, seaworthiness and the
fitting-out of the ships to be used as transports. The Commissioner of
Victualling, who was a member of the Navy Board, decided on the supplies and provisions needed for each voyage; the task of supplying and
delivering these was then contracted out. The Navy Board had extensive
experience of issues associated with transporting troops to distant parts of
the world. They laid down requirements concerning the ventilation, cleaning and fumigation of the convicts' quarters, the supply of clothing, beds
and bedding, the provision of space for a hospital, the employment of an
approved surgeon, the level of rations, medicines and anti-scorbutics and
all other essential requirements. From 1832, the Admiralty decided to
assume direct overall responsibility for transportation.

The master of each convict transport was required to keep a comprehensive log, listing not only navigational issues and the consumption of
stores and supplies, but also unexpected or notable events at sea. The log
also noted any unusual occurrences concerning the prisoners and any

STORES FOR USE OF PRISON, OR HOSPITAL.

Combs, large	40	No.
„ small	40	„
Razors	10	„
Hone	1	„
Strop	1	„
Soap	115	Lbs.
Scrubbing Brushes	55	No.
Bedding	270	Sets.
„ Spare	23	„
Knives and Forks, of each	39	No.
Water Pails, large	4	„
„ small	4	„
Kegs (three-gallon)	39	„
Slates	160	„
Slate Pencils	200	„
Primers	34	„
Hammocks	30	„
Airing Stoves, with Chain for swinging them	4	„
Box, for Solitary Confinement	1	„
Harness Casks, with Padlocks	3	„
Kits	39	„
Air Tubes		„
Illuminators	2	„
Prison Doors	1	„

ARTICLES FOR THE SECURITY OF THE CONVICTS.

Handcuffs	40	Pairs.
Extra Rivets	7	Dozens.
Bazzles, with Chains	240	Pairs.
Oak Blocks, with Iron Plates and Rings	1	No.
Stakes	1	„
Hand Hammers, with Handles	1	„
Chisels	2	„
Punches	2	„

RELIGIOUS BOOKS.

Bibles	46	No.
Testaments	69	„
Common Prayer Books	59	„
Psalters	59	„

CLOTHING FOR USE DURING THE VOYAGE.

Flannel Shirts	230	No.
Raven Duck Overalls	230	Pairs.
Shirts	230	No.
Stockings, Worsted	230	Pairs.
Needles	460	No.
Thread } for repairs	4½	Lbs.
Canvas	115	Yards.

CLOTHING FOR USE ON ARRIVAL IN THE COLONY.

Jackets	230	No.
Waistcoats	230	„
Trowsers	230	Pairs.
Shirts	460	No.
Caps, Woollen	230	„
Neck Handkerchiefs	230	„
Stockings		Pairs.
Shoes	230	„

Padlocks	9	No.
Packing Casks	7	„
Stencil Plates	1	Set.
Marking Ink	4	Bottles.
Wrappers	22	No.

FOR THE GUARD.

Water Kegs	6	No.
Kits	6	„
Covering for Arms	1	„

requests from the surgeon concerning their health and welfare. One copy of this log was to be lodged with the governor of the relevant colony in Australia. The other had to be submitted to the Admiralty authorities when the master returned to England. The surgeon was also required to keep a journal of all matters related to the health of the prisoners and to submit copies in the same way as the master. While this may sound like a rigorous code of requirements, their management and supervision, especially while the ships were at sea, was virtually non-existent in the early days of transportation. This meant that they were often largely ignored or evaded.

It was inevitable that the convicts transported to Australia in the early years were to some extent guinea pigs; death rates were, unsurprisingly, intolerably high from the 1790s through to 1815. Terms and conditions required from the early contractors were markedly less demanding than those drawn up later, after experience had thrown up a host of problems associated with transporting convicts over such large distances. The contract agreed for the Second Fleet, which left Portsmouth in January 1790, for example, stated that the contractors, Messrs Camden, Calvert and King, would transport, clothe and feed the convicts for a straight fee of £17 7s 6d each, irrespective of how many died en route. The awful death toll on the Second Fleet meant that—although they had already been contracted for the Third Fleet—no further contracts were awarded to this firm.

It has to be said that the authorities were not necessarily callous men. Once they had gained experience of what convict transportation to Australia actually involved, they took vigorous steps to improve conditions on the voyage. Over time, they were able to report average death rates per voyage that varied between 1 in 85 in the early days and a much more creditable figure of around 1 in 180 at the end of transportation.

One practice the authorities successfully imposed was the making of deferred payments. This meant that while the contractors received a major part of their fee when the prisoners were embarked at the outset of the journey, the residue was held back until the prisoners were delivered safe and sound at their destination. Additionally, masters and surgeons were assessed by the governor of the colony when they arrived in Australia. If they were commended for their 'Assiduity and Humanity', there would be a bonus for them on their return to England.[2] What is uncertain is whether the governor was really in the right position to make a fully informed judgement on the officials' efficiency and effectiveness.

WHO GUARDS THE GUARDS?

Even the prospect of a financial bonus did not persuade every master to treat convicts with decency and compassion. William Hingston, master of the *Hillsborough* between 1798 and 1799, was particularly notorious, even though the contractors were to receive a bonus of £4 10s 6d for each convict who arrived safe and sound in Australia, in addition to a fee of £18 per head for each prisoner embarked. Such inducements cut no ice with Hingston, who systematically starved his prisoners, shackling them so heavily that they could not move about the deck during the day. At night, confined below decks, he placed them in double irons. Typhus broke out just after the ship had left Langstone Harbour near Portsmouth, with the result that one in three prisoners on this most ill-starred of voyages were dead when the ship arrived at Australia. Yet, no action was taken to make Hingston accountable for his negligence.

The conditions required of the contractors became increasingly stringent over the years. Within these, the companies sought to maximize profits, while keeping their costs to the minimum commensurate with the terms of the contract. To assist in this, they frequently—and illicitly—loaded their vessels with goods for which they knew there was a ready and profitable market in Australia. Nor was it unknown for the masters of the convict ships to stint so much on the food supplies provided during the voyage that there was plenty left over; this could also be sold off at a healthy profit when the ships berthed in Australia.

On the transport *Atlas*, for example, which left for Australia in 1801, conditions below decks were appallingly cramped because the master, Captain Brooks, had taken a large quantity of rum on board. Much of this was then stowed in the quarters theoretically allocated to the prisoners. He intended to sell this when he arrived at Sydney, hoping to make a useful personal profit, but to his chagrin he was not allowed to land the rum. No action was taken against him, however, and after acting as master on several more convict ships he went into semi-retirement and ended up as a respected justice of the peace in Sydney.[3] Private trading was expressly forbidden in 1817.[4]

Effective supervision during the voyage only really occurred once a naval warrant officer, subject to naval discipline and directly answerable for any neglect, was placed in each ship as a surgeon-superintendent. Three ships —*General Hewart, Three Bees, Surrey*—reached Australia in 1814, suffering from the effects of scurvy and typhus, and experiencing high death rates. This led to an inquiry which influenced the Transport Commissioners a year later to adopt the system of surgeon-superintendents. This was put on a regular basis in 1815, after which there was a marked improvement in the conditions on board the convict ships.

One man who can take much credit for the improvements was William Redfern (c.1774–1833), himself a transported convict. A naval surgeon, he had played a minor part in the mutiny at the Nore (a Royal Navy anchorage), off Sheerness in Kent in 1797, for which he was initially condemned to death, but then reprieved and sentenced to transportation instead. He went on to become an acclaimed surgeon in Sydney. He was doctor to, and a friend of, Governor Macquairie, who in 1814 instructed him to investigate and report on the appalling conditions on board the three convict transports mentioned above. Redfern's thorough and momentous report marked a watershed in the organization of the voyages and the treatment of the convicts because its recommendations were listened to in both Australia and Britain. It emphasized the need for effective ventilation, as well as frequent swabbing of the decks, regular cleaning of the 'heads' or latrines, the use of lime and 'oil of tar' as disinfectants, and the fumigation and systematic exercising of the prisoners. He had also urged that every transport ship should have a naval surgeon aboard with the brief to act both in a medical capacity and as a government agent, able to scrutinize and report on how the master conducted affairs without fear of being browbeaten or victimized. Redfern was very insistent that it was a naval surgeon with his knowledge of life at sea that was required, rather than a novice or civilian surgeon 'between jobs' of the sort that was too often provided by the contractors.

Redfern's recommendations were largely adopted and proved to be successful; certainly there was a remarkable fall in death rates on the convict transports. The number of these ships trebled from 1816–20 compared with the previous five years, but the average death rate fell to only one in 122 and this figure continued to improve. It is hard to determine how much the employment of accredited naval surgeons equipped with some 'muscle' influenced this, but the role of the surgeon-superintendent was upgraded from warrant officer status to commissioned rank— arguably demonstrating official recognition of their importance.

The instructions and regulations concerning all aspects of the transportation of convicts to Australia were constantly updated and improved. Changes are reflected in the set of instructions issued in 1832. The surgeon-superintendent was instructed that he must on no account leave the ship once the guard had been embarked. He was provided with a copy of the contract applied to the particular voyage on which he was engaged and a list of the stores with details of how these were to be apportioned among the prisoners. Surgeon-superintendents were also given powers to ensure that the master adhered to the terms of the contract and that no one—officers, crew or guards—engaged in private trading.

The surgeon-superintendent had no jurisdiction over navigational matters or the handling of the ship, but his job involved developing a relationship with the master and also the officer of the guard. Together they were required to ensure that the ship was run as efficiently as possible and that the reasonable needs of the prisoners were attended to. On a day-today basis, there must have been many issues that placed the surgeon-superintendent at odds with the other officers on board.

Security and safety were of paramount importance at all times, and even everyday questions, such as which convicts should be exercised when and in what numbers, must have been a fruitful source of disagreement. In the event of a dispute with the master or the officer of the guard which could not otherwise be resolved, the surgeon-superintendent was instructed to request the arbitration of any senior naval officer where one was available, for example, at a port of call. Such provision proved to be of little practical use, however, as it might take a considerable time to locate an officer of the rank of post-captain or above, let alone to present a contentious issue for his decision. Delay in dealing might, or might not, lead to a valuable 'cooling off' for all the parties concerned. There was, of course, no guarantee that the naval officer would be in possession of all the relevant information or that he would necessarily adjudicate in favour of the surgeon-superintendent. It might happen that the latter was in the wrong.

Most masters kept themselves aloof from the convicts. For this reason, the surgeon-superintendent was the representative of authority with whom the latter had most dealings. This was an unenviable role, requiring the surgeon-superintendent to be an honest broker in an inevitably fraught situation—the involuntary conveyance of felons across the sea to a distant destination. The surgeon-superintendent was not only in charge of the convicts' well-being but also, while invested with official authority, cast in the role of advocate for the prisoners against neglect and abuse from officers and crew. Unless all concerned were determined to live and let live, the relationship between the surgeon-superintendent and the ship's officers and crew and the guards on board was almost bound to be problematic. However, it is clear that co-operation did take place on most voyages, amicably or not. The years during which concientious surgeon-superintendents were on the convict ships are noted overall for the relative cleanliness, good health and low mortality of the convicts.

VESSELS AND VOYAGES

The ships themselves became more capacious and speedier as the 'convict years' progressed. Voyages became faster, with lengthy stops at places such as Rio eliminated. Speed is, of course, still relative, but whereas the

This watercolour drawing of Dr William Bland by Richard Read, 1845–9, was based on a daguerrotype and exhibited in Sydney. Bland, a naval surgeon, was transported for seven years for murder in 1814 after killing a man in a duel. He received a pardon, becoming the first full-time doctor in New South Wales as well as a prominent public figure.

First Fleet took a maximum of 252 days to reach Botany Bay in 1787, some ships by the 1830s were completing the journey in less than 110 days. The fastest recorded voyage of this era was that of the *Emma Eugenia* in 1838—a very creditable 95 days. By the 1850s, approximately 90 days had become the norm.

The vessels used to convey the convicts were almost all minimally converted merchantmen, but most were fast and seaworthy, unlike the prison hulks that simply rotted at their moorings. The convict ships had partitioned quarters between decks for the prisoners and a variety of security devices, such as heavy grills and gigantic padlocks, on the hatchways at night. In most cases the convicts' quarters, known as the prison, had little headroom and was foetid and airless. The ships were crowded, not only with a seething mass of humanity, but also with provisions, stores and livestock. Berths were arranged in rows like bunks and stacked against the hull, lacking the relative freedom of hammocks to move with the roll of the ship. In these conditions rats, cockroaches, body lice and other unwanted parasites found a happy and stable hunting ground.

Until at least 1835, the calculation of harbour dues encouraged ships to be designed with hulls that were narrow and deep, rather than broad in the beam. Such a practice was of little concern for ships carrying an inanimate cargo, but it could make life at sea a living hell for prisoners. Ships with a narrow beam could roll ferociously and wallow sickeningly in heavy seas, with horrifying effects in the stinking, confined quarters below decks. Violent, apparently random, stomach-churning oscillations were accompanied by a terrifying cacophony, which must have convinced even the most hard-bitten felons that their time had come. Powerful waves would crash against the hull, setting the ship's timbers groaning and squealing in protest. Water inevitably penetrated into the sleeping quarters as the planks making up the hull contorted and partly opened up with the relentless pressure of the crashing waves. Masts were prone to judder and creek, sending ominous convulsions through the hull. Every so often a resounding crash might ring out as a spar, yard or other item of the rigging was detached by the wind and plummeted down on deck and crew. All this and more had to be endured by convicts, many of whom had never seen the sea before they were convicted and who knew they were effectively trapped in the event of the ship foundering.

When ships lay becalmed in the doldrums, other, very different problems arose, defying the attempts of most ships to keep up standards of cleanliness. The heat could be almost palpable, searing, crushing, inescapable and vastly compounded between decks, especially on the lower decks. Although wind-sails might be fitted over the hatchways, there was often quite simply no air moving, whereupon the prisoners, and all on board, festered in an enervating, interminable fug. Pitch used for caulking the seams of the ship's timbers could melt and fall onto the helpless, supine prisoners below, who were allowed no more than a quart of stinking, warm water per day to quench their raging thirsts. The mixture of sweaty, close-packed humanity, unspeakable filth sluicing in the bilges and the reek of such livestock as had not yet been slaughtered must have created a nauseating miasma to which, it can only be assumed, those on board became accustomed.

A major problem was caused by the ballast, packed on the floor of the hold in all but the smallest ships. The ballast, usually composed of sand, shingle or small boulders, was intended to provide stability and act as a counterweight to the height and weight of the superstructure of hull, masts and rigging. Over the months and years, however, all manner of detritus and filth permeated downwards through the hull to the bottom of the hold and into the bilges. Here it accumulated in unwholesome pools and eddies, sloshing around with the motion of the ship and smelling repulsively rank. The reek from the bilges permeated every nook and cranny between decks and was something that everyone on board had to eat, sleep and live with. From the 1820s, new ships tended to have iron bars or full water casks for ballast which were much easier to remove for cleaning purposes. Unfortunately, most convict transports continued to use the traditional type of ballast for years to come.

British naval ships had a reputation for their cleanliness—in part because the labour involved in systematic swabbing, scrubbing and scouring was thought to be a useful way of encouraging discipline and pride in the ship. As contemporary medical thinking of the time held that many illnesses were transmitted by foul air, such cleansing was also thought to purify the air and discourage disease. Some surgeons, such as the famous Dr James Lind, the Scottish naval surgeon associated with preventative measures for scurvy, were less convinced of the wisdom of constant regular and thorough swabbing out, especially between decks. Lind believed that the dampness resulting from the difficulty of drying out such places properly was harmful to the health of those on board. Surgeon-superintendents on the convict ships were, of course, naval men. Some may have been keen, even fanatical about achieving the appearance of cleanliness. Others were less zealous in this regard. In reality, most of the convict ships are likely to have been about as clean as practicable, given the contemporary knowledge of dirt and disease and the means available to cope with it.

DEALING WITH DISEASE

The surgeon-superintendents were required to prohibit the embarkation of any convicts who had infectious diseases, or those whose state of health would suggest that they might not survive the journey or could endanger others. They did not always do this as effectively as they should; for example, the ill-health of prisoners when they embarked was blamed for the death of six out of 250 prisoners on the *Prince George* in 1837.[5] That this low figure was thought serious enough to warrant an investigation is an indication of how far standards in the convict transports had improved by that time. However, a surgeon-superintendent was not permitted to reject a prisoner simply on the grounds of old age or bodily infirmity. He had to feel sure in his own mind that the taking of a particular prisoner on board might threaten the health of others on board. It is interesting to note that in 1848, Harvey Morris, surgeon-superintendent on the *Bangalore*, went to great lengths in his journal to blame their unusually large number of fatalities on the poor health of the prisoners when they were taken aboard.[6] Was his outburst an attempt to shift the blame from himself?

The surgeon-superintendent on the *Andromeda*, George Fairford, noted his concerns about the selection procedure in his journal for June to December 1830. He pointed out that both the surgeon of the hulk and the convicts themselves were concerned about the outcome; both pre-ferred to conceal symptoms of disease, and underhand tricks to achieve this were not uncommon. Fairford also noted that it was difficult even for a specialist to discover specific signs of illness in the poor condition of so many convicts:

> The squalid look of the generality of Irish convicts, at least those on board the hulk while I was there, make it difficult from the mere look, to discrimi-nate, so as to pick out every case of sickness. Many therefore were approved who ought never to have been brought forward for examination and even some of whom I rejected were embarked—a piece of disingenuity not found out until too late to be remedied. In a few days the numerous daily applica-tions for torpid bowels taught us to anticipate a sickly voyage.

John Edwards, surgeon of the *Henry Tanner* which left Britain in June 1814, also expresses concerns about the health of the convicts accepted for the transports. He blames the legacy of conditions endured on the hulks, making his point in a somewhat laboured fashion:

> There is one case (of fatality) which is only remarkable for having arisen before the vessel left Harbour and thereby showing the existence of predis-posing and existing causes on board ... I have little doubt of such predispo-sition accompanying many of those embarked, rendering them less able than men in perfect health to undergo with impunity the privations of a long and uninterrupted voyage.[7]

The surgeon-superintendent on board the curiously named *Pestonjee Bomanjee*, Dr Colin Arnett Browning, started a journal on 29 September 1846. He describes the relationship with prison doctors as a constant source of friction on the ship. In theory, the doctors had to work with surgeon-superintendents to ensure that only those convicts fit enough to undergo the rigours of the voyage were embarked. For their part, prison doctors were anxious to rid themselves of seriously ill or persistently demanding convicts and they were not too fussy about how they did it. If they could be palmed off onto an unsuspecting surgeon, who would shortly be leaving for several months, all well and good. Browning writes:

> On the 5th day of October 1846, two hundred male prisoners were, at Woolwich, received on board ... from Millbank Prison for conveyance to Norfolk Island but whose destination was, before the ship sailed, changed to Van Diemen's Land. Previously to their embarkation, the whole of these prisoners were examined by Dr Bailey, Medical Superintendent of the prison, and were certified to be in a fit state for entering on a voyage to the colonies. Before their removal from prison, they were likewise inspected by myself accompanied by the Assistant Surgeon of the Establishment and one of these I had to reject...

> As far as I could discover from observation, the men being dressed in their new clothes and made to appear to the best advantage—and from the earlier reply to my inquiries, there was nothing on which I could find any special objections to the embarkation of any of them... Several appeared to be considerably advanced in years, a few to have lost their teeth and these therefore but ill-provided with the means of masticating hard biscuit and tough salt beef ...

Browning also indicates the scale of the problem, acknowledging that unfitness for the voyage went further than the actual convicts. 'Respecting the soldiers (of the guard themselves), it was observed that some of them were in a state of health that ought to have excluded them altogether from the vicinity of a convict ship.'

Browning's journal is interesting for its specific details on conditions of the time. He disapproves of Woolwich as a place for embarkation because of the prevalence of cholera in that town. Prisoners from Wakefield gaol were identified as particularly debilitated and unsuitable for registration. Unfortunately, there is no record of how Browning's critical comments were received in official circles or, indeed, whether any of these points were acted on as a result of his report. In making waves while possessing little influence, Browning probably found scant sympathy or support from the authorities. Interestingly, Browning employed a clerk on the voyage, who had previously been employed in a bank. The clerk wrote up Browning's journal in a minute but immaculate hand, which makes it an absolute joy for modern eyes to read.[8]

While significant advances in medical and surgical knowledge took place in the first decades of the nineteenth century, systematic training was still wanting. Methods of diagnosis and prognosis also seem limited by today's standards. Nothing was known about microscopic pathogens, for example. Some treatments were available to convicts, however, and it is interesting to consider the specific items carried in the medical chest of a typical surgeon-superintendent. A range of drugs to strengthen a body weakened by disease and fever—not to mention the ubiquitous practice of 'bleeding' patients—was essential. An especially favoured drug, raised almost to the level of a panacea, was cinchona, otherwise known as Peruvian bark, which contains quinine. Having been found very helpful against malaria, quinine was prescribed for a host of other conditions without the slightest evidence that it was effective. Surgeons also made considerable use of cathartic or purgative drugs, such as jalap, medicinal rhubarb and castor oil. James's Powder was among the diaphoretics, employed to assist patients in sweating out impurities, and emetics were widely used. Opium and its derivatives, especially laudanum, were used largely as sedatives and analgesics. Syphilis was a common affliction among prisoners and others on board, and a well-prepared surgeon would consequently stock various substances containing mercury, although this, when applied, might have dire consequences for the patient.[9]

Those unlucky enough to be stricken with serious illness on board a convict ship might well encounter drugs known as epispastics. These usually contained the dried, powdered cantharides beetle, misleadingly known as 'Spanish fly'. When applied to the skin, these substances raised a large and painful blister which was believed to neutralize the existing inflammation.

Opium and cinchona may have been efficacious drugs, but doctors in the age of transportation failed to produce lasting relief from many of the convicts' conditions. For all that, many prisoners and crew members did seem to recover and the journals of the surgeon-superintendents, not unnaturally, make constant reference to their successes, for example, the large number of crew members considered fit enough to return to work or prisoners allowed to rejoin their fellows. The health regime and the food on board the convict ships were as good as those in Britain's contemporary prisons and certainly superior to what was provided in the hulks. For much of the nineteenth century, the diet and relative cleanliness of convict ships was no worse—and often markedly better—than the living conditions endured by many of Britain's working population.

The log of the *Cressy,* which sailed in 1843, illustrates the conditions treated by surgeon-superintendents and the frequency with which they occurred. The surgeon, James Lawrence, identifies the convenient catch-all 'catarrh' as the most common affliction, followed by scurvy and diarrhoea. Only one fatality is recorded on this voyage.[10]

The *Isabella,* which sailed to Australia in 1831–2, provides examples of how medical conditions were treated.[11] The surgeon-superintendent's journal between November 1831 and spring 1832 gives valuable information about the physical complaints and diseases with which he had to deal. Diarrhoea was by far the most common complaint (at least 30 patients required treatment); it was followed in frequency, interestingly, by cases of constipation—a paradox possibly reflecting on the ship's catering and cleanliness. Scurvy (pages 179–82) became a problem as the journey went on, with 13 cases mentioned, while other conditions requiring the surgeon's attention on several occasions include boils, rheumatism, catarrh and colic. Unusually for a convict ship, there were only three recorded cases of venereal disease.[12]

A somewhat different pattern emerges on the *Adelaide,* which undertook the journey to Australia between July 1849 and January 1850. Diarrhoea is again the most frequently treated condition, but the next most common complaint is described as 'catarrh' and, thirdly, 'phlegm'; constipation scarcely features. The surgeon-superintendent also makes several entries for 'dyspepsia' and rheumatism. During this voyage, he saw 412 patients in total, of whom 114 were put on the sick list. In his journal's summing up, the surgeon-superintendent comments:

> The comparatively healthy state of the convicts ... may in a great measure be attributed to the attention in the first instance (previous to the embarkation of the guards and convicts), to the purification of the ship's holds.

The *Adelaide's* surgeon-superintendent was clearly a stickler for cleanliness and he mentions requiring chloride of lime to be used as a cleansing agent, both before and during the voyage. He made every effort to ensure that the ship was well ventilated, with plenty of suitable liquid available to drink; he also endeavoured to see that the prisoners were kept as busily occupied as was possible during the daylight hours. Interestingly, his first seriously ill patient was not a convict at all, but one of the guards who was suffering from cholera, which he was thought to have contracted at Chatham before he left.[13]

THE SCOURGE OF SCURVY

Innumerable mentions of scurvy are made in the journals. Scurvy was an insidious disease that killed thousands of people every year; it was common among poor people on land, but particularly prevalent among mariners. Deaths at sea from scurvy almost certainly exceeded all deaths from shipwrecks, other diseases and battle combined. An estimate suggests that scurvy killed over one million sailors between 1600 and 1800. For each person killed by the disease, three or four were debilitated or incapacitated. Improvements in navigational instruments and the design and seaworthiness of ships only exacerbated the problem of scurvy at sea, as they resulted in ships undertaking longer voyages and staying away from land for a greater length of time. Like most diseases stemming from nutritional deficiency, scurvy was also a scourge of public institutions, such as hospitals and prisons.

Scurvy arises from a lack of vitamin C or ascorbic acid in the diet. Unlike most mammals, humans do not synthesize vitamin C in their bodies; they must therefore obtain it from a diet that includes fresh fruit and vegetables, its richest source. Although scurvy may be fatal if not treated, the onset of the symptoms is slow and can be reversed by consumption of vitamin C at virtually any point in its progress. After about three months without vitamin C, the sufferer begins to feel tired and listless. Within a further two months, the skin is affected and at six months, haemorrhages occur in the legs, producing ulcers that will not heal. In a few weeks more, the victim's gums soften, swell and turn purple, teeth become loose and the breath begins to stink. Problems with the heart and difficulties with breathing may occur around eight to nine months.

Medical historians have brought belated recognition to the work of Dr James Lind (1716–94) in respect of scurvy. Lind, a Scottish naval surgeon, conducted a series of experiments in 1747, which provided indisputable evidence of the anti-scorbutic properties of oranges and lemons. A doggedly determined man, Lind believed that the Admiralty

Case 32

Purpura Petechialis at Natherland

Rhilter point ascending the skin of a limb
as complete as far as to the Bone.
Points here and there communicating

Congested

Shade
183

Sanguinis

Legs indolent shining tense and painful communication

Tumours varying from the size of a Filbert to that of a Bean
without attention or colour of the Cutis

Case 9.

Prep. No 6

(Case 25)

Beautiful light purple with great
Constitutional disturbance, involving
are tenderly hot Legs.
"White report in the same
what happened to the purple
"Livre — complexion by
Does a Alkaline habit?

Sheet
No 7.

Purpura Hemorrhagica

Dark blue purple which ultimately convert the entire leg without
much Constitutional disturbance — though the boldest cases —
Legs are very various —

failed to value seamen's lives sufficiently to provide them with adequate clothing and food, or lacked the will to understand and tackle effectively the large and widening range of diseases they contracted. Drawing on empirical research, Lind developed an understanding of the dietary factors involved, realizing that plenty of citrus fruits and fresh victuals, ideally including green vegetables, were vital for sailors' health. He actually thought that beer was the best anti-scorbutic of all, but it was heavy and bulky and could not be preserved for long at sea. For purposes of storage and carriage, Lind recommended crushing citrus fruits and condensing the juice into a syrup. In corked bottles this syrup would keep for years, and it could be reconstituted simply by adding water. Lind also advocated sauerkraut, or pickled cabbage, for anti-scorbutic purposes where fresh vegetables were not available.

Despite earnest endeavours to publicize his findings, Lind did not have influence in high places. Citrus fruits were expensive, and cheaper and less effective substances were used instead. Several decades after Lind's pioneering work, fellow surgeons with better social connections finally succeeded in persuading the Admiralty of the efficacy of citrus fruits in combating scurvy. In 1795, a year after Lind's death, the instruction went out that all Royal Navy ships on active service should carry lemon juice to be issued on a daily basis to prevent scurvy. Dr Mahon, the enterprising surgeon of the *Barrosa* in 1842, wrote an essay on the disease with meticulous watercolour illustrations of its effects.[14]

EPIDEMICS AT SEA

The presence of hordes of rats, usually the black or ship rat (*Rattus rattus*), was accepted as an unavoidable hazard of life at sea. There could be hundreds of them, even in convict ships which were relatively small, and they constituted a considerable health hazard. They often gnawed their way through sturdy wooden casks in the hold, contaminating supplies and transmitting disease. On occasions, they even rather foolishly ate their way through the side of ships' hulls.

Typhus, often called 'ship fever', 'gaol fever' or 'camp fever', was a dreaded disease and a mass killer. Originally considered to be several diseases because of the different environments in which it broke out, it was eventually established as a single condition that thrived in crowded and unhygienic conditions. We now know that the pathogens of typhus, the transmission of which are facilitated by rats and lice, are the micro-organisms *Rickettsia prowazekii.* They are passed from person to person, mostly by the human body louse or on occasions by the head louse.

Body lice depend on humans to shelter them and their eggs in their clothing, to warm them with their bodies and provide food for them with their blood. For these reasons, convict ships containing masses of closely packed humanity, who only changed their clothes rarely when it was cold, provided ideal conditions for the spread of the typhus pathogens. They are ingested by the lice with blood meals from infected persons. As infected lice move from one host to another, they defecate on the victims' skin; the infected faeces then enter the body if the host scratches the abrasion made by the insect's bite, or by any other open lesion. Symptoms include a rash of pinkish spots and intense, prolonged fever; those who die usually do so because of heart and brain complications. Ironically the lice, acting merely as vectors, always die, whereas many of their human hosts manage to survive.

The naval surgeon James Lind, whose work in connection with scurvy has already been mentioned, also took up cudgels against typhus, insisting that naval sailors should be regularly stripped, scrubbed, shaved and issued with new clothing. As a result of his recommendations, ships of the Royal Navy became largely free from typhus. The disease lingered on some convict ships, however, usually brought on board by convicts who had until recently been housed in prisons or on hulks.

The journal of the *Andromeda,* running from 30 June to 30 December 1830 and kept by the ship's surgeon-superintendent George Fairford, illustrates the concerns surrounding another highly contagious disease, namely, smallpox. The ship's steward succumbed to it early on in the voyage; during the passage from the Thames to Cork he had to be hastily put ashore, while rapid preventative measures were taken on the ship: 'His bed and blankets were destroyed—his clothes well scoured and the half deck repeatedly washed with soap and water then sprinkled with chloride of lime and well ventilated.'

Cholera was another much feared epidemic disease. It is caused by a virulent bacterium that lives in dirty water, and it afflicted a number of convict voyages, with one of the outbreaks occurring on board the *Fanny* in 1832. The surgeon-superintendent was Francis Logan and in his journal, he voices his opinion: 'By what means cholera was brought on board the *Fanny* would be difficult to say, but it was probably by a sailor from Blackwall, who came on board late the night before the ship sailed in a state of intoxication.'[15]

Those who contracted cholera fouled themselves with explosive, uncontrollable diarrhoea. They expired in excruciating pain with convulsive muscle spasms that led their bodies to twitch for hours after death. Bedding, clothing, water sources, almost anything microscopically fouled can transmit the disease, which can spread with terrifying speed. The journal of the convict ship *Hashemey*, in 1848 and 1849, also provides useful background on the impact of cholera on the convict ships. The source on this vessel was suspected to be two prisoners already infected who brought cholera with them from, respectively, Pentonville and Parkhurst prisons. The surgeon-superintendent concerned, Dr Colin Arnett Browning, produced a paper entitled 'The Appearance and Prevalence of Cholera in the *Hashemy*'. He submitted this to the Director-General of the Medical Department of the Navy. Browning was clearly not a man who felt the need to curry favour, and he made a number of trenchant criticisms of current practice. He argued that confinement in a prison or a hulk, with its frugal diet and sedentary regime, was a very inadequate preparation for a demanding voyage by sea. He explained that the frequency with which prisoners exhibited symptoms of catarrh and bronchial problems was because of the inadequate clothing issue on the convict ships. He went on to query the wisdom of convict transports setting forth on such an arduous passage during the winter months.[16]

The journals of the surgeon-superintendents are truly dominated by bladders and (especially) bowels. Time and time again, they mention the treatment of patients with dysentery—one of the most pervasive of the dangerous diseases to which human beings are subject. It is a waterborne disease, usually contracted by ingesting water or food contaminated with faecal matter. Crowded and less than scrupulously clean convict ships, in which prisoners were massed together without adequate sanitation, provided favourable conditions for the disease to spread. On the *Andromeda*, in 1830, George Fairford observed that space in the hospital quarters on board was strictly limited. Some chronic cases in there required constant medical attention with the result that many of the prisoners with dysentery had to remain in the prison—a situation requiring considerable forbearance on the part of the healthy convicts. Fairford was sure that this had contributed to the spread of the disease:

> Formerly these ships were fitted with water closets, which having a constant supply of water, could be kept clean and wholesome all the 24 hours. In this ship, these were exchanged for large iron buckets with covers loosely fitted, which could not be emptied and cleaned out during the night… How far the effluvia from these buckets might have contributed to cause the disease in the first instance I am not prepared to say but I think it may fairly be taken for granted that they would have some effect on increasing the virulence of the disease…[17]

It is hard to know just how prevalent dysentery was on transport ships, however, as its symptoms may have sometimes been mistaken by the surgeon-superintendents for those of chronic diarrhoea, and vice versa.

The convict transports were, of course, hired by the naval authorities. They brought their approach to cleanliness to bear on the contracts for the preparation and operation of these vessels. Where there had been outbreaks of contagious disease, the ship had to be internally stripped and disinfected. This involved the ballast being taken out, the hold washed and scrubbed with fresh water and clean ballast put in. A thorough caulking of the ship's timbers then took place, after which the hatches were battened down, fires were lit in the hold and between decks, and gunpowder charges were ignited in controlled explosions. Then the decks were washed down repeatedly with warm vinegar. All this must have had the effect of purifying the air, if only temporarily. Although the naval authorities appreciated the link between dirt and disease, it took time for rigorous standards of cleanliness concerning the bodies and the clothing of the prisoners to become standard procedure on convict vessels.

EAT, DRINK AND BE MERRY

By today's standards, the quality of food supplied to the convict ships was abysmal. The salt beef and pork were stowed in casks and often putrid by the time the convicts received it. Surgeons had the job of checking the provisions and they constantly bemoaned the fact that casks had been opened and repacked with significantly fewer pieces of meat, or that casks of 'salt beef' and 'salt pork' opened during the voyage were found to be full of stinking, rotting meat.[18] Other profitable deceptions employed by the contractors who supplied convict ships included making false bottoms for the casks and lacing their contents with a number of large bones. Undesirable foreign bodies were often discovered inside, including nails and other metal objects, dead and rotting rodents, horses' hooves and pieces of soiled clothing.

Any shortfall in the supplies provided for a convict voyage was usually the result of peculation by those employed in the commissariat or by the contractors, in some cases both. This not only swindled the Exchequer, but also inevitably affected the quantity and quality of food distributed to the prisoners. The pieces of salt beef and salt pork often consisted largely of bone and gristle, and they were sometimes so hard that even prolonged boiling failed to soften them. The beef was sometimes derisively referred to as 'salt horse'—precisely what some of it was. Winded nags from Ireland and elsewhere were slaughtered and then illicitly dismembered, boiled and pickled in salt; the resulting portions were simply stowed in the casks by the suppliers and passed off as beef or pork, to the considerable profit of all involved. Ironically, some mariners and even convicts seemed to prefer the pieces of 'salt horse' because they were generally reckoned to have a better flavour.

Even if the substance purporting to be salt beef or pork justified its description, it often proved so unyielding to knives and teeth that its only function was to be carved and polished into a variety of ornamental items (pages 83–85). These could command worthwhile prices and some enterprising convicts quickly became skilled enough to produce at least half-decent items of scrimshaw. The pieces of beef shrank by as much as 45 per cent on being cooked, seriously reducing what the prisoners actually received to eat. Pork shrank less when cooked, but it gave off a repulsive smell followed by a thoroughly loathsome, rank taste. Butter and cheese were often rancid and stinking, while peas, in spite of being boiled for eight hours or more, were derisively likened to grape shot, in texture if not in appearance.

The infamous ship's biscuit (compressed bread, with no resemblance to modern biscuit) started life hard. However, ever-present dampness and the activities of weevil grubs converted the inside to a granular consistency, even if the outside appeared solid enough. Hardened career sailors nonchalantly consumed their ship's biscuit complete with the invisible blackheaded grubs, averring that these imparted a not unpleasant, coldish taste to the biscuit. Hungry as they may have been, it is unlikely that the convicts were at sea long enough to acquire the taste for weevil-infested biscuit. There was a partial solution: a sharp tap of the biscuit on a hard surface must have caused the plump little grubs to emerge and wriggle off to safety. Unfortunately, the tap usually also caused the biscuit to disintegrate. One not unknown practice was for fish to be caught and placed in the bags containing infested biscuit. The idea was that the maggots, grateful for a new and more succulent source of food, would vacate the biscuit in favour of the fish, which, of course, would soon become putrid.

Water quickly became unwholesome at sea. Casks were taken on board full of supposedly fresh water, primarily for cleaning purposes but also for drinking. However, the water had often already been in cask for a considerable time. It gradually became green, opaque, smelly and slimy, harbouring a variety of aqueous insect life. The technique of desalinating seawater had been known for a couple of centuries, but the Admiralty had shown little interest.

Burgoo was a thick porridge largely composed of oatmeal. Easy to cook and cheap to provide, it was extensively used at sea, but generally disliked because it was so frequently on the menu. Other delicacies included coffee composed of burnt peas and sweetened with treacle, and a dish called lobscouse. The latter consisted of salted meat stewed with vegetables, spices and crumbled ship's biscuit.

The surgeon-superintendent's journal of the convict transport *Vimeira,* which sailed from England on 1 September 1865, provides valuable evidence of the provisions to be found on board a convict ship in the latter days of transportation. It gives an exhaustive list of all items purchased before the ship set sail. They include biscuit, rum, sugar, chocolate, tea, pork, split peas, beef, suet, raisins, flour, rice, oatmeal, mustard, pepper, vinegar, lemon juice, wine, ground coffee, vegetables, butter, treacle, sago, pickles, condensed egg, bottled porter, Scotch barley, pearl barley, caraway seeds, 'farinaceous foods', biscuit powder, port wine, preserved meats and preserved potato.[19]

The fare available on the convict transports may have lacked variety and nutritional balance. Nonetheless, it was probably as good as, and it was certainly no worse than, that enjoyed by many of the agricultural and urban poor of the time. William Cobbett, who travelled around Britain and wrote up his observations in *Rural Rides*, published in 1830, commented that the average agricultural labourer counted himself lucky if he got meat once a week. James Kay's survey of cotton workers in Manchester in 1832 came to very similar conclusions.

Some surgeon-superintendents allowed themselves comments on the food provided at sea. Andrew Henderson, serving on the *Emily*, which arrived at Van Diemen's Land in November 1842, is scathing:

> Two pounds of beef one day and a pound and three quarters of pork the next: with the beef a small ration of flour; with the pork a smaller portion of pease—it is really horrible; no human stomach could bear it on long voyages [i.e. voyages of six months continuance without adding decent vegetable matter]—were it not for the daily quota of rum (raw) to assist digestion; which ultimately must injure the soundest constitution.

Henderson criticizes the practice of allowing the guards the privilege of making cakes of their oatmeal by mixing it with flour and 'slush' (the fat skilled off the top of the water in which the meat had been boiled in the galley). However, he did approve the practice of boiling salt meat in salt water and has kind words to say about what he describes as the 'pudding', containing as it does suet and raisins. He concludes by noting that variety in the diet 'would seem to agree with the generality of human stomachs and hence act as a preventive of scurvy.'[20]

Despite some horror stories and the weight of popular mythology, convict ships sailing to Australia became significantly safer and healthier after 1815. The death rate on board these vessels, sometimes falling to as little as one per cent, made them statistically a great deal safer to travel in than the ships that had carried convicts to the American colonies in the eighteenth century. For this improvement the government, the Admiralty and the surgeon-superintendents must take the credit, even if transportation constituted a flawed form of punishment.

8

The Surgeon's Tale

FOR A PERIOD of about 80 years, ships conveying convicts left England and Ireland bound for the Australian mainland, for Van Diemen's Land and Norfolk Island. Through all this time, shipboard routines remained substantially the same, and so did the personnel who oversaw or performed them. On board were the officers, the crew—many of them old shellbacks, veteran sailors hardened to all the travails that life at sea could throw at them—and guards to control the prisoners in potentially volatile situations. Many voyages to Western Australia in the early nineteenth century also contained 'Pensioner Guards'—emigrants who, under a government-assisted emigration scheme,

This surgical instrument case of Dr Gillespie, a naval surgeon, is compact and easily portable. The surgeon would probably have kept a larger collection of medical equipment on board in a heavier wooden chest.

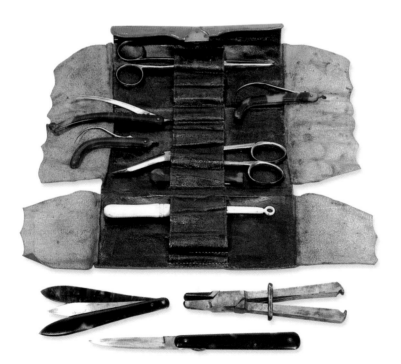

were on their way to settle in that state and who assisted with guard duties. Such pensioners and other warders were often accompanied by their wives and families, enduring some of the hardships that the convicts suffered. A surgeon, later re-designated 'surgeon-superintendent', was employed to look after the physical well-being of all on board, and there was usually an instructor to assist with the education of the convicts.

The surgeons in the First Fleet, and some of those who sailed subsequently in the early years of transportation to Australia, were sometimes on the way to take up medical posts in the colonies. They were required to minister to the convicts and those aboard as required, but in a fairly informal way during the voyage. Others were appointed, subject to official approval, by the contractors, according to clauses laid down in the charter arrangements. In the absence of evidence to the contrary, it is unlikely that the selection of these men was very rigorous. The post of civilian surgeon in a convict ship was probably not eagerly sought after. It was demanding, the situation and the conditions uncongenial, the pay poor and the status low. Most of the private surgeons were presumably novices eager for experience, or embittered veterans unable to find more prestigious work. Initially, at least, their calibre was low. Some may have been debtors or rascals, eager to put the greatest distance possible between themselves and Britain; many were drunkards. However, the supervision and accountability of the surgeons was to improve significantly over the years.

When transportation to Australia started, the supervision and management of both medical arrangements and surgeons was in the hands of the quaintly named Commissioners of Sick and Wounded, a body noted neither for its energy nor its effectiveness. In 1806, this aspect of its work was transferred to the Transport Board, which usefully included a member who was a physician. It was the Transport Board that introduced the system of designated surgeon-superintendents. In 1817, the Commissioners of Victualling took over the task of medical supervision of convict transport, and in 1832, this was transferred to the Admiralty. A new post of Physician of the Navy was established and then, with the fervour for titular aggrandizement that characterizes mandarins, the same post was renamed 'Inspector-General of Naval Hospitals' in 1841 and 'Director-General of the Medical Department of the Navy' in 1843.

The negative experience of the Second Fleet and the generally low quality of the surgeons employed by the contractors served to convince the authorities that properly accredited naval surgeons should be used. From 1792, it became the stated intention to place a naval surgeon in each convict transport for the duration of the voyage. The surgeon was answerable only to the Admiralty and his brief was to supervise the health of all on board and report on any abuses by the officers and crew. However, he was in a difficult position at this time, lacking control over how the master ran his ship or about issues of navigation, even where these impinged on the welfare of the prisoners. For all that, it was a foolhardy master who totally ignored the observations and suggestions of a diligent and scrupulous naval surgeon.

ROLES AND RESPONSIBILITIES

The first convict transport ship to convey an accredited naval surgeon was the *Royal Admiral* in 1792. His presence seems to have had a beneficial impact on prisoners' health on the ship. At first, these surgeons were simply styled 'superintendents' and they were volunteers, often working alongside a surgeon appointed by the contractors. As warrant rather than commissioned officers, they could find themselves at a disadvantage in disputes with the masters of the ships and the commissioned army officers in charge of the guards. Neither masters nor officers of the guard saw why they should take advice, let alone orders, from someone they regarded as a social and professional inferior.

While an effective case had been made for the routine employment of naval surgeons, the onset of the wars with Napoleonic France in 1793 meant that such men were fully occupied working in fighting ships; there were few to spare for convict transports. Of a total of 18 convict ships that left Britain for Australia between 1792 and 1800, the first six had surgeons on board, and on these the death rate was one man in 55 and one woman in 45. Of the next six ships, just two carried surgeons, and the death rate in this group of ships was one man in 19 and one woman in 68. The final six transports had no proper medical supervision, and on these one man in six died and one woman in 34. Such evidence was pretty conclusive and the number of surgeons being employed did gradually increase despite the demands of war. In 1814, just before the Napoleonic Wars ended, the Royal Navy employed 14 physicians, 850 surgeons and 500 assistant surgeons.

The success of surgeon-superintendents depended on rigorous commitment to a range of important responsibilities. Control of rations was an important part of the job, ensuring that each prisoner received his fair share, that it was available at the appointed time and that it was properly cooked. Getting convicts to eat it was a different matter. The surgeon-superintendent on board the *Sir Charles Forbes* in 1825, perhaps a Scot, comments ruefully about his convicts, 'As they were mostly Englishmen, I found it difficult to persuade them to use oatmeal as an article in their diet.' He believed that their refusal to eat oatmeal contributed to their frequent constipation.[1] Surgeon-superintendents were also required to be present when each cask of provisions was opened, to note in their journals the condition of the contents and any deficiencies in quantity or quality. Since peculation was rife among the suppliers and in the victualling yards, the journals are full of comments about poor quality and short measure.

Every prisoner was to be seen daily, and those who were sick had to be individually examined at least twice daily. Surgeon-superintendents were obliged to ensure that each prisoner received an ounce of lemon juice and sugar every day, that they were clean in their persons and that their quarters were kept as hygienic and well ventilated as possible. They were expected to make some provision for the schooling of the prisoners, especially the younger ones, and, in the absence of a chaplain, to read

This hand-coloured lithograph of c.1830–7 depicts two naval surgeon-superintendents cutting a dash on the quayside. The increased respect accorded to naval surgeons is indicated by their change in status from warrant officer to commissioned officer.

divine service on Sundays. All this amounted to a pretty onerous responsibility for a conscientious man. Additionally, surgeon-superintendents were required to produce a substantial number of regular returns and to complete their journals fully.

The surgeon-superintendents had a rather thankless task, made no easier with the issuing of a somewhat brusque instruction on 1 November 1836. Signed by W. Burnett, Physician General to the Admiralty, it announced that:

> The Surgeons Superintendent of Convict Ships are particularly desired to notice, that they will be required to render a regular Sick Book, with the Journal, and the Nosological Synopsis now added thereto, in a complete and Scientific state, together with a certificate from the Medical Storekeeper at Deptford, as to the condition and number of their Surgical Instruments, in all respects the same as if employed in King's Ships and that in the event of any failure in these particulars, the Certificate necessary from this Department, to entitle them to receive their Pay and Allowances will be withheld. [A nosological synopsis is an analysis of the diseases that were treated on the voyage.]

To add to their responsibilities, the surgeon-superintendents were instructed in 1823 to attempt reformation of the convicts in their care. Official eyes were keen to direct prisoners' minds along remedial paths, hence the requirement for schooling and worship. Unsurprisingly, those who thought that the prisoners could be reformed were anxious to start the process at the earliest possible opportunity. James Carmichael, surgeon-superintendent of the *Samuel Boddington*, alludes to classes being held for the convicts on a voyage in 1845–6:

> Every attention was paid to promote the moral improvement of the convicts in persuading and encouraging those who were able to read through books and religious tracts supplied for their use and inviting those who could not read to endeavour to learn as much as possible during the voyage…[2]

Reading matter was made freely available on board convict ships. It included bibles, religious tracts and other morally uplifting works—tracts such as *Exercises against Lying* and *Dissuasions from Stealing*. It is hard to imagine items of this sort being eagerly seized upon by the minority of prisoners who were sufficiently literate to read them. It is even harder to believe that these unctuous publications could have generated feelings of contrition in convict hearts, or persuaded prisoners to put their sinful ways behind them. On the other hand, much of the voyage was boring and a literate prisoner might well have resorted to reading anything available to while away the time—even pious tracts.

The sticks of discipline at sea (pages 138–42) were balanced with spiritual carrots: those who had responded particularly well to such ministrations might find themselves presented with copies of religious books on their arrival in the Australian colonies.[3] The effectiveness of these evangelical activities in the long term is hard to establish. Not surprisingly, surgeon-superintendents took a pragmatic attitude. One of them, Dr Haslem, sailing on the *Mariner* in 1816, was not optimistic about his role in the cure of souls, stating bluntly that the prisoners under his care were so degraded that any reform was quite simply impossible.[4] Others argued that even if disease could be virtually eradicated on board the transport ships, moral pollution could not, as the physical circumstances thrust criminal novices into close and sustained contact with the most hardened recidivists. Nevertheless, attempts were made to rehabilitate the prisoners with instructional classes during the voyage as John Rodmell, surgeon-superintendent on the *Medina*, which sailed for Australia on 19 July 1823, points out: 'A school was established in the Boys' Prison and very considerable progress was made by those in attendance, not only for reading and writing but arithmetic. A plentiful supply of pens and ink, paper and slates were furnished for their use.'[5]

THE SURGEON-SUPERINTENDENTS

Those who became surgeon-superintendents were largely selected on a rota basis by the Admiralty from the list of unemployed half-pay naval surgeons—quite extensive in times of peace, but less so during wars. When his name appeared, the naval surgeon would be offered a post, which he was entitled to refuse. If he accepted and performed his duties well, however, he might be given the opportunity to continue in the convict service. Several men thus decided to undertake a number of voyages, despite the all-too-evident drawbacks of the job. One such was Robert Espie, who was to act as surgeon-superintendent on convict ships to Australia in 1816, 1820, 1826, 1834 and 1836.

One major problem was that instructions in the early days ignored the question of how surgeons and surgeon-superintendents were to return to England or Ireland. The return passage could cost nearly as much as they had earned on the outward leg, obliging the Admiralty to authorize a payment of £100 towards their return. Some of them exploited this concession by finding a merchant vessel bound for Britain which required the paid services of a surgeon. These often returned by a circuitous route, allowing the surgeons the opportunity for a spot of sight-seeing while being, in effect, paid twice over. Eventually officialdom became so exasperated at funding the pleasure cruises of peripatetic surgeons that they were required to take passage and return home by the first available direct ship; formal documentation was then requested to prove that this stipulation had been observed.

Generally the private and naval surgeons used on convict ships were unlikely to be the pick of their profession. Surgeons as a whole lacked the status enjoyed by physicians; they were frequently satirized as 'sawbones', rough-and-ready men, little better than butchers, who performed amputations, set fractures, lanced boils, treated piles, and purged and bled their patients, most of whom were from the poorer classes. Sometimes a young man would obtain a modicum of knowledge as an assistant to a physician on shore and then enlist as a surgeon's mate in the Royal Navy in order to widen his experience. Other surgeons on half-pay might exploit their contacts to obtain more congenial work using their professional skills in a civilian medical capacity. Naval surgeons with social 'influence' were much more likely to be fully employed at sea or in a shore-based capacity even during peacetime. The most prestigious posts for naval surgeons were not at sea, but in naval hospitals, such as Haslar, near Portsmouth. Here they received more generous payment than their seagoing colleagues with, of course, fewer natural hazards to contend with and free board provided. It was not simply a bed of roses, however. Hospitals in the eighteenth and nineteenth centuries, naval ones included, were notoriously filthy and uncaring institutions, often staffed by ill-trained, callous and frequently drunken nurses.

In spite of the numerous drawbacks experienced while serving as a surgeon or surgeon-superintendent in a convict ship, there were plenty of men only too eager to serve in that capacity.[6] One particular file in the National Archives consists of letters to the Lords Commissioners of the Admiralty, written between 1829 and 1833. These request, sometimes almost plead, for the applicant to be given an appointment as a surgeon-superintendent. They are often accompanied by supporting testimonials,

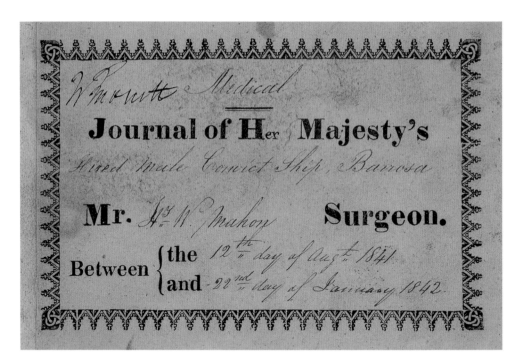

Journal of H_{er} Majesty's

Mr. *H^y W^c Mahon* Surgeon.

Between { the 12th day of Augt 1841
and 22nd day of January 1842

The cover of the medical journal for the convict ship Barrosa, 1841–2 (ADM 101/ 7/8). Although the surgeons were issued with a standard format journal, the contents were idiosyncratic—some are sparse, others full of details about shipboard life. They are invaluable sources for grasping the reality of convict voyages.

in some cases from very senior and eminent naval officers. Several letters, such as that from William Borland, indicate that the supplicant is temporarily unemployed, although the reasons why they are 'between jobs' are usually glossed over. They provide fragmented but fascinating pictures of real people, some of whom were clearly absolutely desperate for employment. It is intriguing to speculate about what is left unsaid in these letters, as well as to marvel at the outrageously bullish claims that some make in support of their applications. The author of a particularly fulsome letter, one Robert Dixon, described with such exuberance both his vast breadth of relevant experience and the enormous esteem in which he was held by professional colleagues that one can only wonder how a man of such calibre could possibly be left seeking employment. Another applicant complains that he has spent over six months contacting the Admiralty for an appointment as a surgeon-superintendent, during which time, to his certain knowledge, other surgeons junior to him have received seagoing appointments. We can only speculate what sins of commission or omission led to this man being repeatedly passed over, or indeed if he ever achieved his ambition.

Some degree of control over appointments was maintained—those who aspired to work in the Royal Navy had to be examined before employment—but the oral testing was somewhat perfunctory and few applicants failed. Unsurprisingly, this led to significant disparities in the knowledge, experience and competence of naval surgeons. Those trained at the Scottish universities of Edinburgh, Glasgow and Aberdeen received the very best of medical and surgical knowledge, but others would have learned the ropes as apprentices at sea, as supernumeraries on hospital wards, or even by attending private lectures and demonstrations on medical and surgical matters held in cities, such as Edinburgh, Dublin and London.

JOURNALS AND JOTTINGS

The journals of the surgeon-superintendents are a very rich source of evidence about life on board convict transport ships. Despite official instructions on the scope and contents of these journals, they vary considerably in presentation, style and substance. As a result, logs or journals often provide fascinating reading, although, as Robert Hughes observes, 'The duller reading they make, the better the voyage for the prisoners.' These documents are rarely dull, however, even if they are frequently almost indecipherable. They record the often humdrum and mundane ailments and incidents to be expected in people closeted at sea for such a length of time, most of them under conditions of restraint. At their best, the journals provide vivid impressions of the actual voyage to Australia experienced by tens of thousands of prisoners during the 'convict years'.

The individual flavour of the journals gives clear insights into the personality and professionalism of the surgeons concerned. Some reports are terse and minimalist, their authors displaying indifference verging on callousness, coupled with thinly veiled contempt for those in their charge. Such men appear concerned only to collect their pay and to keep the discharge of their duties to the absolute minimum. William McDowell, who officiated in the *Lady East*, is an example of the 'minimalist' school of surgeon-superintendents. His journal, covering the period 16 September 1824 to 4 May 1825, is much briefer than the norm, which he excuses by a decision to describe only the more 'particular and severe' cases, dismissing as unworthy of attention 'a considerable number of trifling diseases involving the bowels'. His patients, living with the consequences in a poorly ventilated, confined space, may not have thought such complaints were 'trifling'.[7] Yet the professional preferences of many surgeons are reflected in the journals; the surgeon of the *Pestonjee Bomanjee*, for example, which left for Australia during April 1852, seems almost obsessed with haemorrhoids.[8]

One of the most eccentric journals was produced by the surgeon-superintendent on board the convict transport *Agamemnon* in 1820. This man, a Dr Hall, wrote his journal entirely in Latin for reasons best known to himself, but possibly reflecting his lofty contempt for the business he was undertaking, and for which, after all, he was being paid.[9] The result must have severely taxed the patience of those who had to inspect the reports he made, although unfortunately their reactions are not recorded.

However, many reports reveal highly conscientious and compassionate surgeons, clearly determined to put their professional skills at the disposal of the prisoners, guards, crew and any passengers. Relations with the ships' masters, their officers and guards could also be positive as well as sources of tension; the experience of John Rodmell, surgeon-superintendent on board the *Medina*, a chartered vessel which sailed for Australia on 19 July 1823, proved to be a happy one: 'The Officer of the Guard and the Master of the Ship were at all times ready to attend to and carry into effect any measure that I might suggest for the benefit of the convicts...'

Rodmell's journal includes several intriguing details, such as his approval of new stocks of underwear supplied to the convicts, made from kersey. This coarse woollen cloth, although itchy and uncomfortable to wear, would have provided convicts with valuable warmth on board ship: 'The supply of Kersey drawers furnished lately I consider a valuable addition to the articles of clothing, particularly for convicts leaving England during the winter.'

Frequently the reports of these same, highly motivated men give detailed and intimate insights into shipboard life and routine. They were clearly fascinated by, and felt the need to relate, various unusual and untoward events that inevitably occurred during the voyages, even if this information was not strictly required by those to whom they reported. The journals are not always easy to use because many are almost totally illegible, but most can be deciphered with patience and a few are a joy to read, both for their calligraphy and their content. Matthew Burnside, surgeon-superintendent in the *Providence* which sailed to Australia between

November 1825 and May 1826, for example, provides a meticulous, detailed and legible journal, although unfortunately he restricts himself mainly to medical matters.[10] A contemporary of his, Charles Cameron, officiated on the *Midas*, sailing between June and December 1825. His journal is legible and comprehensive and especially interesting because the convicts were female. Female-only convict ships were in a minority.[11]

In addition, there were surgeon-superintendents who felt strongly about the system and used the opportunity to voice their concerns. One such, Thomas Reid, travelled on the voyages of the convict ships *Neptune* (to Sydney in 1818) and *Morley* (to Hobart Town and Sydney in 1820). Reid wrote his accounts in *Two Voyages to New South Wales and Van Diemen's Land* (1822), which he dedicated to Elizabeth Fry, drawing on his own direct experience to express his strong opposition to transportation. Although he was highly praised by the captains for his care of the prisoners, Reid refused to participate in any further convict transport.

Considering that the work of surgeon-superintendents was not held in high esteem, at least in the early days, nor was it particularly lucrative, the best of these men display an admirably selfless diligence and sense of duty. Their journals are also remarkable, in some cases, for an evident *joie de vivre*, enhancing and enriching our understanding of what transportation meant to those immediately involved.

The National Archives has over 600 journals compiled by surgeon-superintendents, most of which can be examined at first hand. We cannot know how much some of the surgeon-superintendents dissembled, attempting to justify themselves or shift blame on to others if things had gone badly, or seeking to ingratiate themselves with higher powers. At the back of the official pro-forma journal is a section for 'General Remarks'— often the most interesting part of the journals, containing comments or observations of a more informal character. However, not all surgeon-superintendents chose to use the official journal.[12]

A SOUND MIND IN A HEALTHY BODY

Morgan Price became something of a veteran, acting in the capacity of surgeon-superintendent on several convict ships to Australia. His first voyage was on the transport *Brampton*, which left for New South Wales in 1823. Evidently not a man overly concerned about good relations with his colleagues, he describes a flaming row that broke out one night between the Captain of the Guard and the Master, in which the captain drew his sword. Although those involved were restrained and the crisis blew over, Price clearly deplored such an event occurring early in the voyage, as well as in full view of the prisoners. By submitting an entry about this fracas in his journal, he set the cogs in motion for an official inquiry. Price was definitely something of a stormy petrel; the journal also reveals his role in an extremely acrimonious dispute with the victualling authorities at Deptford, concerning a substantial consignment of rum, which could not be properly accounted for.[13]

Price's fearlessness in making waves surfaced again in 1835, when he served as surgeon-superintendent on the *Hector*, sailing to Van Diemen's Land. He criticized the vessel, which was transporting female prisoners, for being much too small, and then went on to berate the poor quality of seamanship which accounted for what, according to Price, was the unusual length of the voyage. He commented unfavourably upon the inadequate ventilation, and complained that several prisoners and their children had been kept on board far too long before the ship sailed, with harmful effects on their well-being, while others had been forced to endure a difficult voyage down the coast from Scotland in a 'small sloop' before joining *Hector*, experiencing needless suffering as a result.[14]

On the voyage itself, however, surgeon-superintendents were empowered to give orders to the master of a convict ship on matters seriously affecting the health and welfare of the prisoners. James Carmichael, surgeon-superintendent of the *Samuel Boddington*, recorded such an incident in his journal for the voyage from August 1845 to January 1846.

> I was induced to require that the ship should be put into Cape of Good Hope which was complied with on the 7th December, after having been 72 days at sea and about 10 of the prisoners, who had been complaining of evident precursory symptoms of scurvy, were completely free from the slightest sign or symptoms after 7 days refreshment at the Cape of Good Hope.

An example of a similar stop appears in the journal of Henry Walsh Mahon, surgeon-superintendent on the 730-ton barque, *Barrosa*. It left Sheerness on 30 August 1841 to make its second voyage as a convict ship, achieving the passage in 136 days. Mahon's journal reveals him to be conscientious, perceptive and vivacious. Some of the convicts were suffering from sickness and debility during the early part of the voyage, and Mahon required the ship to put in at Tenerife for fresh supplies of food and water. Prisoners who had money were allowed to buy the rather odd combination of fruit and onions from local bumboats that plied their trade alongside the ship, under the supervision of a non-commissioned officer, whose job it was to ensure fair prices and good quality. Back at sea, Mahon was pleased to see that the prisoners were fascinated by the appearance in the sea of huge numbers of Portuguese-men-of-war—members of the *Physalia* genus, often mistaken for jellyfish and capable of inflicting painful, even deadly, stings. Mahon believed that external stimulus was highly beneficial for the prisoners, diverting attention from present discomfort and future anxiety.

In this painting by Jean-Baptiste Debret (1822–8), a floating food vendor sells his wares to the crew of a merchant vessel off the coast of Rio de Janeiro. The scene reflects the continuous cultural interchange among sailors, traders, immigrants, convicts and slaves.

The voyage of the *Corona*, which reached Western Australia on 26 December 1866, is retold in a delightfully atmospheric account; it specializes in understated comments, such as 'ship rolling very much', 'heavy squall, ship lurching heavily' and 'prisoners seasick'. They leave the reader to imagine the conditions below decks, where the prisoners were necessarily

restricted in a cramped space, while the ship wallowed sickeningly early in its voyage. Retching miserably or vomiting uncontrollably, many of these poor devils had probably never before seen the sea, let alone been on it. Physical suffering combined with the traumas of the trial and sentence and their enforced estrangement from everything familiar and reassuring, including their families, must have convinced many of them that they were descending into the jaws of Hell itself.[15]

William Smith was the surgeon-superintendent aboard the *Merchantman*, which sailed to Western Australia, arriving on 30 September 1864. The journal is unusual in that Smith chooses to provide a list of the offences for which the approximately 270 prisoners on board (average age just over 30 years, the oldest being 64 and the youngest 17[16]) had been convicted. As might be expected, offences such as 'larceny' and 'robbery' feature very prominently, but some others are rather more piquant. They include counterfeit coining, having a mould for coining, military manslaughter, military insubordination, desertion, assault with intent to ravish, being at large before the expiration of a sentence, and several cases of arson and more specifically of 'firing a stack' or rick-burning, a form of rural protest. Smith clearly has a particular interest in the crimes of those in his care, also citing in his journal details of misdemeanours that took place during the journey. These included 'William Thompson, accused and found guilty of committing an unnatural offence' (exact nature unspecified, but he received 36 lashes for it), William Barker, given three days solitary confinement for 'making use of improper language', and an unnamed prisoner found in felonious possession of onions and bacon, who had his allowance of wine stopped for a week.

To the conscientious surgeon-superintendent, concern for the prevention of illness was as great as dealing with its manifestations. One such was Charles Linton, who sailed on the *Guildford* in 1827; his journal mentions the number of convicts who, when first embarked, were suffering from chilblains. Linton's tone is generally measured, but his anger was certainly roused on the issue of ventilation.

> The width and height of the *Guildford* between decks was very favourable for keeping the prison well ventilated... I had considerable difficulty, however, in getting the windsails mounted and kept properly trim and attended to during the voyage ... from the criminal want of helpful activity in the master and his mates from whom I received very little official assistance of any kind

during the whole voyage. I consequently was obliged on all occasions of the most trifling nature to attend to every minor circumstance of detail myself in order to see the arrangements for the preservation of health attended to and executed.

John Tarn, surgeon-superintendent aboard the *Georgiana* in 1831, also commented on the importance of airing the accommodation below decks to reduce the spread of disease and infections:

> The general healthy state of the ship during the voyage may be attributed to the regulations invariably adhered to in fine weather ... viz ... that of having the whole of the convicts on deck during the day. By so doing the prisons became thoroughly ventilated and dried and all accumulation of effluvia was effectively prevented. Great attention was also paid to cleanliness both in the persons and the habits of the convicts, and dryness was promoted by the frequent use of stoves for that purpose.[17]

The surgeon-superintendents' duties, responsibilities and powers were clearly delineated, and there must have been times when his requirements conflicted sharply with those of the master on matters affecting the navigation and operation of the ship. The ability to work together for the good of the ship and all aboard was an essential ingredient of a successful surgeon-superintendent, but he was operating in a potentially volatile situation. An intolerant master, jealous of his knowledge and experience in nautical affairs, or an over-zealous surgeon-superintendent could easily provoke mutual antagonism and misunderstanding. The surgeon-superintendents could—and did on many occasions—go straight to the Admiralty with recommendations that had not been achieved on the voyage. For example, they made pleas for more guards, better clothing for convicts and sailors, improved diets, effective discipline and more supplies. The wonder is that the journals do not more frequently allude to these difficulties; in reality, many surgeon-superintendents may have felt that it was politic to omit such problems in reports to their superiors. That Linton was prepared to give praise where he thought it was due is evident from this passage: 'The whole of the provisions which were served out to the prisoners during the passage to New South Wales were without exception of excellent quality.'[18]

John Mould, sailing on the *Sir John Peel* between August 1844 and January 1845, shared Linton's concern with ventilation on board ship. He also approved of physical activity in the fresh air as the best way of

	Gal	Cwt	lb	oz
Cort. Peruv. Opt:			15	
Camphora			12	
Crem: Tart:			3	
Confectio Card:			6	
Cera Flava			10	
Corn. Cerv. C. pp't			2	
Canthard: Pulv:			60	
Opium Crude			20	
Sal. Cathart: amar:			2	
— Glaub:			2	
— Nitri			2	
— Tartari			1	
— Ammon: Crud:			1	
Tart: Emetic:			20	
Flor. Sulphur:			1	
— Cham Pulv:		50		
Rad. Ipecac. pulv		50		
— Rhabarb: pulv:			1	
— Jalap: pulv:			10	
— Valerian			20	
— Serpentar Ung:			12	
Calomel. pp't			20	
Merc. Corrosiv. Sublimat:			20	
— Præcipit: rubr:			15	
— Emetic Flav:				6
Argent. Vivum			2	
Ung. Cærul. Fort:			20	
Sp't Vini Rectific:	100			
— Lavend. Compos:			6	
— Nitri Dulc:			6	
Vitriolum Cæruls:			6	
— Alb:			10	
Sacc. Saturni			50	
Magnesia Alba			12	
Cons. Rosar. Rubr:			10	
Elect. Lenitiv:			26	
Caustic. Lunare			3	
Lapis Calaminaris ppt			20	

	Gal	Cwt	lb	oz
Manna Optima			10	
Luna			10	
Alum Com:		1		
— Ustum			2	
Sapon: Venet:			2	
Acet. Distillat	10			
Tart. Solubil:			20	
Pulv: Doctoris Jacob. reum				
Elix: Vitriol. Acid:			20	
Pulv: Rad. Colum:			15	
Cuprum Ammon:				12
Flor. Zinci			20	
Vitrum Antimonii			1	
Pulv: Rad. Jellitie			6	
Lint			2	
Tow			5	
Nux Mosch:			8	
Sp't Corn. Cerv:			12	
— Terebinthin	26			
Vinum Antimon:			8	
Salvia			10	
Herb pro foliæ			4	
Ol. Spirit. Cinnam:				4
— Menth Piperitid			1	
— Ricini			16	
— Oliv. Optim:	100			
Aloe Soccot. Optim:			10	
Acet. Jellitie			10	
Gum: Arabic. pulv:			1	
Ipecacuanha			10	
Moschus Chin: Opt:				2
Extract. Saturni Goulard:			16	
— Cathart:			10	
— Cicutæ			1	
Emp. Commun:			2	
— Mercuriale			12	
— Vesicator:			30	
Ung. Basilic. Flav:			2	
— Nigr:			2	
Cerat. Epulotic:			3	
Tinctura Thebaica	260		10	

A typical inventory of medical instruments used on the convict ships in the 1780s (1/639). It includes apparatus for trepanning, a process of cutting discs of bone from the skull. The prospect of undergoing such surgery at sea is distinctly unnerving.

keeping healthy—an interestingly modern prescription.

> At least a partial amount of the health of the prisoners may be attributed to
> strict attention having been paid to keeping the Prison as dry as possible, at
> the same time that it was thoroughly clean and well-ventilated and to this end
> the deck was dry-holystoned whenever the weather would permit … all
> moisture was carefully scraped up, and windsails were sedulously employed
> while the use of chloride of lime … was not neglected. [19]

The holystones referred to were made of softish sandstone and were used
by sailors for scouring the decks of ships, after which the deck was hosed
down with saltwater, creating a smooth, blanched appearance. The name
'holystone' is supposed to have derived from the fact that the sailors
looked as though they were performing a devotion when they were on
their hands and knees scrubbing the deck; small holystones were called
'prayer books' and the larger ones 'bibles'. Another explanation is that the
first stones used in this way were plundered from the church of St
Nicholas at Great Yarmouth. 'Windsails' were long tubes or funnels of
sailcloth with wings at one end; they were suspended from a stay in the
standing rigging in an attempt to direct fresh air below deck.

Browning, surgeon-superintendent on the *Prestonjee Bamanjee* in
1846, was clearly a conscientious and painstaking man. He refused to
allow any meals to be served until he himself had inspected and pronounced on them. He was another great believer in the virtue of exercise
and activity for the prisoners, advocating:

> …attention to exercise both of mind and body. The major bodily exercise
> consisted in walking the deck and in their being marched in regular order and
> in their successive divisions, around the upper deck, as frequently as the state
> of the weather and other circumstances in prudence allow.

In his journal, Browning also turned his attention to the question of diet
and prophylactics:

> Any opportunities of determining between the comparative merits of crystal-
> lized citric acid and lemon juice as anti-scorbutics has been very limited but
> such as they were, they dispose me to adhere to my former conclusion and
> continue my preference for the citric acid, and the occasional use of pickles.
> The introduction of potatoes is a great improvement to a seagoing diet. The
> pepper supplied for use was cayenne. It ought, in my judgement, to have been
> black pepper and that was confirmed by Dr Jones, of the flagship at the Cape,
> that it was black pepper of which he had occasion … in reference to the diet
> of prisoners, to recommend.

Browning concludes his journal on a rather smug note: 'I cannot easily imagine a body of men, disbarking [*sic*] at the termination of a long voyage, in a better state of health and fitter for presently entering in the performance of manual labour.' Clearly he had not been so sanguine all the time the ship was at sea, as this somewhat querulous entry makes it clear: 'By far the most trying portion of my duties related to the soldiers' wives, nearly the whole of whom were the most *self-willed, disobedient* and *unruly* [his emphasis] body of women that ever came under my immediate observation.'[20]

WOMEN AT SEA

The surgeon-superintendent of the *Lady of the Lake*, William Evans, provides a very comprehensive journal dated 2 May to 6 November 1829. He served on this 243-ton female convict ship, embarking at Deptford in May 1829. The small vessel was heavily laden with women and children, both convict and free travellers, as Evans was quick to point out. 'Eighty-one female prisoners and seventeen children is the largest number ever sent to New South Wales in so small a vessel, and here I may observe, she was the smallest ship ever taken up to convey convicts.'

The female convicts were taken on board at Woolwich and they received several visits there from two Quaker ladies, a 'Mrs Pryor and Mrs Lydia Irving'. He commends these reformers, who brought both practical articles and books for spiritual guidance, as being almost 'indefatigable in endeavouring to impress upon the prisoners the necessity of abandoning their evil ways and becoming useful members of Society.'

The female convicts were now placed six in each hold, with a specially chosen monitor to supervise them. They were to maintain good order, to see that the berths were properly cleaned and to ensure that those under their charge received the correct rations. The monitors were also to read the Bible to the prisoners. In return for carrying out their duties satisfactorily, they were each to receive the rather scant reward of a sovereign on reaching Australia. The implication would seem to be that their real reward was of a more spiritual kind. For their part, the prisoners appointed as cook and cook's mate were allowed to sell dripping. This accumulated on the surface of the water in which the meat was boiled and it was eagerly bought by manufacturers of soap in New South Wales.

Despite the care that Evans attempted to take of his charges, tragic accidents inevitably occurred. One such that he describes involved a young girl of 18, Christiana McDonald, who on 30 September 1829, 'fell overboard in endeavouring to save her cape... The ship was going through the water at the rate of eight knots at the time. The helm was instantly put down and a boat was lowered but she sank almost immediately... '

Children, inevitably, were among the casualties of such a long period at sea. They often suffered from the lack of appropriate sustenance, such as Maria Dix, an infant of 13 months, who died of 'atrophy, arising in some respects from want of proper food having been deprived of its milk diet on embarking at Woolwich...' Margaret Coddington was even younger than Maria, being only a baby of nine months when she died of 'marasmus'—a wasting away of the body due to nutritional deficiencies.

All in all, it must have been a great relief to surgeon-superintendents and convicts alike when the destination was, at least metaphorically, in sight. Evans' journal describes how the ship drew near to the coast of Australia on the morning of 31 October 1829, and he was finally relieved of his responsibilities.

> The pilot came aboard about 8 pm at the entrance of the River Derwent, and on the following day we came to anchor in Sullivan's Cove, Hobart Town... On the 4th November, the prisoners were inspected by His Excellency the Lieutenant Governor, who was pleased to say that he was perfectly satisfied with their appearance and with their management during the voyage and on the 6th November, they were all landed and consigned to the service of settlers with the exception of three...

Evans appears to have been an earnest and courageous man. While apparently concerned to maintain a thoroughly professional relationship with those under his care, he was also prepared to risk unfavourable notice by stating that such small ships should not be used on such voyages, because of the harmful effects on their human cargo.[21]

> I may here be permitted to observe that a ship of the small poundage of the 'Lady of the Lake' is by no means adapted to carry female prisoners; from being constantly wet between decks and the hatches being obliged to be put on thereby causing a great deterioration of the atmosphere in the prison...

The journal of the *Kinnear*, which sailed from Kingstown Harbour, Dublin, to Hobart between 2 May and 14 October 1848, is also of interest for its entirely female complement of prisoners, all of whom had been housed previously in Grange Gorman penitentiary in Dublin. John Williams, the surgeon-superintendent, emerges as a thorough, professional and unemotional man. He has a keen eye for the convicts, noting their individual circumstances and physical defects. One woman, Mary Nowlan, is described as 'a slightly made woman [who] exhibited an exceedingly large head, an overhanging forehead and had a singularly repulsive countenance, approaching the idiotic.'

Williams' journal illustrates how women were susceptible to conditions on board ship, which might exacerbate various gynaecological complaints or complications with pregnancy or childbirth. On 10 July 1848, for example, a woman named Elizabeth Larkin died, to be later buried at sea. She had been very poorly since embarkation, when she was suffering from debility and an exceptionally heavy menstrual discharge, which she put down to the shock of hearing her sentence. Another woman, Mary Clougherty, was successfully treated for syphilis by the application of mercury, but more serious was the case of Catherine Young. She first appears in the journal on 15 July 1848, when she gave birth with great difficulty and had to be treated with 30 drops of laudanum. She then became severely constipated until gaining relief after castor oil was administered—a pretty drastic remedy. She appeared to recover, but was taken ill again and died on 6 August.

Drugs offered a brief palliative for the patient, but were often ultimately unsuccessful. Ellen Nalley, recorded as having difficulty in giving birth, recurs in the journal as suffering from external piles which bled frequently, profusely and painfully, as well as severe constipation. Repeated doses of laudanum seem to have cured her problems, although modern medicine would be concerned about the liberal use of such opium-based prophylactics. This took various forms, but laudanum, which included some alcohol mixed in with the opium, was one of the most popular. A less successful outcome occurred with Catherine McNamara, who is first mentioned in the journal on 22 June and becomes an almost constant feature until her death in September. She is first noted for curiously having a hysterical fit on catching sight of a Roman Catholic priest on board the *Kinnear*, and this seems to have precipitated a physical and mental decline. After severe seasickness, she complained of gastric affliction, flatulence, loss of appetite, depression and a recurring delusion that the ship was sinking and she was going down with it.

Williams, intrigued, speculates that such symptoms were caused by the appalling, although unspecified, crimes that McNamara had committed, which were now preying on her mind. She became insane and made a number of attempts to take her life, constantly announcing that she wished she was dead. Before she finally died, she had descended into a state of what Williams describes as 'helpless imbecility'.

Williams was clearly an intelligent surgeon-superintendent, and his journal contains some cogent observations on how to keep the ship clean and healthy:

> I shall explain the general economy of the ship, ventilation, cleanliness, etc and in particular the use of 'Chloride of Lime' to whose disinfecting and purifying properties I attribute the high degree of health that prevailed amongst the many women, congregated together in such a small space …This invaluable solution has the immediate effect of destroying putrid and offensive effluvia arising from animal and vegetable decomposition … and is capable of being applied with equal facility and economy … for the destruction of noxious smells, deleterious gases, the disinfection of convict ships, reservoirs of urine and excremental matter, the purification of stinking bilge water; in short, in the total destruction of every species of infectious effluvia and offensive odour on board ship…[22]

The author of the surgeon-superintendent's journal of the *Sir Robert Peel*, running from 29 August 1844 to 18 January 1845, was one John Mould. In his concluding 'general remarks', he, too, expresses concern about prevailing illness among his charges—interestingly, more apparent among the troops, who had been longer on board ship, than the convicts. He also expresses belief in the modern holistic relationship of mental and physical wellbeing, particularly where potentially 'hysterical' women were involved:

> The remark is forced upon me that much of this sickness depended on the indolence and untidy habits of these people… The berths or standing bed-places, which are built for the women, are great hindrances to ventilation, besides being harbours for filth and, if fever should occur, each one formed a little centre of contagion… The women and children, especially the Irish, are constantly lolling, so that, unless they are daily inspected with candle and [lantern], dirt of every kind accumulated in their corners and beneath them. The expense of these fittings might be saved and these evils avoided by obliging all to sleep in hammocks, a spare cot or two being allowed for such as parturient women should such sick be embarked; for nothing could well be more inconvenient during a labour than one of the present bed-places…

The specific concern for Irish convicts is not unique among the journals. John Grant Stewart was the surgeon-superintendent on the *British Sovereign*, which sailed from Ireland in October 1840. His report includes observations about the poor health of the many prisoners on board, who had been almost totally dependent on potatoes for their diet. He also allows himself some harsh words about the largely English land-lords whose insistence on the payment of rent by their impoverished Irish peasant tenants meant that the latter were forced to grow crops for sale rather than consumption. Those who could not pay their rent were evicted from their holdings as a result, and many starved when the potato blight struck; the lucky ones managed to get away from Ireland. As several among the Royal Navy's top brass owned large amounts of land in Ireland, it took some courage for Stewart to make a such a statement.[23]

EXPECTING THE UNEXPECTED

Back at sea, Henry Walsh Mahon, surgeon on the *Barrosa* in 1841, seemed to welcome anything that broke the monotony of the voyage for the pris-oners. He was pleased to see, for example, that the prisoners were fasci-nated by the appearance of huge numbers of Portuguese-men-of-war.

Mahon was clearly not one to sit back and let matters run their course. The voyage had not been proceeding for long before he felt it safe to declare that the convicts were in good health, and he then turned his attention to preventative measures. He attempted to identify those among the prisoners who had neither had smallpox nor been vaccinated against the disease. Only in 1798, some 40 years earlier, had a modest country physician named Edward Jenner published his findings on vaccination. His inoculation of people with matter from cowpox pustules excited deri-sion in some circles, as might have been expected, but its success was assured; by 1801, at least 100,000 people had been vaccinated in England, and the practice was well on the way to almost universal acceptance. Five prisoners were found among what was—literally—a captive audience. All were vaccinated, but Mahon then rather abruptly concluded his observa-tions, declaring that they all failed to exhibit the signs that the cowpox had 'taken'. Three months into the voyage the dreaded symptoms of scurvy made their appearance and the remainder of his journal is taken up with extraordinarily detailed analyses of the cases concerned.[24]

Particularly unusual conditions were sometimes encountered by the surgeon-superintendents and for Mahon, perhaps inevitably, this was certainly true. In his journal, he records a prisoner suffering from 'squinting and stammering', and another with a 'pistol wound'. He performed an operation that successfully dealt with the squint, but the stammering proved harder to treat. Mahon carried out an operation on the patient's uvula, which was encouragingly followed by the man speaking with complete fluency for the whole of the following day before disappointingly reverting to his usual hesitant manner of speech. The 'pistol wound' was the result of one of the guards accidentally (or perhaps stupidly) discharging his firearm, not knowing that it was loaded, and hitting one of his comrades. The injury was serious enough for the patient to be admitted to the military hospital at Hobart Town.[25] Elsewhere the convict David Barritt, described in the surgeon-superintendent's journal as a 'poor, thin, miserable creature' suffering from phthisis, was recovering well from a course of treatment for his condition when he, and 15 other prisoners, were severely scalded while taking the tea to their messes for breakfast. Such were the minutiae of problems, some predictable and others completely unexpected, with which the surgeon-superintendent was expected to deal.

The surgeon-superintendent of the *London*, which set sail in November 1850, notes the unusually high number of his prisoners suffering from 'inflammation of the eye'. He ascribed this to their previous confinement in Mountjoy prison, which employed the notorious 'separate system' under which each prisoner spent most of the time working in his cell. What little exercise was available was taken wearing a mask, while talking was not allowed; some prisoners were driven insane by such a regime. As a result, the convicts had got used to living and working in poorly lit conditions. On the first few weeks of the voyage, when they were brought up from below for exercise, they had to wear caps with visors to minimize the glare of the light, but the light was still too bright for many of them, hence the inflammations.[26]

A curious event occurred on the *Robert Small* when it transported 300 convicts to Fremantle in Western Australia. The ship left Britain on 1 May 1853, with Harvey Morris as surgeon-superintendent. Ten deaths were recorded on the voyage, by no means exceptional in itself, but it emerged that the ship had sailed with its ballast composed of a mixture of sand and

Dutch clay. The latter was a black, peat-like substance with a very high organic content. This caused it to putrefy once the tropics had been reached and to emit a highly noxious gas. The ship was forced to put into Rio de Janiero to offload 150 tons of this ballast. An inquiry was later held at Fremantle where it was argued that the effluvium given off by the original ballast was responsible for many of the cases of illness on board, and possibly some of the fatalities. The inquiry also revealed that Morris, deliberately or through neglect, had only recorded in his journal about a third of those who had reported to him as being sick.[27]

The surgeon's log of the *Clara*, which sailed to Fremantle in the early months of 1864, is interesting; it is the only one seen that gives a station list in the event of a fire, plus a similar list for use during an attempted breakout among the prisoners. There is also a laconic reference to the crew members who would man the starboard and port-side guns in such an eventuality.[28]

FROM SAIL TO STEAM

The surgeon-superintendent A. Watson, of the transport ship *Racehorse*, noted in his journal for April to August 1865 that the ship was towed down the Thames from East India Dock to Gravesend by the steam tug *Willington*. The tug was a new kind of vessel, a product of applying steam power to marine propulsion. They probably came into use in the 1810s and the Royal Navy bought its first tugs in 1822, using them for towing ships of the line and other large vessels into and out of harbour at times when the wind was unfavourable. The Navy showed some reluctance to use steam power because, among other reasons, it was thought that smuts and cinders would dirty the sails and pristine scrubbed decks of its sailing men-of-war.

Contemporaries believed that sailing ship technology could be developed further—the truth of which was revealed in the great clipper ships, built from the 1840s to the 1860s. Steam's rise to ascendancy at sea was slow, and it is interesting that, in 1865, Dr Watson found the sight of the steam tug at work unusual enough to warrant mention in his journal.

1799
Saturday —
September 21st

and for a considerable distance, they frequently fly into the ship, I believe
when pursued by a larger fish, they are in this respect very unfortunate, for
when pursued by large fish, and fly, they are frequently are caught by birds
on the watch for them, and to avoid which if they take to the water, it
is frequently into the mouth of their first pursuer they drop — This morning one of them flew in on the forecastle from which I have taken the
following drawing. a number of Canattas were likewise speared and
taken — one of which I have taken a drawing of — as appears on the next
page, they are a large handsome fish but sometimes very pernicious to those
who eat of them.   — Latt: Observed — 11 — 49. N.

The Flying Fish.

After inspecting the fabric of the ship and its fitments in accordance with the instructions of the Director of Transport Services, Watson noted that *Racehorse* took on a guard of 49 men, accompanied by 30 women and no less than 72 children—probably more trouble than the entire complement of convicts. He travelled by railway—that revolutionary application of steam power to land transport—to Chatham to inspect the convicts before they embarked. Watson goes on to record a series of errors, among which was the failure of the contractor to supply the required bread and vegetables before the ship sailed and a navigational oversight which caused the ship's anchor to foul the harbour moorings.

In his journal, Watson was an assiduous recorder of precisely those small shipboard incidents which, although trivial in themselves, give a vivid sense of everyday life at sea on the convict ships. For example, a sentry at the main hatch, who allowed a lamp under his charge to go out, was placed under guard on bread and water, and then put on 'watch and watch'; he also had his grog stopped for a week. The first punishment was a real deterrent because it required the offender to go on watch every four hours. It was a psychological and a physical torture because it meant that he was unable to have any continuous sleep during the designated period.

Even worse, from the point of view of some men at sea, was the loss of their grog. In 1687, the Royal Navy had introduced a ration of one pint of neat rum a day for men and half a pint for boys. In 1740, Admiral Vernon (1684–1757), known as 'Old Grogram' because he seemed inseparable from a boat cloak made of that material (a composite of silk and mohair), reduced the allowance of rum by diluting it. The watered down rum was known as 'grog', and even in its weakened state it certainly helped to relieve the rigours of life at sea. Another guard, who had supplied a prisoner with a clasp knife, was ordered on 'watch and watch' and had his grog stopped for 14 days. A surgeon-superintendent hostile to alcohol recorded the death of one of the crew from hepatitis; he put the death down to drinking too much grog over a long career at sea.

'BLOW THE WIND SOUTHERLY'

The journal from the *Lady of the Lake*, which sailed between May and November 1829, records how fires had to be brought below decks even in July, when rain made quarters extremely damp and the strong southwesterly breezes caused many convicts to suffer bouts of recurring sea-sickness. The weather was an ongoing concern of everyone on board ship and journals constantly refer to it. Within a week or two of the ship's departure from Britain, the surgeon-superintendent Dr Watson commented on the marked improvement in the overall health of the convicts, probably due to the relative abundance of fresh air and a controlled dietary regime.

However, it was not all plain sailing. For a period in late July and August, the weather was sultry and humid, progress slow, the health of those aboard suffered and tempers frayed. By contrast, once under the influence of the south-east trade winds, the increased speed of the ship and the fresher air boosted the health and the spirits of all on board. On the 16 October 1829, a hurricane was encountered during which the ship had to heave to. Huge seas washed over the ship and water cascaded into every part of the hull, soaking and saturating everybody and everything and making life a total misery. Resulting from this were innumerable cases of catarrh, pneumonia, rheumatism and dysentery.

Despite such trials, Watson was able to record that a month into the voyage, the convicts were generally in much healthier condition than when they had embarked. He added that 'I attribute the healthy condition of the convicts to the circumstance that their prison has been kept clean, dry and wholesome, and that they have passed a good portion of their time on deck.'[29] It is likely that regimes on well-run convict ships were considerably better than those experienced in most of Britain's prisons.

We have tried in this chapter to give something of the flavour of the journals of the surgeon-superintendents. Besides a wealth of historical information, these journals are full of tragedy, comedy, curiosity and human interest—all the ingredients that feed our imagination and bring the experience of the voyage uniquely to life.

9

The Promised Land

THE LENGTHY voyages to Australia were stressful experiences for all on board convict ships, including the many guards, officers and free settlers who sailed with the prisoners. Despite natural apprehension and some regret, there must have been a general sense of relief at the sighting of land, and many surgeon-superintendents' journals record that the convicts disembarked in good spirits. The relief of the convicts on the *Albion* in 1828 was apparent to the surgeon-superintendent Thomas Logan, who described their 'liveliest satisfaction' and 'animated eagerness to behold their future country.' Not all of them had the opportunity, however. One of the *Albion*'s convicts, William Crew aged 25, had suffered from dysentery throughout the voyage; Logan made many entries commenting on his health and expressing genuine concern. Tragically, the young man died the day after the *Albion* arrived in Sydney. Despite this death, Logan was still able to record that 'this morning the convicts, 188 in number, were landed in good health... I was delivered of my charge, with the satisfaction of finding that no cause of complaint was alleged by anyone against me.'[1]

The reports of the surgeon-superintendents were verified, hence their concern with complaints that might affect their fees (page 168). The governor of New South Wales, Lachlan Macquarie, known as the 'Father of Australia', gave his seal of approval to the *Atlas* surgeon-superintendent's account in November 1819, confirming 'I have perused the foregoing journal.'[2] During the period before disembarking, the convict Joseph Mason summed up what many others must have been feeling: '[all was] conjecture and surmise as to our future destiny; a state of suspense which was to continue for some time.'[3] At least a 'state of suspense' was a far cry from the dreadful experience of those 'wretched people' of the Second Fleet, who were described on arrival in 1790 by the *Sydney Cove Chronicle*.

Final formalities could provide a chance for

The entrance of Port Jackson and part of Sydney show a sizeable, apparently thriving town in this painting of 1823. The crossing of the Blue Mountains in 1813, followed by the discovery of a prosperous hinterland, fostered Sydney's growth: it was declared a city in 1842.

expressions of mutual appreciation between convicts and their surgeon. John Hampton, for example, who went on to become the Governor of Western Australia between 1862 and 1868, sailed as surgeon-superintendent on the *Sir George Seymour* to Van Diemen's Land in 1845. His report on the voyage was striking:

> I have been for years familiar with the convict service at sea, have gone out to this and the neighbouring colony in charge of emigrants, male and female convicts, and served in the highly disciplined ships of war, yet I never met with anything to equal the uniform orderly good conduct of the prisoners on board the *Sir George Seymour*.[4]

Hampton had clearly made an impact on the convicts under his care, and the prisoners reciprocated the sentiments in a remarkable and moving letter of gratitude.[5]

Honoured Sir

As our debarkation will shortly take place, permit us to express the deep sensations of gratitude we feel to you for your humane, affable, kind and generous treatment of us during the voyage.

Whether we consider your affectionate regard to our comfort and health, or the admirable and mild discipline with which you have ruled us, and the almost paternal care with which you have watched over us, or the strict impartiality and justice which you have so signally manifested to us on all occasions, we cannot find expressions sufficiently comprehensive to convey the deep obligation we feel ourselves under you.

We well know addresses like this are frequently mere matter of form, but we earnestly beg you to believe that every sentiment herein expressed is the heartfelt and sincere feeling of each individual whose name is hereto attached.

In conclusion, allow us to express our sincere and earnest prayers and wishes for the health, happiness, and prosperity of yourself, your lady, and family.

Your grateful and obedient servants
(Signed by all the Exiles)

Such glowing praise for Hampton is in stark contrast to his later reputation. He has been described by Robert Hughes as a 'dismally cynical opportunist ... who wrote a whitewashing report on the convict population' and the 'odious and corrupt governor of Western Australia'.[6]

PROCESSING THE PRISONERS

When the convicts finally reached their destination, the necessary paperwork for their transfer had to be completed by colonial officials before disembarkation. In 1824, prisoners arriving in Sydney from Dublin on the *Hooghley* were handed over to the governor of Hyde Park Barracks.

They were mustered by the Colonial Secretary and then directed to be distributed throughout the Colony. These men, taken collectively, appeared healthy strong and well satisfied—facts that speak volumes in favour of those under whom their misfortunes had placed them.[7]

The convicts then underwent a lengthy ritual of documentation, which included details of their religion, literacy, occupation, place of birth and age. Physical descriptions were catalogued, describing build, colour of hair, birthmarks, scars and tattoos. Documents known as indents or indentures were written to transfer the prisoners formally from the custody of the master of a transport ship to the governor of the colony receiving them. Such processing made the convicts the most well-documented people in the British Empire.[8]

As the years progressed and New South Wales became more established, a routine for dealing with new convicts was established. The newly disembarked prisoners were sent to Hyde Park Barracks, the main depot for receiving convicts. Here, most were 'assigned out' to work for different masters, mainly free settlers, although convicts with skills which the authorities valued, such as carpenters, were kept in barracks and put to a variety of official tasks. The system of assignment worked satisfactorily as long as the employer was reasonable and the convict also behaved. In such circumstances, convicts were provided with essentials such as clothes, food and shelter, and working conditions were little different from those of an employee at home.

The assignment system was always controversial. Economically it was efficient and viable, especially for valued trades such as carpenters, blacksmiths and stonemasons, who were often employed on the government works programmes. Problems arose from the autonomy enjoyed by the employers in their relations with those who were assigned to them. For some convicts, the conditions under which they lived were considerably better than if they had remained in Britain as free labourers. Understandably, this was a cause of considerable resentment. In 1842, assignment was replaced by the probation system, which required the prisoners to undertake hard labour with nominal pay. On the basis of good behaviour, however, they could eventually obtain a ticket of leave and then a pardon.

CHANGING PLACES

During the period 1787 to 1868, prisoners from Britain, Ireland and parts of the Empire were sent to different destinations in Australia. As well as Botany Bay, penal colonies were established offshore on Van Diemen's Land, in Victoria (part of New South Wales until 1851) and in Western Australia, evolving at different times and for different reasons. Free settlers were part of the reason for the shift and for some of the changes in policy that shaped the lives of convicts after their sentences were served.

We do not know how far Britain initially planned to send free settlers as well as convicts to establish the Australian colony. By the time the Third Fleet arrived in 1791, it was evident to Captain Arthur Phillip that Sydney needed the impetus of farmers and emigrants able to reap the benefits of their own labour. The problem lay in attracting such free settlers; by 1800, only 20 had gone to New South Wales. One alternative was to offer

Hyde Park Barracks in Sydney, c.1820, by Joseph Lyceum. The Barracks' architect was Francis Howard Greenery, a pupil of the eminent John Nash. The structure was considered Greenery's greatest success, accommodating 800 newly arrived convicts.

grants of land as well as the use of tools to deserving convicts, who had served their sentences. These 'Emancipists', it was thought, might then become independent, set examples to others and in turn employ convicts, who would work on the farms. James Ruse, at Parramatta in 1791, was the first ex-convict to receive a grant of land. By 1792, an assortment of officers, guards and Emancipists were cultivating 1,000 acres of land, and a further 4,000 acres had been set aside for farming. The 'assignment system', in which convicts worked for farmers and masters, was sustainably cheap; the cost of convict upkeep was passed on to private individuals, rather than being the responsibility of the British government. In addition, the assignment of convicts provided a form of social control, as the new arrivals could be removed from their gangs and dispersed far away from their former 'evil associations'. The prospect of cheap, readily available labour also had the advantage of attracting more free settlers to Australia.

However, the seeds of conflict between Emancipists and the new settlers were being sown. Before 1810, Emancipists were given land grants, although they were excluded from the political and social life of the New South Wales colony. During the period between 1810–21, when Lachlan Macquarie was governor, attempts were made to alter this situation. Many

Emancipists became wealthy and formed a class of high social and economic standing. However, to many of the newly arrived free settlers (the 'Exclusives'), the prestige of some Emancipists sat uneasily with their sense of superiority. After all, the Emancipists were ex-convicts and as such were perceived as a threat to the economic and political prospects of the settlers. The settlers argued that criminality was being rewarded. Further, as the offspring of convicts might inherit the same proclivity to crime, they, too, should not be entrusted to hold official positions. Subsequently lobby groups were formed with the intention of denying ex-convicts, as well as their children, equality of rights. Such discrimination drove many Emancipists to seek homesteads elsewhere.

New South Wales and Van Diemen's Land accounted for the bulk of the convict population, containing over 81,000 and 67,000 respectively. Others were sent to Moreton Bay, Norfolk Island and, after 1850, to Western Australia. Much of the convict population in New South Wales had established themselves as landholders and tradesmen before free immigration, and there were many success stories among its emancipated convicts. An exceptional example was Richard Dry, convicted in Dublin in 1787 for political activity and transported to Van Diemen's Land. Dry was given a grant of 500 acres in 1818; by 1827, he was working 12,000 acres with 4,000 cattle and 7,000 sheep.

Lieutenant Governor Arthur took the entire management of the convicts' assignment in hand as soon as he arrived in Van Diemen's Land in 1824. Although Van Diemen's Land became a penal colony for some of the worst offenders, it was initially established in 1803 as a supplementary island colony to New South Wales. The different systems in New South Wales and Van Diemen's Land were to lead to differences in the growth of the two colonies.

Van Diemen's Land, later known as Tasmania, became a separate colony in 1825. As with the mainland, private masters employed convict labour, but under more demanding conditions. The regime that emerged there owed a great deal to the dedicated and meticulous work of George Arthur during his 12-year governorship, between 1824 and 1836. He gave his name to Port Arthur, which he designed as a penitentiary where particularly difficult convicts were held under tough conditions; the place was intended, among other things, to refute claims that transportation was a 'soft option' for criminals.

A charcoal sketch of the Eagle Haw Neck from Tasman's Peninsula, 1852 (MPG 1/689). The lamps and posts were used for surveillance on this isthmus of less than 100 yards width. One convict attempted to escape disguised as a kangaroo, but had to surrender when troops were about to shoot at the beast.

Convicts first arrived in Western Australia in 1827, when a small group was sent from Sydney to establish a British presence. The region began its life as a free colony in 1829, but it had willingly started taking limited numbers of convicts in 1850 because of chronic shortages of labour. Most convicts were transported to West Australia between 1850 and 1868, although in later years this practice was fast becoming an anachronism. The last convict ship left Britain for that colony in October 1867. Those sent to Western Australia had either been specially selected for their good behaviour after serving part of their sentences in British prisons, or were Irish Fenians, viewed as political prisoners. The regime under which they lived was a relatively liberal one and their presence was far less controversial than in the more brutal systems operated to the east.

No female prisoners were sent to Western Australia. During the 1840s, Western Australia was financially depressed, and some merchants and landowners felt that penal settlement might assist the colony. In 1848, Lord Grey, Secretary of State for the Colonies, included Western Australia in his circular about the reception of exiles, and the following year it was determined that the colony would become a place where convicts could be sent.[9] It was agreed that a limited number of convicts would be sent out along with military pensioners and their families, as well as free women in an attempt to balance out the sexes. The local government in Perth had requested the need for male labour to work on public works, such as roads and buildings.

By the early 1860s, it was becoming clear in London that transportation to Western Australia was a needlessly expensive option. It was also a pointless one, given that there was by now considerable spare capacity in the British prisons (page 249). The continued presence of transportation to Western Australia was extremely unpopular elsewhere on the continent. New South Wales began to evolve during the 'convict years' into a group of British colonies. In 1841, New Zealand separated from New South Wales, and in 1851, Victoria (formerly known as the Port Phillip District of New South Wales) also broke away. Attempts at settlement in Victoria were made in 1803, although the only convicts sent directly from Britain were some 1,750 convicts known as the 'Exiles', who arrived between 1844 and 1849.

Although transportation to New South Wales was abolished in May 1840, free settlers in Melbourne asked for some shipments of reformed convict exiles four years later. They needed help with a serious labour shortage in the Port Phillip District. The end came shortly afterwards, however, as a result of migration from Van Diemen's Land and the discovery of gold. These developments witnessed an influx of free labour into the region, and convict ships were turned away. Complete abolition of transportation to New South Wales was finally achieved in October 1850.

THE END OF THE LINE

The debate over whether punishment should act as a deterrent to crime or be the first step towards rehabilitation continued in the colony and in Britain. From the start of transportation, a view had persisted which held that too liberal and lenient an approach was taken towards convicts. This view still existed 50 years later, reflected in correspondence from the Colonial Office during the 1830s. 'His Majesty's Government have determined to adopt the principle of subjecting [the convicts] to different degrees of severity, according to the Magnitude of their offences.' It was

A Chai

Convicts going to work n.

Gang,

N. S. Wales.

made clear that the worst offenders would be sent to penal settlements while others whose crimes were defined as 'less enormous' should be given severe labour in the chain gangs.[10]

Convicts committing serious offences in Australia were dispatched to its notorious penal colonies—Van Diemen's Land, Newcastle, Port Macquarie, Moreton Bay and Norfolk Island. These purpose-built settlements, whose sole purpose was to punish criminals, became well known for their brutal treatment. Van Diemen's Land was established in 1803, but it was not until 1818 that regular shipments of convicts from Britain were sent (the *Indefatigable* arrived there in 1812 with 200 male prisoners). The years between 1803 and 1818 saw convicts from New South Wales come to the island and, as with Norfolk Island, the colony quickly established a reputation for cruelty.

The severity of the punishments in some of the colonies contrasted with the positive attempts at reform made on many of the voyages. The good work achieved on board ship seemed, not surprisingly, to be in danger of being lost, faced with the daily rituals of cruelty and humiliation. The point was noted by the Reverend T.B. Taylor, who wrote to Lord Stanley, the Colonial Secretary, 'From the opportunities I have had of conversing with men of all dispositions, I have arrived at the conclusion that they [the convicts] are one and all losing that conviction of moral and religious responsibility which, in a greater or lesser degree, they possessed during the voyage.'

Taylor was extremely critical of the barbarous conditions inflicted on the convicts, a situation exacerbated by a physical environment in which hardened re-offenders could mix with less serious criminals. In his view, this could only perpetuate the cycle of vice.

> The comparatively innocent and the thoroughly degraded are thrown together; novices are at once initiated into the mysteries of crime... With these scoundrels the English farm labourer, the tempted and fallen mechanic, the suspected but innocent victims of perjury or mistake, are indiscriminately herded. With them are mixed Chinamen from Hong Kong, the aborigines of New Holland, West Indian Blacks, Greeks, Caffres and Malays; soldiers for desertion; idiots, madmen, pig-stealers and pickpockets. At night

the sleeping-wards are very cesspools of unheard of vices. I cannot find sober words enough in which to express the enormity of this evil.[11]

When convicts were brought before magistrates for committing offences, they tended to be relatively minor. Many were accused of being 'drunk and disorderly', while others were charged with insolence, petty stealing, disobedience and absence without leave. Punishments included periods of hard labour, extension of existing sentences, or flogging. Any page from the special police returns of convicts sentenced by the magistrates of Van Diemen's Land reinforces this point as the offences take on a particular familiarity.[12]

Name	*Offence*	*Sentence*
Mary Mitchell	Drunk	Six months' hard labour in the wash-tub factory, Launceston
Margaret Brown	Repeated drunkenness	Twelve months' imprisonment in crime-class factory, Hobart
Mary Connolly	Drunk	Ticket of leave supended and House of Correction
William Mortimer	Intoxicated while driving master's cart	Three months' hard labour
Alexander Brown	Indolence, negligence and absent all night	Twelve months' hard labour on chain gang
James White	Stealing one pair of ear-rings from three-year-old girl, and representing himself to be free	Hard labour for three months
Margaret Kyle	Stealing two bottles containing three pints of rum—property of her master	Sentence extended by two years
Thomas Shoesmith	Indecently exposing his person in a public street	Hard labour for three months

The list contains many convicts who were no longer wanted by their masters, as well as those who had absconded or were insolent.

Caleb Banks	Master refuses to keep him	Returned to Government
Angus Macdonald	Absconding	Sentence extended by six months
Charles Brady	Insolence	Two months' hard labour
Peter Carie	Disobedience of orders	Cell for seven days
George Williams	Useless as a farm servant	Returned to Government

Some convicts amassed a list of offences, such as those above, during the course of their sentence. These would re-appear when they appealed for conditional and free pardons. Records of such appeals show the comments made by the Principal Superintendent, as well as extracts from police records on the convict's past offences. The decision to grant a pardon was made by the Lieutenant-Governor on the basis of this information. Some of the appeals were straightforward. Typical of these was that of William Evans, who had served 17 years in the colony without any offences. His appeal was approved, as was that of Robert Graham, who had been serving a life sentence. Robert had served only 16 years, but during this period

No. 15.—General Special Return of Convicts in the Principal Superintendent's Department, sentenced at *Hobart Town* and *Launceston, Van Diemen's Land,* &c.—*continued.*

Name, Police Number, and Ship.	In whose Service, or how Employed.	OFFENCE.	Date of Trial.	Sentence, and by whom.	How recommended to be disposed of, and General Remarks.
Week ending 13 May 1837—continued.		HOBART—*continued.*			
198; Ann Mackenna; Edward; house servant. 7 yrs., 1 yr., 1 yr., 6 mths.	Mrs. Clare, Macquarie-st.	- - Absconding from her service on the 13th of April last, and remaining illegally at large until the 10th instant, when she was apprehended by Constable Gibbs in the house of William Wright, of Watchorn-street.	11 May 1837	- - Existing sentence of transportation extended 12 months.	- - Principal superintendent, and Alexander Murray, esq., J.P.	- - Confirmed, and to be detained in the female house of correction for three months at the wash-tub. (signed) J. F.
552; Margaret Bartle; Westmorland; plain cook and house servant. 14 yrs.	- - Mr. Dixon, Macquarie-st.	- - Suspicion of having stolen a 1 *l.* note.	—	- - Case of felony; dismissed, but recommended to be detained in the house of correction for three months before assignment, and then be assigned in the interior.	- - Principal superintendent.	Confirmed. (signed) J. F.
879; Wm. Gemmill; Georgiana (2.); labourer. 7 yrs., 3 yrs.	- - Hulk chain-gang.	Fighting - - - - -	—	- - Present sentence in chains to be extended three months.	- - The principal superintendent.	- Confirmed, and to be sent to Grass-tree Hill chain-gang. (signed) J. F.
242; Frederick Edwards; Surrey life. (2.); stonemason.	- - Stonemason, Custom-house.	- - Absent from his duty, and being under the effects of liquor.	12 May 1837	- - To be kept to hard labour in chains at his trade for three months.	- - ditto -	Confirmed. (signed) J. F.
1655; Morrice Howling; Isabella; boy. 7 yrs.	- - Marine department, Government brig Isabella.	- - Having a quantity of tobacco in his possession, without being able satisfactorily to account for the same	13 May 1837	- - To be kept to hard labour on the roads for six months.	- - ditto -	- - Confirmed; Campbell Town road-party, and then to be sent to Morven for assignment. (signed) J. F.
379; Samuel Newton; Layton (2.); labourer. 7 yrs.	- - - Labourer, prisoners' barracks.	Being drunk - - - -	—	- - To be kept to hard labour for three months on the roads.	- - ditto -	- - Confirmed; Sandy Bay road-party; then to prisoners' barracks for assignment in the interior. (signed) J. F.
		LAUNCESTON:			
749; Alex. Frazer; Layton (2.); gentleman's servant. 7 yrs., 2 yrs.	- - King's Meadows' party.	Absent without leave - -	5 May 1837	- - Six weeks' hard labour; Morven road-party recommended.	- - William Franks, esq., J.P.	- - Confirmed, and afterwards to be assigned. (signed) J. F.

he had been 'favourably recommended by four gentlemen.'

Many convicts had a catalogue of offences against their names and were not approved for a pardon. However, bad behaviour was not necessarily a decisive factor in preventing pardons as long as they had behaved during the past year. Andrew Conran, for example, had been tried in Dublin in 1815 and had accumulated a list of offences by 1837. These included six charges of being drunk and disorderly, riotous conduct, absence from muster and divine service, and stealing Crown property. Despite this tally, Conran did receive his conditional pardon. Ralph Ellis from Worcester was sentenced to life in 1823 for highway robbery. During the 14 years of his sentence in the colony, he was insolent and disobedient on numerous occasions. He mixed with some 'notoriously bad characters', was charged with cattle-stealing and was absent from muster and church. The report recorded that 'I think his character rather suspicious and therefore that he is safer with his ticket of leave' rather than his pardon.

However, for some there was no concession at all. Joseph Furnival from Stafford, for example, had served 15 years of his life sentence for burglary. He neglected his duties, disobeyed orders and was drunk and disorderly on several occasions. For his second offence of disobeying orders, he was given 50 lashes and 25 for the third offence. This did not deter him, however, and he continued to disobey orders on three further occasions, for which he received periods of working on the chain gang. In addition, he was punished six times for drunkenness, receiving stolen goods, assaulting his wife and beating Thomas Mowbray. In all, Furnival was given at least 100 lashes and spent many months labouring on chain gangs. His appeal was not approved.[13]

In 1822, a penal colony was established on the west coast of Van Diemen's Land at Macquarie Harbour for re-offenders from New South Wales. However, in due course the harbour became difficult to control, and it was closed down in preference for a new settlement at Port Arthur on the southeast coast of the island. Some 67,000 convicts were sent to Van Diemen's Land, including more than 14,000 Irish prisoners over a 50-year period. In 1834, Point Puer was established on the island to rehabilitate boy convicts. In 1835, approximately

This document of 1827 is a return list of convicts who offended at Launceston Hobart, and Van Diemen's Land (CO 280/83 f. 68 v). The offences listed would appear to be fairly minor, although one convict's retribution is a not-insignificant 12-month extension of her sentence.

800 convicts were working in chain gangs at the notorious penal station at Port Arthur. After 1842, the worst offenders from Van Diemen's Land were transported to Norfolk Island (see below), and the last convict ships arrived in Van Diemen's Land in 1851. Transportation was officially abolished there in 1853, and on 1 January 1856 the colony became known as Tasmania. The new name signified closing the door on its penal past.

Newcastle, 98 miles north of Sydney, was the first secondary penal colony established in 1804 and it operated its harsh conditions until 1824. Newcastle was succeeded by Port Macquarie, approximately halfway between Sydney and Brisbane on the east coast, but the colony was closed nine years later following criticism of its harsh methods. Convicts from here were transferred to Norfolk Island, later notorious for its excessive discipline and brutality. Moreton Bay, in southeast Queensland, was for centuries inhabited by Aboriginal tribes. It became a penal settlement in 1824 to accommodate Sydney's worst convicts. An attempt to end transportation to Moreton Bay, because of the severe regime, was made in 1839, although convict ships still continued to be diverted there from Sydney. Transportation to all of the eastern colonies came to an end and the last direct ship for Moreton Bay left Britain in 1850.

THE AUSTRALIAN ALCATRAZ

Those regarded as the most hard-bitten and least remorseful convicts were sent to Norfolk Island—the largest of a group of small islands about 900 miles northeast of Sydney, and the nearest thing to an actual prison that Australia had to offer. Not the slightest attempt was made to reform the prisoners there. They were merely terrorized and brutalized by the treatment they received, and those who inflicted it were brutalized as well.

Norfolk Island was originally settled in 1788 and abandoned in 1814. It was reopened in 1824 by the British government for the secondary punishment of some of the most hardened convicts. In such a brutal environment rebellions, not surprisingly, were a recurring feature. The leaders of an 1834 mutiny at Van Diemen's Land were tried and 30 of them were condemned to death. Of these, 16 then had their sentences commuted to life imprisonment on Norfolk Island. The story goes that when the condemned men received this news, those to be hanged flung their hats in the air, cheering their good fortune, while those who were reprieved plunged to the depths of despair, fervently begging to be hanged instead.

The brutal conditions in certain penal colonies, most notoriously those on Norfolk Island, have been well documented. Governor Thomas Brisbane made it clear when he stated that 'felons on Norfolk Island have forfeited all claim to protection of the law.' As a foretaste of what might be expected on Norfolk Island, James Lawrence recorded en route that there were 75 convicts in irons, without clothes, in a small prison with hardly any air to breathe. Another prisoner, Laurence Frayne, convicted of theft in Dublin in 1825, had been re-convicted for repeatedly absconding. For this he had been cut to ribbons by extensive flogging; his shoulders were reduced to a state of decomposition, 'the stench of which I could not bear.' Maggots crawled in his back and he was denied bandages.[14]

On arrival at Norfolk Island, utter hell awaited many convicts. No free settlers lived there, so no assignment system existed: convicts worked instead in gangs from sunrise to sunset. Officials relied on informers, and there was never a shortage of these. Floggings were common, and Laurence Frayne received more in the colony for his part in an attempted rebellion. He was given 50 lashes on his back, and once that had scabbed over he received another 50. A few days later he received yet another 50 lashes, this time on his buttocks, then another 50, four days later. He was jailed for a week and then received a further 200 lashes over a period of a few days. Frayne was not exceptional. In the 1830s, William Riley received 1,000 lashes and 11 months solitary confinement in the space of two years, while Michael Burns had 2,000 lashes in less than three years.[15] Commenting on the suicide rate, William Ullathorne, the Catholic Vicar-General of Australia who visited the island in 1834, noted that 'so indifferent had even life become, that murders were committed in cold blood, the murderer afterwards declaring that he had no ill-feelings against his victim, but that his sole object was to obtain his own release.' That release was execution.

Not everyone was in favour of the harsh regime that had been put in place. There were critics of the punishments meted out in some of the penal colonies. In a Report on Convict Discipline in 1837, concerns were expressed about the extent and the purpose of such punishments:

> It is a gross mistake to consider convicts as being generally insensible to their degraded person; they ... harden themselves against severity and contempt. But I have never talked to one with anything approaching to kindness or

sympathy, that he has not evinced deep emotion; and no one can dispassion-
ately consider their general demeanour in church without being convinced
that they are still accessible to good impressions. The misery (and it is a cry-
ing misery) is that the circumstances in which they are placed outside that
sacred building are such that scarcely any impressions made can be permanent and available.[16]

The most outspoken critic and reformer was Alexander Maconochie. He
began his career in the Royal Navy, rising to the rank of captain, then, in
1833, was appointed as the first Professor of Geography at the University
of London. He went to Van Diemen's Land in 1837, at the request of Sir
John Franklin the Governor, to compile a 67-point questionnaire on the
treatment of convicts. The Home Secretary, Lord John Russell, ordered
Maconochie's first report to be made public in 1838, with the result that
an intended private document became public. Russell was a strong critic
of transportation and this report provided him with the ammunition he
required. The report was scathing in its attack on the treatment and
exploitation of convicts, comparing farmers who employed convicts with
slave-owners. Robert Hughes, commenting on the significance of this
report, has observed, 'If any moment can be said to mark the peak and
incipient decline of transportation to Australia, this innocuous act
marked it.'[17] There was uproar on its publication among the free citizens
of Van Diemen's Land, who felt insulted at the comparisons with slavery.
They were also aware that they relied on the repressive regime for cheap
labour and this report aimed at undermining and exposing that abuse.

Three years later, Maconochie was appointed superintendent of the
penal settlement at Norfolk Island—a post unlikely to have attracted a
huge rush of applications—and it is in this role that he is best remembered. A severe critic of the brutal penal system he found there,
Maconochie seized the opportunity to put some reforming ideas into
practice. In his Report on the Management of Transported Convicts,
1845, he wrote:

> Whatever the precise remedy for the moral evils which have hitherto resulted
> from Transportation, the precise disease which has caused them is, beyond
> all question, the taint of Slavery (the predominance of physical coercion, and
> the comparative absence of persuasive motive) which has throughout char-
> acterized it... Men will do for liberty what they will not do for lashes.[18]

Maconochie did not advocate a lenient approach, but he wanted an end to cruel and vindictive punishments which, he was convinced, made an ordinary convict bad and a bad one infinitely worse. Reduced to essentials, what he did was to encourage the prisoners to shorten the length of their sentences by piecework. His new regime involved two stages of treatment. One was punishment for past crimes, which convicts must meet with 'manly penitence', and secondly, training for the future, which they could embrace 'with hope'. This system would be based on marks awarded to convicts according to their conduct on a daily basis, as evaluated by the overseers. Prisoners would advance from punishment to probation, and from probation to release. The convicts' fates were in their own hands. They received wages only for work done, and with these wages they had to buy their food and other necessities. They earned marks for the work they did and these marks built up into units which earned reductions in the length of their sentences. The sentences themselves were divided into three periods. The first was a demandingly strict individual regime; the second was membership of a peer group in which all the members benefited from hard work and mutual support; the third was conditional freedom. Other measures which intimidated and humiliated prisoners were abolished. In its immediate impact, Maconochie's penal experiment was remarkably successful. During his four years in charge at Norfolk Island, only 3 per cent of the 1,450 prisoners discharged in that time are recorded as having received further convictions.

The world was not ready for Maconochie, however, and criticisms of his 'new system' followed. 'In the course of a few weeks his [Maconochie's] imagination appears to have increased in fertility,' observed one contemporary.[19] As one might expect, there were many who were eager to debunk everything that Maconochie stood for. Stories began to circulate that Norfolk Island was really nothing more than a restful retreat in which the convicts enjoyed lives of pampered and cosseted ease, and happily thumbed their noses at authority. His efforts met with resistance at every step—from colonial administrators in Australia to civil servants and politicians in London. The British government did not appreciate his ideas and Maconochie was recalled in 1844. After his replacement, Norfolk Island degenerated into a regime of cruelty and recrimination, exhibiting the worst of repressive penal practice.

Yet even these entrenched institutions were subject to change and eventual decline. The last ship conveying prisoners sailed for Hobart in

Van Diemen's Land on 27 November 1852. At the end of 1853, it was formally announced that no further use would be made of the island as a penal colony. The rundown of penal activities on Norfolk Island began in 1854, and was completed in May 1856. The Penal Services Acts of 1853 and 1857 almost ended transportation, although those convicted of smuggling counterfeit coins were still theoretically liable to transportation for life as late as 1975.

CRIME AND PUNISHMENT

A question that arises from the diversity of settlements, forms of punishments and the system of transportation itself is the extent to which convicts were successfully reformed. Once they had served their sentences and were free, would enforced removal from an underworld of ghettos and partners in crime break the cycle? The ability to escape depended on a number of factors, including where the convicts were based and the prevailing level of magisterial control.

Free settlers arriving in Australia resented the influential roles in local society and the economy assumed by significant numbers of ex-convicts. Within 20 years of the establishment of the New South Wales colony, some of its richest inhabitants were ex-convicts who had become merchants or bankers. Second only to them in affluence was a petit bourgeoisie of other ex-convicts, who had become successful shopkeepers, publicans and tradesmen. Contrary to received opinion among critics of transportation, the official grant of a 30-acre farm to ex-convicts guaranteed no more than a frugal livelihood. Opponents of transportation noted that many rich ex-convicts had gained their wealth by exploiting convict labour, operating on entirely the same terms as those who emigrated there as free colonists. This was seen as an institutionalized reward for wrongdoing.

Another cause of criticism at the time of Governor Lachlan Macquarie was the emerging practice of employers paying wages to the convicts they hired. As if their earning money was not bad enough, those overseeing convicts' work often gave them fixed tasks which may certainly have involved hard work but, contrary to the rules, could be completed by early or mid-afternoon. Enterprising convicts could then do extra work for an employer or conduct their own business, further evidence of how criminality could be made to pay. Likewise arousing the ire of critics was the protection afforded to convicts by the New South Wales courts against mistreatment by their masters. Convicts possessed rights under British law and technically, under the assignment system, a master could not punish an individual convict. Instead, he could charge and send him to a magistrate, who would decide the punishment. Back home in Britain, a master's infliction of corporal punishment and other cruelties on domestic servants and employees was still perfectly acceptable in official circles. Why, it was asked, should the privilege of protection be extended to those who had committed serious crimes, in contempt of society's norms? When Governor Macquarie, believing that New South Wales owed its development to the efforts of the convicts, made three ex-convicts into magistrates, the chattering classes back in England exploded with outrage.

By the 1820s, assignment had become the main method of convict organization. The well-behaved convicts were generally assigned to either the government or to masters under the assignment system, which remained in place until 1840. In a report on the conditions of convicts in Van Diemen's Land in 1837, the following questions and answers were offered:

> *What Distinction is made in the Treatment, Discipline or Assignment of Convicts sentenced to seven, fourteen, twenty-one or life?*
>> No distinction is made … but prisoners who have misconducted themselves during the voyage are not assigned until after probation on the roads.
> *Is regard paid to their former station in society, or good character on the voyage, or previous guilty habits in England?*
>> No, not generally; the men are assigned according to the kind of work they are required to perform; in the event of any man of notoriously bad character, good care is taken to whom he is assigned.
> *What means are taken and how soon after the arrival of the convicts to procure situations for those who are allowed to work as mechanics, etc or to enter Domestic Service?*
>> On the day they are landed the Board of Assignment attend and nominate the convicts to their respective services, appropriating such mechanics to the Government as are required.[20]

New South Wales and Van Diemen's Land were effectively open prisons, depending not only on punishment, but also on rewards for good behaviour. Such incentives included granting free passage for wives and children, as well as a system of pardons and tickets of leave, introduced by Governor King in 1801. Even on Norfolk Island, Maconochie recognized the need for families to be together—essentially an argument for the prevention of homosexuality—stating that, 'Married men when transported should have a fixed means afforded them, involving some sacrifice on their parts, of having their families sent after them. Much misery and immorality would be thus spared on both sides.'[21]

The issuing of pardons to convicts before their full sentences had been served was the responsibility of the governors of New South Wales and Van Diemen's Land. In essence, there were two types of pardon: conditional, meaning that the convict could not return to Britain until his or her original sentence had expired, and absolute, which restored the convicts' full rights as British citizens and allowed them to return home. Pardons could be issued for good behaviour, for informing on others or for services rendered to the government.

The ticket of leave system was intended to limit government expenditure by reducing what was paid out to feed and house convicts engaged in public works. It enabled prisoners, after satisfactorily serving a minimum part of their sentence, to make a living of their own under the terms of a kind of parole. While they could be recalled to bond labour if they re-offended, the opportunity to make their own way was so tempting that the vast majority of those in receipt of tickets of leave employed their skills in lawful fashion. For critics, this was simply another example of rewarding wrongdoers and therefore of encouraging people to commit serious offences 'punishable' by transportation.

The assignment system aroused strong feelings throughout its existence. The historian A.G.L. Shaw has argued that it was by no means working badly on the eve of its abolition, quoting Charles Darwin's comments after his visit to Australia in 1836: 'As a means of making men outwardly honest, of converting vagabonds, most useless in one country, into active citizens of another, and thus giving birth to a new and *splendid country*, it has succeeded to a degree perhaps unparalleled in history.'[22] It did not last, however. After 1840, the British Government introduced a system of probation where convicts were assigned to a probation gang. The probation gangs were used to build public works such as roads, bridges and public buildings. Depending on their behaviour, the convict advanced through the different stages of probation.

The assignment system was certainly open to abuse by exploitative masters and insolent or idle convicts. The worst type of convict, including those who re-offended in the colony, were thus assigned to hard labour in the chain gangs, under constant supervision. Typically, many convicts failed to learn from their punishments; they were in continual trouble during their period of sentence. Others fell back into bad habits after receiving free pardons. In the former category was John McKey, transported for life for assault and robbery; he arrived in Van Diemen's Land in 1826. Between 1830 and 1837, he was variously convicted of being drunk, of assaulting and beating Sophia Nightingale and finally of murder, for which he was executed and gibbeted in Hobart. An example of the latter was George Richardson, sentenced to life at York in 1811. He sailed on the *Indefatigable*, which brought the first convicts direct to Van Diemen's Land in 1812. Richardson received a conditional, then a free pardon in 1818 and 1821 respectively.

The Ticket of Leave Passport for convict Thomas Griffith, 13 May 1845. These documents were granted before sentences had expired, but they required convicts to seek employment and to report regularly to the local magistrates.

D. 17.

TICKET OF LEAVE PASSPORT.

No. *45*

The Bearer *Thomas Griffiths*
Convict by the Ship *Asia (IV) 1834* holding a
Ticket of Leave No. *44/355* for the District of *Paterson*
which is deposited in the Police Office at *do*
and whose personal Description and Signature are on the other side, has obtained the permission of His Excellency the Governor to *proceed to the Darwin River in the service of Mr David Ryan*

for *twelve* months, from the date hereof, conforming himself in every respect, according to the regulations laid down for the guidance of Convicts of his class.

Given at the Office of the Principal Superintendent of Convicts, Sydney, this *thirtieth* Day of *May* One Thousand Eight Hundred and *forty five*

Registered
Thomas Ryan
Chief Clerk.

Within two years, however, he was convicted at Hobart for stealing 56 sheep and was executed in April 1823.[23]

WOMEN'S FACTORIES

Troublesome women prisoners were often sent to work in an all-female factory, and were given accommodation nearby. The first such factory, where women made rope, was constructed at Parramatta in 1804. Other women were assigned to work for free settlers or emancipated convicts as domestic servants. The children of female convicts—both those who had travelled from Britain and those born on board ship or after arrival— would either stay with their mothers or be placed in an orphanage. There were plenty of them. Many women at the female factory in Parramatta found themselves either pregnant or having to look after young children; their lives alternated between working and visiting the 'lying-in' hospital. It was impossible for women to avoid the attentions of a population that consisted largely of men, and for the sake of self-preservation most had to accept a man—and the attendant consequences—in due course.

The Parramatta factory was also famous for a number of riots. In 1827, the authorities stopped the inmates' bread and sugar rations; this sparked off a revolt, with around 100 women breaking out and marching to the town to seize provisions. Four years later, several hundred women again protested at having their hair shaved. In revenge, they seized an unpopular overseer and shaved her head, then threatened to go to Sydney and shave the head of the Governor and also to demolish the press of the *Monitor* newspaper for portraying them as 'the worst and vilest of their sex'. The following year, soldiers were called to quell 'extremely unruly' behaviour. 'The women ... threw a shower of stones [at us]. It will never do to show them any clemency... I have no doubt but all the officers who saw their riotous conduct will be convinced of the necessity of keeping them under the hand of power.'[24]

Parrametta was by no means unique. There were similar disturbances at the female factory at Launceston in 1841, when 85 women barricaded themselves in a section of the factory; armed with knives, bricks and bottles, they beat off police attacks.[25] Other factories included the Cascades female factory near Hobart, which opened in 1828 and was overcrowded with women and children from the first day. Whilst the brutality in female factories did not match that of some of the male regimes, there was a close monitoring of the women and the death rate among the convicts' children was high. Elizabeth Fry, the penal reformer, had visited female prisoners on the hulks in England and campaigned for improved conditions. Fellow Quakers James Backhouse and George Walker established the first Religious Society of Friends when they went to Van Diemen's Land in 1832. Their mission was to enquire into the condition of the penal settlements in Australia and the welfare of the Aborigines and the free settlers.

THE ONES THAT GOT AWAY

The majority of prisoners faced up to their sentences on arrival and got on with serving their punishment. However, there is always the attraction of escaping in any prison system, and some did attempt this. These brave souls faced the choice of going inland and trying to survive in the inhospitable conditions, where they would have to endure ferocious heat, as well as contending with hostile Aborigines, unknown wildlife and a lack of food. Alternatively, they could head out to sea. This option meant stowing away on a ship, or stealing a boat and taking a chance on what lay ahead. Some convicts were allowed to stow away on American whaling ships, whose crews had little sympathy with the convict system.

The case of Mary Bryant has been well documented.[26] A sailor's daughter from Cornwall, she was sentenced to seven years' transportation for stealing a cloak. In Australia, she married another Cornish convict, William Bryant, who fathered her second child. Having acquired some tools and navigational instruments, William hid them in his hut and bided his time. The moment came on a March night in 1791, when he, Mary, their two children and seven other convicts stole the governor's six-oar cutter and set sail along the coast, surviving on edible plants and fish. They were eventually blown out to sea until they landed on one of the many islands of the Great Barrier Reef. Here they replenished themselves, stocked up their boat and set sail again. Some two months later they arrived at Koepang in Timor, eventually to be arrested by the Dutch and shipped first to Batavia. Here William and his son, Emmanuel, died of fever. The others, including Mary and her daughter, Charlotte, were shipped back to England via the Cape. Charlotte died at sea and Mary eventually reached London, where she was imprisoned in Newgate.

Following pressure on the Home Secretary Henry Dundas from the writer James Boswell, Mary was given an unconditional pardon and allowed to return to Cornwall in 1793, at the age of 28.

Those who took the alternative escape route and headed inland faced the serious dangers of hostile terrain. The 'Chinese Travellers' were escapees who believed China was only a few hundred miles north of Parrametta. The first Chinese Travellers set off from Rose Hill in 1791; they finished up dazed, lost and starving in the bush, and were easily recaptured. Other convicts, hearing rumours of other settlements nearby and believing that China was just over the horizon, also escaped. Those that managed to survive the rigours of the country returned to the colony to further punishment.

Runaways became known as 'bolters', and then evolved into the popular image of the anti-authority hero, the bushranger. Groups of marauders had formed during the earliest years of the colony and they were very difficult to capture. The number of bushrangers was increased by escaped prisoners from Sydney, who had been re-convicted and subsequently sent to Van Dieman's Land as punishment.

Bushrangers were the most persistent disturbers of the peace in Australia and, although the number of bushrangers was small compared to the large number of convicts, their activities became the stuff of legend. Initially, bushranging in New South Wales was a nuisance, but it was not on the scale of that in Van Diemen's Land. Nonetheless, the bushrangers became such a problem by 1814 that Governor Lachlan Macquarie offered an amnesty to those who turned themselves in. The amnesty failed to secure a mass surrender. Instead it aroused panic in Hobart, prompting Lieutenant Governor Davey to declare martial law and hang as many outlaws as he could catch.

Two famous bushrangers who emerged in this period were Michael Howe and Matthew Brady. Howe had a gang of 28 men and was fond of portraying himself as a hero. His favourite targets were those landowners with a reputation for treating convicts badly. He waged war against the colonial authorities, raiding military garrisons and settlements on the outskirts of Hobart and gathering recruits as he went. Howe's downfall came in 1818, when he was beaten to death by bounty hunters. They cut off his head and carried it back to Hobart Town, where it was put on public view.

Manchester-born Matthew Brady had been sentenced to seven years' exile in 1820 for stealing a basket with some bacon, butter and rice. In 1824, Brady and 13 other convicts escaped from Macquarie Harbour in a whaleboat. His gang robbed travellers and outlying settlers, gaining wealth and reputation in the process. Brady, inevitably, was betrayed and shot in the leg by government forces. He was eventually captured and placed in Launceston gaol, where he was hanged on 4 May 1826. Despite such a public deterrent, many other bushrangers remained at large.

Notices appeared in newspapers with lists of escaped convicts who had evaded capture, and also warning of the activities of bushrangers who plundered and robbed farms. *The Australian* of 4 August 1825 wrote that, 'Mr Maziere's overseer has had to go to Newcastle for a supply of provisions, he having been robbed of everything except the clothes he wore. Mr Lymant's farm has also been plundered by them.' More reports followed in November of that year: 'Between the bushrangers and the native blacks, the settlers seem to have a very sorry time. They are constantly called upon to keep a very sharp look out and to repress one or other of these pests.'[27]

The early bushrangers were convicts who had escaped from assigned service in the penal colonies of New South Wales and Van Diemen's Land. After the discovery of gold in the 1850s, bushrangers increased their activities, with many ambushing gold shipments. The bushrangers of this later period were often native Australians rather than convicts who had been transported from Britain.

Despite images of the convict as immoral, drunken, idle and irredeemably steeped in vice, thousands of convicts brought many skills and positive qualities to Australia between 1787 and 1868. They produced hundreds of stories of adventure, adversity, disappointment, hardship and success. They also produced ballads, many of which survive today. Significantly, they forged a founding history of modern Australia. Despite the bushrangers, the bolters and the re-offenders, the majority of convicts did reform; they became free men and women, and changed their lives for the better. Courageously, they seized the chance to start again in a different environment and found, or developed, opportunities in their new country. There were convicts who, when they had the chance, chose to return to Britain—but many others stayed on in Australia. In one of history's curious turns of events, transportation worked for many convicts, although seldom in the ways that the British government had planned.

Towards the End of Transportation

IN BRITAIN, experiencing the social and economic turmoil associated with the Industrial Revolution, the period 1780–1850 saw a seemingly inexorable increase both of crime and of the prison population. In 1820, about 13,700 people were committed to trial for serious offences; by 1840, the figure had increased to 27,200. The number of prisoners almost doubled between 1820 and 1840. The entire gamut of punishment seemed incapable of making a significant impact on these figures and this provoked sometimes anguished debates over crime and penal policy. The purpose, relative usefulness and nature of the regimes in land-based prisons and in hulks were scrutinized; the advantages and disadvantages of transportation were deliberated over, as was the efficacy of hanging as the ultimate deterrent. Reforms did take place, but they lacked any coherent, long-term strategy and were largely reactions to the rapid growth of crime.

The government took over total responsibility for the hulks in 1815, but criticism of the hulks continued despite various reforms. (So, too, did that of the prisons, and indeed most aspects of the penal system.) In 1832, a Select Committee condemned the whole concept of hulks as penal institutions and argued that they did little or nothing to deter crime. However, it was also acknowledged pragmatically that it was cheaper to keep a convict in a hulk than in a prison and that hulks provided a cost-effective alternative to new prisons, as indeed did transportation. In some circles, however, transportation continued to be supported on economic grounds: it disposed of people who would otherwise have been a charge on the poor rates and who were unlikely ever to return from punishment to resume their criminal or otherwise undesirable ways in Britain.

The debate was widespread and lively, albeit prejudiced and extremely subjective as such public expressions of opinion have always tended to be. Towns and cities across Britain, London in particular, were seen as hotbeds of crime, but there was also concern about the rapid escalation of criminal activity in rural areas. Furthermore, rising political agitation struck fear into the hearts and minds of the wealthy and powerful, for whom crime and political subversion were natural companions. The period between 1820 and the mid-1840s saw a number of issues which

*A faded photograph of the area around Sydney, 1876 (*COPY *1/33 f.279). The city had continued to develop and expand, but by this time, of course, the transportation of convicts had ceased.*

galvanized mass political action, accompanied by the threat or reality of popular violence. These issues included agitation for reform of the electoral system, widespread opposition to the 'New Poor Law' of 1834, and the emergence of the Chartist movement, the aims of which had they been implemented would have brought about fundamental changes in the balance of political power. In this situation, strengthening the powers of the police and criminal justice system seemed to some the only effective response to the dangerous forces of anarchy.

Many who voiced their opinions on crime and punishment believed that those who were transported welcomed their sentences as a reward, a once-in-a-lifetime opportunity to make a new start. The *Quarterly Review* in 1828 opined that the 'entire removal of the individual to a new scene of life affords at once the only security to society against his future crimes and the contagion of his habits, and the only chance left to himself for regaining decency and respectability.'[1] Some ex-convicts themselves added to the debate, dividing unhelpfully between those who considered it an appalling, inhumane punishment and others who positively relished the new beginnings in New South Wales or Van Diemen's Land. Some who had experienced transportation further confused the issue by stating that the threat of punishment, no matter how severe, was no deterrent to the determined professional criminal. Sydney Smith, the well-known clergyman and essayist, fulminated over the apparent inadequacies of transportation as a means of punishment. As far as he was concerned, it allowed the 'heart-broken pauper and the abandoned profligate [to be] converted into ... a jolly-faced yeoman.'[2]

Such views found support in several popular ballads which presented transportation as a great adventure. 'The Jolly Lad's Trip to Botany Bay', for example, dating from around the 1790s, hails from Birmingham; one of its verses runs like this:

> *Now many a bonny lass in Botany may be seen,*
> *Who knows but she might be an Indian queen?*
> *Deck'd out with diamonds see the British fair.*
> *A fig for transportation, little do we care.*[3]

Presumably written by someone blissfully unacquainted with the realities of transportation, the experience sounds more like a trip round the bay in a pleasure steamer than enforced exile to a barren land, thousands of miles away.

In 1813, the *Edinburgh Review*, a highly influential periodical, emphasized the flaws of transportation from a very different standpoint:

> The reality is that the miserable wretch, after rotting in hulks for a year or two, is crammed with some hundreds of his fellows into a floating prison, or maybe a pest-house, in which, if he survives the risk of famine, pestilence, mutiny, fire, shipwreck and explosion, he is conveyed ... to a life of alternating slavery and rebellion ... [with] exquisite suffering [and] uniform misery... All this passes at the opposite extremity of the earth, from whence it operates no more upon the inhabitants of England than if it were passing on the moon.[4]

DETERRENCE AND ECONOMY

The end of war with France, in 1815, was followed in Britain by a severe economic depression, an increase in crime and a rapid rise in the number of convicts being transported to the Australian colonies. The increased number of convicts arriving there could not all be employed privately and so government expenditure rose, not only on conveying convicts to the colony, but also on maintaining them and finding work for them once they were there. Back at home, transportation was condemned as a waste of money and of resources. Why should (primarily) young men be transported to work on projects, such as road and dock-building, in Australia, rather than put to similar work back in Britain—avoiding the cost of transportation at the same time?

Alarm bells rang among civil servants, and the Home Office, wrestling with escalating crime, tried to pressurize the Colonial Office to make transportation more of a deterrent. In effect, officialdom wanted the impossible: an effective punishment with minimal cost. During the period between 1815 and 1830, the whole concept of transportation to Australia came under sustained attack from an unholy alliance of critics across the political spectrum, united only by their opposition to the practice continuing. Some were opposed to transportation *per se*; others wished it to be a much more ferocious punishment, fear of which would keep even the least deferential, most criminally inclined elements of the population under control.

Central to the argument was the issue of whether transportation provided an effective form of punishment or not. Some people believed that it created a criminal fraternity, experiencing common hardship, developing a subculture of shared values and disseminating expertise. Convicts with money or influence could even avoid having to undertake hard labour, while enjoying a lifestyle considerably superior to that of the bulk of the British population.

In an attempt to assuage the force of this criticism, the government set up a commission of inquiry under John Thomas Bigge, which reported in 1822. Its brief was to establish whether the regime in New South Wales could be made more rigorous. Bigge did his job conscientiously and made a number of recommendations, which were largely accepted; they provided a flexible framework on which convict affairs were run until transportation to New South Wales ceased in 1840. As far as possible, convicts should be assigned to prosperous free settlers in the rural areas to get them away from the undesirable influences of the towns. Privileges such as wages and tickets of leave had to be worked for, rather than being matters of right. Accurate records of all offences committed by convicts in the colony had to be kept. Any property that convicts brought to New South Wales should be confiscated and returned only when its owner could demonstrate a reformed character. Convicts would no longer receive land when they became free. As A.G.L. Shaw stated in *Convicts and the Colonies*, 'Deterrence and economy, the two watchwords of British penal policy after the Napoleonic Wars, still held sway in the 1830s. Even if transportation did not seem to deter English criminals as much as the government wished, any possible alternative seemed sure to be more expensive and by no means certain to be any more effective.' However, these were almost certainly incompatible objectives.

The government hoped that the reforms following Bigge's inquiry would increase the perceived severity of transportation as a punishment. However, serious anomalies still existed around the system in which convicts were assigned to employers (pages 234–7). Most of the latter were more concerned about maximizing their profits than with supervising the reform of their convicts, or keeping them under strict control. Some prisoners had to graft under the most demanding of work schedules. Others, especially the very large numbers who were shepherds, got away with very little being required of them. The manifest unfairness of this, not surprisingly, provoked adverse comment.

A new element in the critique of transportation emerged in the 1830s, when the assignment of convicts to private employers was denounced as tantamount to slavery. Britain had become pre-eminent among the European nations engaged in slavery in the eighteenth century, generating enormous wealth from the trade, especially in ports along the country's Atlantic coast, such as Bristol, Liverpool and Whitehaven. The practice of slavery began to attract criticism in the last quarter of the eighteenth century, leading to the formation of the very influential Anti-Slavery Society in 1823. Their activities eventually led to the abolition of slavery throughout the British Empire in 1833, whereupon many of the moral arguments used against slavery were brought to bear on transportation. Although these arguments lacked the depth of popular support given to the anti-slavery campaign, they became part of the wider battleground for Liberals and Conservatives, following the 1832 Reform Act, which extended the franchise to the urban middle classes. Archbishop Richard Whately, a leading opponent of what he described as the slave society of New South Wales, wrote *Thoughts on Secondary Punishments* in 1832, describing his views on the issue.

CONVICTS AND CITIZENS

The debate on whether or not transportation deterred or effectively punished wrongdoing rumbled on with varying degrees of intensity and venom through to the 1850s. Another concern was its impact on the burgeoning colony itself. It was said that many would-be emigrants to Australia were deterred by the colony's reputation for drunkenness, generally dissolute behaviour and lawlessness, most of which was blamed on escaped convicts or those who had served their sentences, but had not turned their backs on their criminal or anti-social ways. The stories that circulated may have been exaggerated and sensationalized, but as bad news always attracts more attention than good, an impression was created which proved very difficult to expunge.

The popular press of the day, refusing as ever to let the truth compromise a good story, published stories to support these claims. One involved a felon who, despite his conviction, managed to pay for his wife to join him in Australia, whereupon she arranged for him to be assigned to her as a servant. This brazen couple allegedly prospered in Sydney on the proceeds of previous criminal activities. Reports were made that other reprobates and spongers committed crimes in Britain in the confident belief that capture and conviction guaranteed them a free passage to an Antipodean Shangri-La.

Many of the free settlers who established themselves in New South Wales saw their own positions and prosperity wrapped up with the growth of trade and industry. They argued vehemently that the only way to progress towards a more favourable climate for economic development was to end transportation. This ignored the fact that those ex-convicts who gained a stake in the new Australian society often became fervent believers in the rule of law and, in many cases, were to make major contributions to the development of Australian society.

The establishment of colonies so far from Britain was a process that was inevitably fraught with difficulties. Transportation became etched into popular culture and was viewed in a pejorative way, being blamed for many of the social problems that afflicted the early decades of settlement in Australia. Squalid, shanty-type housing, drunkenness, prostitution, violence, lawlessness and contempt for authority were all features of Australia in convict times, but they have been emphasized at the expense of many positive, less sensational developments. A new community in

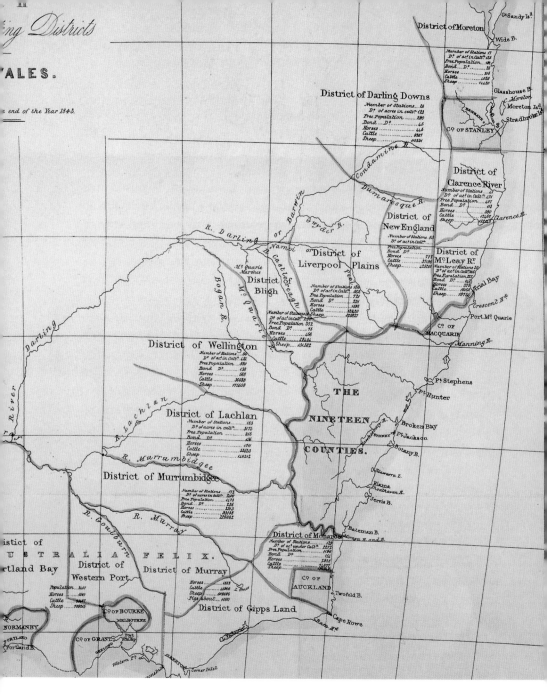

A sketched map showing the 'Squatting Districts' of New South Wales, 1844 (MPG 1/120). These were large tracts of mainly undeveloped land occupied by early European farmers, who often clashed violently with the Aboriginal peoples of the area.

which there is a large component of unwillingly transplanted young men and many other rootless individuals is bound to be an unstable one—the developing West in the United States provided abundant evidence of that.

REFORM OF THE PRISONS

Changes were afoot in Britain, too, as overdue attempts were made at national prison reform. William Crawford became the first Inspector of English Prisons in 1835. He then travelled extensively in the United States, visiting a range of penal institutions, and had been impressed by their versions of both the separate and the silent systems. In the first, the prisoners slept, ate and worked in their individual cells and during their short periods of outside exercise were hooded so they could not be recognized by their fellows. The second involved the prisoners being employed in large numbers in a sizeable workshop under conditions of the strictest silence, which made them feel isolated and prevented the development of a prison sub-culture. He produced a report which gained enthusiastic support from the Home Secretary, Lord John Russell, and it was largely as a result of this that a sizeable new penitentiary was completed at Pentonville in North London in 1842. Incorporating both systems, it became a model for prison design and discipline which was copied not only in England, but in many parts of Europe and the USA. Aristocrats, including the tetchy old Duke of Wellington, clergymen, magistrates, politicians and the simply curious flocked to see the virtues of silence and solitude encapsulated in bricks and mortar. A vigorous prison-building programme followed. By 1848, 54 further prisons had been opened, often considerably smaller, but built along similar lines: rows of single cells arranged in tiers and in separate blocks radiating from a central hub like spokes of a wheel. The regimes were harsh, however. At Pentonville, the men were marched from their solitary cells disguised with masks, and in chapel, at exercise and in the workshops where they laboured for most of the day, they were prevented from communicating with one another.

In the prisons operating on the Pentonville model, it did not always prove possible to keep the inmates fully employed. If they were kept in solitary confinement in their cells, they often exhibited tendencies to unacceptable behaviour or to mental derangement. Either of these might cause them to be punished and such punishment could take the form of physically arduous and mentally destructive activity, such as the treadmill and the crank, the latter being an apparatus in which a prisoner turned a handle attached to a heavy revolving box containing gravel. That such tasks were demeaning and pointless fully justified them in the eyes of some observers. When prisons were being discussed, there were always some commentators whose starting point was the existence of a core of incorrigible and totally irredeemable offenders, who were innately criminal and for whom no punishment could ever be bad enough.

In 1848, as a result of increasing doubts about the efficacy and relevance of transportation, and bearing in mind the growing weight of opposition to the practice in Australia, the British government embarked on the building of a system of state-operated prisons. It had apparently come to the conclusion, albeit tardily, that it was cheaper to house convicts in prisons at home than to send them overseas. With the prisons came the concept of custodial sentences for all those major crimes, except murder and a handful of others, which had been formerly punished by either public hanging or transportation. Up to this time, most offenders had served sentences no longer than six months and the longest had been three years. Now those convicted of serious offences were despatched to prisons administered by central government and put to hard labour in quarries or on public works. At the end of their sentences, they received a ticket of leave which released them back into the community, where they had to abide by a number of conditions, the infringement of which might involve their return to prison. At the time, there was considerable public hysteria about the fact that 'hardened criminals' were at large in the community rather than in far-away Australia.

Reforms trickled through in the nineteenth century. In 1824, the practice of classifying prisoners was established; the Prison Inspectorate was set up in 1835; and by 1853, the first Penal Servitude Act substituted periods of hard labour for certain sentences, which previously would have been punished with a term of transportation. The Act also allowed a prisoner who behaved well and worked hard to win a number of privileges. Issues involving the reform of prison conditions do not normally generate much public sympathy, but events at Birmingham prison in 1854 excited widespread concern. Between 1849 and 1851, the Governor there had been the self-same Alexander Maconochie who had had such a radical, if short-lived, impact at Norfolk Island. At Birmingham, he had inaugurated a more humanitarian system, but one which again was portrayed as being inimical to effective discipline. This led to him being forced out and replaced by the Assistant Governor, whose ferociously repressive regime led to a national outcry and the convening of a Royal Commission. This took away much local authority control over prisons, but confirmed that solitary confinement, the silent system and hard labour on treadmill and hand crank were to continue as standard practice.

The debate about transportation rolled on as the century progressed. One MP adamantly opposed to the practice was Sir William Molesworth, perhaps best described as an eager 'Young Turk' seeking to make a name for himself. In April 1837, he successfully forced the House of Commons to establish a select committee on transportation. Its brief was to 'inquire into the System of Transportation, its Efficacy as a Punishment, its influence on the Moral State of Society in the Penal colonies, and how far it is susceptible of improvement.' The Molesworth Committee issued its report in 1838, proposing that transportation would be ended at the first available opportunity. In so doing, it reflected the determination of the real powers behind its deliberations: the Home Secretary, Lord John Russell and the Secretary of State for the Colonies, Lord Grey. Both men wished to use the committee's findings to bolster their own convictions that criminal law should be liberalized. Both also wanted to see transportation run down and replaced by custodial sentences within the new domestic penitentiaries.

The committee's report supported Russell and Grey's determination to end the assignment of convicts to private employers as soon as possible. Transportation was deemed to be an ineffective punishment, expensive and likely to harden rather than reform recidivist convicts, while effectively rewarding wrongdoing in others by giving them a fresh start. The committee's members argued that transportation should be replaced by hard labour at home. As a source of labour in Australia, penal colonies undermined the status and efforts of those who had come as free emigrants and discouraged further settlement. As insufficient new workers were arriving, the colony's development was being held back. For this reason, free emigration had to be encouraged as a matter of urgency.

For all this, the committee members were not yet quite ready to abolish transportation itself, despite the one-sided and often lurid evidence which Molesworth and the hand-picked witnesses presented to them. Such evidence aroused a storm of protest in the Australian colonies because of the way he stereotyped those who lived there, both the free settlers and ex-convicts, as drunkards and libertines, suffused with the odium of criminality. Emotive outbursts from Molesworth likening New South Wales to Sodom and Gomorrah understandably roused the colonists to a fever pitch of fury. It was feared that such libels would deter further free immigration, despite the strenuous efforts that had been made by free settlers to differentiate themselves from convicts and ex-convicts.

The Molesworth Committee's report was full of stage-managed rhetoric, but it did help to bring transportation into its last phase. Its desire to end transportation in 1837 was impracticable in the immediate term as the existing prisons and the hulks in England were grossly overcrowded. The Molesworth Committee thus agreed that transportation to New South Wales should be abandoned, but that it could continue on a reduced scale to other destinations nearby where the regimes were much harsher, namely Van Diemen's Land and Norfolk Island, although no convicts were

A poster depicting female emigration to Australia, 1834 (CO 384/35 (10)). It reflects the immense need for female labour, particularly as domestic staff, in Van Diemen's Land. Women with textile skills, such as seamstresses, were also in high demand, as were nurses.

COLONISTS AND CONVICTS.

Australian Colonist, "NOW, MR. BULL! DON'T SHOOT ANY MORE OF YOUR *RUBBISH* HERE, OR YOU AND I SHALL QUARREL."

The caption of this Punch *cartoon of 1864, 'Colonists and Convicts', shows the growing resentment by free settlers, and many ex-convicts, about the continuing despatch of British convicts to exile in Australia.*

sent to the latter after 1839. Transportation to New South Wales ended in 1840, by which time a system of bounties had been inaugurated which encouraged free immigrants to settle there. The *Eden* was the last normal transport ship to deposit Britain's final convicts on Australia's shores. The end of an era had finally arrived.

All convicts now despatched from Britain to the region either went in small numbers to Western Australia or travelled in larger numbers to Van Diemen's Land, where assignment had ceased. They were maintained by the government and worked in gangs on a variety of public projects, but these ran into problems. The economy of Van Diemen's Land was in recession and convicts ending their sentences there found it very difficult to obtain work. The free inhabitants were required to pay much of the cost of the convict labour, but they claimed that they could not do so because of their own straitened circumstances.

THE END OF AN ERA

Politicians back in London did not necessarily have any great sympathy for the plight of voluntary Australian settlers, no matter how upright and honest they may have been. Issues concerning Australia did not normally receive high priority in the political agenda. However, some unwelcome reports did serve to propel transportation into prominence in public debate. There were no women convicts on Van Diemen's Land, and in the mid-1840s, many reports came in of the widespread prevalence of 'unnatural vice', a 'nameless crime', as male homosexuality was euphemistically known. Few things were more likely to create nervous reactions among the politicians of the time than such rumours, and the response from London was urgently to search for somewhere else in the British Empire to take convicts.

Time was running out for the whole concept of transportation. The colonies were asserting themselves and making it quite clear that they would not employ British convicts on public works unless Britain paid for them, which she was not prepared to do. Norfolk Island was abandoned as a penal colony in 1856, by which time transportation was increasingly under question. Society in Van Diemen's Land was in chaos as its free settlers fled to the mainland from what they thought of as criminal anarchy. It had refused to accept any new convicts from 1852.

The Colonial Office in London was under severe strain, considering alternative dumping grounds for its unwanted criminals. Northern Australia was contemplated; New Guinea, the Falkland Islands and Labrador all came under scrutiny and were rejected. It was decided that existing minor penal colonies in Bermuda and Gibraltar could not take increased numbers. An inquiry of Queensland as to whether it would consider the establishment of a convict colony met with a brusque rebuff. While small numbers of convicts continued to be sent to Bermuda, South Africa also made it quite clear that it did not want convicts, nor could New South Wales be persuaded to resume acceptance. Other possibilities—Barbados, Ceylon, Canada, St Helena, Mauritius and Trinidad—were touted and rejected for a variety of reasons, although a new penal establishment was opened at Gibraltar. Perhaps the most bizarre place touted as a possible destination for convicts was Auckland Island, a remote spot well to the south of New Zealand. Happily for any who might have been sent there, this suggestion was quietly dropped.

The Colonial Secretary Lord Grey came up with what at best can be seen as an interim solution for this intensifying problem. Those sentenced to transportation would serve a term in a prison cell in Britain, then a period of hard labour either in Britain or a penal colony, and then indefinite exile in the colony. This scheme was extremely unpopular with the majority of those already living in Australia: they just wanted an end to the system. Early in the 1850s, a number of associations of the type now called pressure or interest groups were established in the various Australian colonies to fight the continuance of transportation. These culminated in the creation of the Australasian Anti-Transportation League. It was argued vehemently that free immigration into Australia was significantly inhibited by the transportation of felons. Free labour was undercut, so it was argued, by the presence of the convicts, who were so numerous and ubiquitous that they made Australia an unfit place for women and children. The British government may have been notoriously purblind, but it could not totally ignore the weight of colonial opinion. In 1853, the impact of this pressure was admitted by Palmerston, then the newly appointed Home Secretary.

The last straw for transportation was the discovery of gold in New South Wales and in Victoria in 1851. Now the idea of sending convicts to a place separated from untold possible riches by a narrow stretch of water was patently absurd. There was a rush, a stampede, to get to the goldfields from Europe; the cost of shipping to Australia went up as a consequence, making transportation an even more expensive operation. Why spend large amounts of money sending felons to Australia as unwilling residents, when large numbers of free men from Britain were prepared to give up everything for the chance to get there?

A CRUEL AND INEFFICIENT SYSTEM

It has to be said that not all those convicted of offences for which the penalty had previously been transportation welcomed the new arrangements. Many felt aggrieved that they had been robbed of the opportunity for a new start in Australia. The 1850s were marked by considerable unrest in prisons partly caused by disgruntled inmates hoping that direct action might bring about a return of transportation. In government circles there were also dissenting voices, some arguing that Britain should not allow itself to be pushed about by colonial opinion. Grey even went so far as to argue that it would make more sense to part with the colonies than to expend resources in their protection and defence while having no effective jurisdiction over them.

Controversy has surrounded the issue of transportation from its inception, through its implementation and eventual end, down to the present day. The transported convicts and the penal regimes to which they were subjected have been interpreted in many different ways. For some, the convict origins of Australia have been a cause of shame. For those who have chosen to ridicule Australia, they have been a source of much misguided, negative and tasteless humour. Others, however, have derived considerable pride in their descent from felons, such as poachers, who fell foul of Britain's class system and the armoury of laws that were created to protect the property of the rich. Yet others point proudly to their descent from eighteenth and nineteenth century inhabitants of mainland Britain and of Ireland who were transported for their political activities, for their fight against injustice.

Many of those who were transported were convicted of offences which seem to us today to be extremely trivial and whose main crime consisted simply in being poor and desperate. There is a paradoxical glamour in such ancestry. Satisfaction is gained by those claiming descent from people whose lowly social and economic status meant that they were often more sinned against than sinning, but whose response to the appalling experience of transportation was a robust one—first, survival, and then carving out a new and better existence for themselves and their offspring. For some of those who achieved this, their reward was the very real one of escape from the social and economic misery associated with the Industrial Revolution in Britain and alluded to so graphically by acute observers such as Friedrich Engels and Henry Mayhew.

Debate continues to reverberate around the nature of Britain's penal system in the period of transportation. For many, the criminal law of the time was unduly biased in favour of the rich and powerful and intolerably severe in its dealings with those, mostly from the disenfranchised majority, whose activities were seen as threatening the social and political hegemony. No real attention was paid, it could be said, to identifying and tackling the causes of criminality—probably too deeply rooted and complicated to be reached by any forms of deterrent punishment. Under a harsh, sometimes cruel and retributive legal and penal system, convicts despatched to Van Diemen's Land and Norfolk Island in particular were subjected to acts of unspeakable brutality, both officially sanctioned and otherwise. However, others critical of transportation could point to the relaxed conditions under which many convicts served their sentences in New South Wales. Frequently a part of their term was remitted, they earned wages and went on to establish successful new lives for themselves. Many hardliners saw little punishment in that.

THE REALITY OF TRANSPORTATION

In exploring what transportation really meant, we have used the records of the National Archives to explore the practice and its historical context drawing extensively on contemporary voices. Issues related to crime and punishment always evoke strong emotional responses, and transportation is no exception. Leaving aside questions of ethics and the efficacy of transportation as punishment and deterrent, we should remember that other factors have been cited as contributing to the decision to create settlements for convicts in Australia. But did these settlements really generate economic success for the colony? New South Wales did not become a significant source of either raw materials for industry or for the fabric of British-built ships. A British presence in Australia did not apparently make any real difference to the balance of forces in the Indian Ocean throughout most of the period that convicts were sent there. After Trafalgar, Britain enjoyed naval supremacy for several decades, enabling her to build up and guard international trading networks with some assurance. No naval bases of significance were developed on Australia's coasts in the days of sailing ships. Transportation was intended to achieve the settlement of Australia. Involuntary though much of that settlement was, the effect was probably quicker than it would otherwise have been, at least until the discovery of gold in Australia.

Transportation carved a niche for itself in British popular culture. Many musical narratives were produced dealing with the subject. The vast majority do so from the standpoint that it was an experience to be dreaded. They often relate the sad lament about a decent young man, the child of poor but respectable parents, who leaves home to be apprenticed in London, but gets into bad company. After committing one or more foolish offences, he is arrested, tried and, while still no more than a youth, sentenced to transportation. In early examples of this genre, the American colonies are cited as the destination, but after 1788, Botany Bay makes its appearance. These ballads mostly have a rather dirge-like quality; they often end with one or more admonishing verses of this sort:

> *My country men take warning e' er too late,*
> *Lest you should share my hard unhappy fate;*
> *Altho' but little crimes you have done,*
> *Consider seven or fourteen years to come.*
> *Now young men with speed your lives amend,*
> *Take my advice as one that is your friend:*
> *For tho' so slight you make of it while you are here,*
> *Hard is your lot when once you get there.*[5]

Or:

> *How hard is the place of confinement*
> *That keeps me from my heart's delight.*
> *Cold chains and cold irons surround me,*
> *And a plank for a pillow at night.*
> *How often I wish that the eagle*
> *Would lend me her wing, I would fly,*
> *Then I'd fly to the arms of my Polly,*
> *And in her soft bosom I'd lie.*[6]

Such songs powerfully remind us of the real consequences of transportation—irrevocably shattered individual lives.

Transportation played a very significant part in British penal practice for two centuries or more. It also made a considerable contribution to Australian economic and social development. Convict labour may be intrinsically less efficient than that provided by paid workers, but in the early stages of the opening up of the Australian continent it was almost the only labour available. It provided early Australian capitalists with an abundance of cheap labour, increasing the profitability of their operations and possibly encouraging further investment. The presence of large numbers of convicts in Australia meant that British governments, accepting a level of responsibility for them, were forced to make substantial investments in the infrastructure of the embryonic colonies. Some of those who arrived as stigmatized criminals stayed on after paying their debts to society. Their talents were used not only to benefit themselves, but also to shape and define an emerging Australian culture and civilization.

Notes

Introduction

1 PC 1/67–92 (1819–1844).
2 HO 47 and HO 13.
3 December 1792, HO 47/15/104
4 August 1790, HO 47/12/107.
5 October 1788, HO 47/7/123.
6 September 1784, HO 47/1/63.
7 September 1789, HO 47/9/65.
8 August 1788, HO 47/7/115.

1 *The Beginning of Transportation*

1 RADZINOWICZ, Sir L. (1948) *A History of English Criminal Law and Its Administration from 1750*, Steven and Sons, London, vol. 1, p. 27.
2 HAY, D. *et al* (1977) *Albion's Fatal Tree: Crime and Society in Eighteenth Century England*, Penguin, Harmondsworth, p. 22.
3 HUGHES.
4 FLYNN, p. 10.
5 HO 42/3; 42/4; 42/5.
6 HO 42/3; 42/5.
7 HO 42/45; 42/65; 42/217.
8 BEATTIE, J.M. (2001) *Policing and Punishment in London 1660–1720: Urban Crime and the Limits of Terror*, Oxford University Press, p. 279.
9 EKIRCH, R. (1987) *Bound for America: The Transportation of British Convicts to the Colonies, 1718–1775*, Oxford University Press, New York, p. 2.
10 HUGHES, p. 42.
11 HO 7/2.
12 TS 45/71.
13 HO 7/2.
14 HO 44/25.
15 HO 7/2.
16 HO 8/9.
17 HO 7/1.
18 HO 42/6.
19 SHAW, p. 130.
20 CO 201.

2 *The First Three Fleets*

1 CO 201/2.
2 10 May 1785, HO 7/1.
3 Sackville Hamilton to Whitehall, 24 October 1786, CO 202/5.
4 ADM 55/40, f. 160, f. 165.
5 Letter, May 23 1789, CO 201/4.
6 SHAW, p. 50.
7 Nepean to Steele, 4 September 1786, T 1/639.
8 Nepean to Steele, 14 November 1786, T 1/639.
9 Chatham Papers, PRO 30/8/171.
10 T 1/639; Navy Board Minute, 20 Jan 1787, ADM 106/2623.
11 Lists of tools and utensils and clothing allowances for the colony are shown in CO 201/2.
12 DEFOE, D. (1724) *A Tour through the Whole Island of Great Britain*.
13 June 10 1787, CO 201/2. *See also* 13 March 1787, CO 201/2 part 2.
14 Phillip to Sydney, 6 August 1787, CO 201/2.
15 CO 201/2 part 2.
16 Phillip to Sydney, 2 September 1787, CO 201/2.
17 BATESON, p. 117.
18 September 1784, HO 42/7.
19 Grenville to Treasury, 6 July 1789, HO 35/10.
20 HO 35/9.
21 Newgate register records, PCOM 2/176; CO 201/4; ADM 106/2347; *see also* REES.
22 http://www.geocities.com/winsome griffin/HenryCone.html.
23 13 and 29 April 1789, CO 201/4.
24 CO 201/4.
25 ADM 1/2395.
26 T 1/665–678; High Court of Admiralty Proceedings of trial, HCA 1/61.
27 BATESON, p. 129; 13–15 April letters from the Cape, CO 201/5.
28 BATESON, p. 129.
29 Long to Bernard, 16 February, HO 35/12 —Treasury Correspondence.

30 Navy Board Records 1749–1806,
    ADM 106/2943.
31 RICKARD, p. 75.
32 HUGHES.
33 FROST, A. (1995) *Images of Botany Bay*,
    Melbourne University Press, pp. 211–23.
34 SHAW, p. 70.
35 *See* sources HO 10/1–55, 1787–1859 *and*
    HO 11/1–21, 1787–1870 for details of
    convicts.

3 *The Trauma of Exile*

1   Letter to Peel, 29 August 1822, PC 1/70.
2   PC 1/67–92 (1819–1844). *See* HO 14
    for the period 1849–1870 *and also*
    ADM 108/10; ADM 108/21;
    ADM 108/22; ADM 108/23;
    ADM 108/25; ADM 108/27.
3   PALMER (1988), pp. 152–3.
4   *See* HO 40, HO 41, HO 44, *and* HO 52
    for Swing disturbances. *See also* TS 11.
    For localities *see* Berkshire TS 11/849;
    Buckinghamshire TS 11/865; Kent
    TS 11/943; Oxfordshire TS 11/1031
    and Sussex TS 11/1007.
5   ADM 101/23/1.
6   Hughes, pp. 131–2.
7   May 1832, PC 1/80 part 1.
8   26 June 1838, PC 1/87.
9   29 June 1839, PC 1/86.
10 10 September, PC 1/67.
11 4 January 1819, PC 1/67; 14 December
    1819, PC 1/67; 3 November 1840,
    PC 1/88.
12 26 November, 1837, PC 1/85.
13 17 August 1842, PC 1/90.
14 11 December 1837, PC 1/85.
15 December 1819, PC 1/67.
16 22 August 1849, PC 1/88.
17 In 1830 the average annual income for an
    agricultural labourer was about £330.
    (Source: WILLIAMSON, J.G. (1982)
    'The Structure of Pay in Britain, 1710',
    Research in Economic History, 7.)
18 May 1834, PC 1/82; PC 1/78; 23
    September 1839, PC 1/78; May 1824,
    PC 1/82.
19 September 1837, PC 1/85.
20 12 April 1830, PC 1/78.

21 ADM 101/71/7.
22 17 August 1837, PC 1/85.
23 17 November 1834, PC 1/82.
24 January 1838, PC 1/86.
25 24 August 1832, PC 1/80.
26 27 June 1815, PC 1/4030.
27 25 January 1819, PC 1/67; November
    1832, PC 1/80; January 1838, PC 1/86;
    December 1840, PC 1/88.
28 18 May 1832, PC 1/80.
29 June 1838, PC 1/86.
30 16 March 1822, PC 1/70; 30 March 1822,
    PC 1/70; 23 August, 1822, PC 1/70.
31 KENT & TOWNSEND (2001), p. 247.
32 September 1830, PC 1/78; February 1834,
    PC 1/82.
33 PC 1/78.
34 September 1830, PC 1/78.
35 May 1834, PC 1/82.
36 September 1830, PC 1/78; 15 December
    1840, PC 1/88; 23 December 1819,
    PC 1/670.
37 September 1832, PC 1/80; September
    1836, PC 1/86.
38 August 1844, PC 1/92.
39 HO 47/34.
40 19 September 1832, PC 1/80.
41 16 March 1837, PC 1/85.
42 14 June 1842, PC 1/90.
43 May 1834, PC 1/82.
44 MT 32/12; HUGHES, p. 142.
45 RICKARD, p. 70.
46 Bromley to Bigge, 1820, CO 201/119.
47 TENCH, W. (2004) *A Narrative of the
    Expedition to Botany Bay*, Kessinger
    Publishing, p. 19.
48 ROBSON.
49 HO 44/37.
50 FIELD & MILLETT
51 *Lincelles* 1862, MT 32/2; *Clyde* 1862,
    MT 32/6; *Norwood* 1862, MT 32/3;
    Racehorse 1865, MT 32/9.
52 CO 386/154 1848–1873.
53 SHAW, p. 229. *See* CO 201 for correspon-
    dence relating to New South Wales.
54 CO 386/154.
55 CO 386/154.
56 KENT & TOWNSEND (2001), p. 248.
57 NICHOLAS, S. & SHERGOLD, P.R.
    (1988) 'Convicts as Migrants', in
    NICHOLAS, p. 54.

4 *Who Were the Convicts?*

1 ADM 101/253.
2 ADM 101/66/8.
3 PALMER (1988), p. 150.
4 SHAW, p. 179.
5 *Phoebe Dunbar* ADM 101/253.
6 PALMER (1979), p. 118.
7 *Asia* ADM 101/5/9; *Mandarin* ADM 101/46/7; *Maitland* ADM 101/46/1; *Woodbridge* ADM 101/75/2.
8 16 October 1842, PC 1/90.
9 *See also* HO 27/68.
10 July 1838, HO 73/2.
11 CO 201/234; HUGHES, p. 356. For different views, *see*, for example, ROBSON, and NICHOLAS (pp. 7–8).
12 *Bencoolan* ADM 101/7/10.
13 *Albion* ADM 101/1/9.
14 TOBIAS. Register of Newgate Gaol, PCOM 2/185; 2/186; 2/199; 21/201. Ordinary's and Surgeon's Notebook, PCOM 2/161. Hulks Account, T 38/331; 38/332; 38/336; 38/337. Petition from Isaac Solomons, HO 17f113. Transportation Register, HO 11/8. Surgeon's Log, ADM 101/74/7.
15 HUGHES, p. 244.
16 OXLEY, D. (1989) 'Female Convicts', in NICHOLAS, p. 92.
17 NICHOLAS, pp. 204–5.
18 BIGGE, John, Report of the Commissioner of Inquiry into the State of the Colony of New South Wales, Great Britain, Parliamentary Papers, vol. 20, paper 448; STURMA.
19 17 July 1803, HO 44/45.
20 MCLACHLAN.
21 *See* BAKER, S.J.; *see also* BAKER, A. (1984) *Death is a Good Solution*, University of Queensland Press, St Lucia.
22 4 June and 4 July 1849, HO 45/2949.
23 RICKARD, p. 68.
24 ADM 101/64.
25 HUGHES, pp. 137–8.
26 ADM 101/55/9.
27 ADM 101/6/7.
28 BATESON, pp. 65–6.
29 RICKARD, p. 70.
30 ADM 101/34/8.
31 ADM 101/45.

32 CO 280/240.
33 *Baring*, 1819, ADM 101/7/4; *Mary* ADM 101/51/5.
34 Hume to Peel, 9 December 1835, HO 44/49.
35 BATESON, pp. 79–80.
36 Ibid., pp. 99, 103.
37 Lord Sidmouth, ADM 101/44.
38 NICOL, J. (2000), *The Life and Adventures of John Nicol, Mariner*, Canongate, Edinburgh (first edition, 1822).
39 NICOLL, pp. 112–4.
40 *See* DAMOUSI.
41 28 February 1845, 25 August 1846, HO 45/1188.
42 *See*, for example, the series MT 32/1–12.
43 HO 73/2 part 2; NICHOLAS, S. & SHERGOLD, P.R. (1988) 'Convicts as Migrants', in NICHOLAS, pp. 74–8.
44 Old Bailey Minutes, April 1856, CRIM 6/8; *Lord Raglan* MT 32/1, MT 32/1.
45 MT 32/1; CO 280/240.
46 CO 280/240.
47 Letter, 21 July 1827, PC 1/4327; letter, 10 December 1827, PC 1/4327.
48 Stephen's minute, 29 January 1831, CO 280/25.

5 *Child Convicts*

1 HOLDEN.
2 SHORE, p. 11.
3 HO 26/1–55; SHORE, p. 133.
4 Ho 73/16, notebook 1.
5 Report of the committee for investigating the causes of the alarming increase of juvenile delinquents in the metropolis, London 1816, p. 5.
6 HO 73/2.
7 Nicholas White, HO 73/16.
8 Notebook IV, HO 73/16.
9 SHORE, p. 8.
10 Ibid. p. 170.
11 21–22 October 1805, ADM 51/4514 part 4, pp. 132–3; 17 December 1805, MPI 1/536.
12 CORDINGLY.

13 John Capper's Report of 27 January 1827, Parliamentary Papers, 1827, vol. XIX, p. 137; CAMPBELL, pp. 131–2.
14 CAMPBELL, p. 133.
15 Ibid. p. 139.
16 HO 73/16, notebook 1.
17 HO 44/12, f. 59.
18 Part 1, HO 73/2.
19 HO 73/16.
20 DICKENS, C. (2004) *Oliver Twist*, Penguin, Harmondsworth, p. 443.
21 *Elphinstone* ADM 101/24/11.
22 PC 1/2717.
23 HO 73/16.
24 HUGHES, p. 408.
25 PC 1/2717.
26 March 1842, HO 8/71.
27 NICHOLAS, pp 81–2.
28 PC 1/2717.
29 HO 10; HO 11; ADM 101.
30 We are indebted to Wendy Bloomfield, the great-great-great granddaughter of Richard Pinnuck, for this information.

6 *Keeping Order*

1 *Clyde* MT 32/6; *Diana* ADM 101/19/6; *Lord Raglan* MT 32/1.
2 MT 32/6.
3 ADM 101/37/6.
4 *Norwood* MT 32/12.
5 *Vimeira* MT 32/10.
6 PC 2/139.
7 CO 280/240.
8 BATESON, pp. 134, 148, 166, 179.
9 SEMPLE LISLE, J.G. (1799) *The Life of Major J.G. Semple Lisle*, W. Stewart, London.
10 *Ocean* ADM 101/57/9.
11 *Isabella* ADM 101/36/4; *Mangles*, ADM 101/47/3; *Ocean*, ADM 101/57/9.
12 *Royal Charlotte* ADM 101/65/4; *John Barry* ADM 101/38/2; *Somersetshire* ADM 101/68/5.
13 7 April 1842, PC 1/90.
14 *Corona* MT 32/11.
15 RICKARD, p. 71.
16 12 December 1815, PC 1/4030.
17 *Lord Raglan* MT 32/1; *Agincourt* ADM 101/1/7; *Racehorse* MT 32/9.

18 HUGHES, p. 265.
19 PEAKMAN, J. (2004) *Lascivious Bodies: A Sexual History of the Eighteenth Century*, Atlantic Books, London, p. 155. *See also* GILBERT, A.N. 'Buggery and the British Navy 1700–1861', *Journal of Social History*, vol. X, no. 1 (1978).
20 *Lord Raglan* MT 32/1; *Merchantman* MT 32/5.
21 HO 44/37.
22 HO 44/37.
23 *Norwood* MT 32/12.
24 Letter to Governor Phillip, 24 August 1789, CO 201/4.
25 *Anson* ADM 101/3/4.
26 GIBBINGS, pp. 23–4.
27 *Anson* ADM 101/3/4
28 CO 280/240.
29 CO 280/83.
30 Surgeon's instructions, Bigge Appendix, 1819, CO 201/118.
31 *Clyde* MT 32/6.
32 HO 44/45.
33 CO 201/119, 76–9.
34 *Grenada* ADM 101/30/5.
35 SHAW, p. 123.
36 GROCOTT, A.M. (1980) *Convicts, Clergymen and Churches: Attitudes of Convicts and Ex-Convicts Towards the Clergy in New South Wales from 1788 to 1851*, Sydney University Press, Sydney.
37 *See* chapter 4.
38 *See* chapter 7.
39 SILLARD; *Mount Stuart Elphinstone* ADM 101/55/9.
40 SILLARD, p. 22
41 Ibid., p. 37.
42 Ibid., p. 75.
43 PALMER (1988), p. 148
44 RICKARD, p. 72–3.
45 HUGHES, p. 155.
46 RODGER, p. 207.

7 *Health, Disease and Food on the Convict Ships*

1 BATESON, p. 12
2 CO 201.20, f. 239
3 CO 201/23.
4 CO 202/8/545.

5 CO 201/23 f.150.
6 ADM 101/7/1.
7 ADM 101/33/7.
8 ADM 101/32/5.
9 ADM 101/12/1; 101/18/6; 101/19/1; 101/43/1; 101/53/6; 101/71/7.
10 ADM 101/18/6.
11 ADM 101/36/4.
12 ADM 101/36/4.
13 ADM 101/1/4.
14 *Aurora* ADM 101/6/7; *Barrosa* ADM 101/7/8.
15 ADM 101/27/3.
16 ADM 101/32/5.
17 ADM 101/2/6.
18 ADM 101/44/4.
19 MT 32/10.
20 ADM 101/25/2.

8 *The Surgeon's Tale*

1 ADM 101/67/6.
2 ADM 101/66/4.
3 CO 201/44; CO 201/118.
4 CO 201/119.
5 ADM 101/52/6.
6 ADM 101/6/186.
7 ADM 101/41/1.
8 ADM 101/59/4.
9 ADM 101/1/6.
10 ADM 101/12/3.
11 ADM 101/53/6.
12 ADM 101/19/1.
13 ADM 101/13/3.
14 ADM 101/32/9.
15 MT 32/11.
16 MT 32/8.
17 ADM 101/29/5.
18 ADM 101/31/4.
19 ADM 101/6/83.
20 ADM 101/59/2.
21 ADM 101/55/9.
22 ADM 101/40/6.
23 ADM 101/13/5.
24 ADM 101/7/8.
25 ADM 101/7/8.
26 ADM 101/255.
27 ADM 101/253.
28 MT 32/7.
29 MT 32/9.

9 *The Promised Land*

1 *Albion* ADM 101/1/9.
2 *Atlas* ADM 101/6/2.
3 KENT & TOWNSEND (1996), p.38
4 CO 280/240.
5 10 March 1845, CO 280/240.
6 HUGHES, pp.548–9; SHAW, p.356.
7 GIBBINGS, p.35
8 HO 10; HO 11; HO 16/1–9.
9 Western Australia, Original Correspondence, 1849, CO 18/52.
10 Phillips to Hay, 26 February 1833, CO 201/234; Hay to Phillips, 25 June 1833, CO 202/29; private letters from Mr Hay, 1830–1836.
11 Naylor to Stanley, CO 280/240.
12 13 May 1837, CO 280/83.
13 CO 280/83.
14 HUGHES, p.462.
15 Ibid., p.480.
16 1837 Report on Convict Discipline in Van Diemen's Land, CO 280/83, Note E.
17 HUGHES, p.491.
18 27 January 1845, CO 881/3/1.
19 CO 280/83.
20 CO 280/83.
21 CO 280/240.
22 SHAW, p.245.
23 CO 280/83.
24 SMITH, pp.54–5.
25 DANIELS & MURNANE, p.20.
26 CURREY; POTTLE; HUGHES, pp.205–9.
27 GIBBINGS, p.43.

Conclusion: *Towards the End of Transportation*

1 SHAW, p.143
2 Ibid., p.140
3 PALMER (1988), p.148
4 *Edinburgh Review*, 1813.
5 PALMER (1988), p.146
6 Ibid., p.148

Bibliography

PRIMARY SOURCES

The National Archives website (http://www.pro.gov.uk) is very informative and can be easily accessed for primary sources relating to convict transportation. The National Archives' sources listed below are in order of their catalogue letters/numbers.

ADMIRALTY

ADM 6/186 Application for employment as surgeons of convict ships 1829–1833.
ADM 55/40 Journal of *Endeavour* kept by James Cook 1767–1771.
ADM 101 series contains some 600 journals from convict ships for which naval surgeons were provided. The journals contain an account of the treatment of medical cases, a daily sick list, the incidence of diseases, and in many cases general comments relating to discipline. Many of these were consulted in the writing of this book.
ADM 104/17 Surgeons; ADM 106/2943 Navy Board Records 1749–1806

AUDIT OFFICE

AO 2/17 Convict Hulk Establishment 1826; AO 3/291 Accounts.

COLONIAL OFFICE

CO 18/52; CO 18/105 1858 Despatches general; CO 24/22 Letters from Sec of State 1838–44; CO 91/219 Report on the Convict Establishment; CO 201 Correspondence, Original-Secretary of State; CO 201/1 Correspondence; CO 201/2 Correspondence 1786–7; CO 201/4/4/15/30 Letters relating to first fleet; CO 201/4/15/30; CO 201/118–142 Bigge's Report; CO 202/5 Various letters from Port Jackson; CO 280/83 Despatches Convict discipline 1837; CO 280/240; CO 386/154 Register of applications for passages to the colonies for convicts' families 1848–1873; CO 700 Map of Port Jackson 1796; CO 881/2/1 Correspondence respecting the 'Convicts Prevention Bill' 16 February 1852 to 7 February 1854; CO 881/3/1 Western Australia; CO 885/2/12 Transportation and emigration; CO 885/2/15 Overview of the transportation system, 1852; CO 885/2/17 A history of the transportation system by T. Frederick Elliot.

CENTRAL CRIMINAL COURT

CRIM 6/8 Old Bailey minutes 1856.

HOME OFFICE

HO 7 Home Office: Convicts 1785–1825; HO 7/1 House of Commons Committee *re* Transportation of convicts to West Coast of Africa 1785; HO 8/11824 Hulks; HO 8/2 1824 Convicts on the hulks; HO 8/71 *Euryalus* March 1842; HO 8/72 *Euryalus* June 1842; HO 10/1–64 Settlers and convicts, 1787–1859; HO 11/1–21 Lists of convicts transported in various ships 1787–1870; HO 12/1 Petitions from convicts' wives from 1849; HO 13 Criminal Entry Books 1782–1871; HO 14/1 Petitions from convicts' wives from 1849; HO 17 f113 Petition from Isaac Solomons; HO 26/1–55 Criminal records for Middlesex; HO 35/7 letters concerning raising of First Fleet 1786; HO 42/5 Petitions and pleas 1784; HO 44/12 Domestic correspondence; HO 44/13 Robert Peel *re* sentencing of convicts; HO 44/25 Cholera ship Canada; HO 44/31 Use of bodies of convicts on hulks for anatomical dissection 1838; HO 44/37 Misconduct of female on *John Renwick*; HO 44/45 Letter in relation to hulks; HO 44/49 Letter *re* state of convict ships; HO 44/45 Religious ceremonies; HO 45/395 Regulations; HO 45/959 Female convicts in Van Diemen's Land 1844–48; HO 45/1188 Matrons on female convict ships 1845–6; HO 45/2927 First arrival of convicts; HO 47 Judges' reports on criminals; HO 73/2 Letters and papers; HO 73/3 1838–38; HO 73/16 Correspondence 1835–37; HO 2949 Rewards for convicts.

MINISTRY OF TRANSPORT

MT 32/1–12 1858–67 Superintendent Surgeons journals to Fremantle.

PRIVY COUNCIL

PC 1/67–92 Petitions and pleas from families 1819–1844; PC 1/2715 *Eden*, 1840; PC 1/2718 *Anson*, 1843; PC 1/2717 *Elphinstone* 1842; PC 1/4030 Convict medical records; PC 1/4327 Henry Savery convict; PC 1/4351 Roman Catholic clergy 1829; PC 2/139 Lists of Scottish convicts.

PRISON COMMISSION AND HOME OFFICE PRISON DEPARTMENT

PCOM 2/161 Surgeon's notebook; PCOM 2/185; 2/186; 2/199; 21/201 Register of Newgate Prison.

PUBLIC RECORD OFFICE, GIFTS, DEPOSITS, NOTES AND TRANSCRIPTS

PRO 22/8 Log of *Endeavour* 1768–1771; PRO 30/22/3B Molesworth 20 June 1838.

TREASURY

T 1/639 1786 provisions for First fleet; T 38/331; 38/332; 38/336; 38/337 Hulks accounts.

TREASURY SOLICITOR (CONTRACTS WITH AGENTS TO TRANSPORT PRISONERS)

TS 18/460; TS 18/488; TS 18/515; TS 18/1308; TS 18/1321; TS 18/1361; TS 45/71.

PUBLICATIONS OF THE HOUSE OF COMMONS

ZHC 1 Parliamentary Sessions Papers *re* convict ship *Euryalus*.

SELECTED SECONDARY SOURCES

BAKER, S.J. (1966) *The Australian Language: An Examination of the English Language and English Speech as Used in Australia, from Convict Days to the Present*, Angus and Robertson, Sydney.

BATESON, C. (1985) *The Convict Ships*, Brown, Son & Ferguson, Glasgow.

BRANCH-JOHNSON, W. (1957) *The English Prison Hulks*, Christopher Johnson, London.

BROOKE, A & BRANDON, D. (2004) *Tyburn: London's Fatal Tree*, Sutton, Stroud.

BROWN, M. (1988) *Australia Bound! The Story of West Country Connections 1688–1888*, Ex Libris, Bradford-on-Avon.

BROWN, S.R. (2003) *Scurvy*, Summersdale Publishers, Chichester.

CAMPBELL, C. (2001) *The Intolerable Hulks: British Shipboard Confinement 1776–1857*, Fenestra Books, Tucson, Arizona.

CHAPMAN, D. (1981) *1788: The People of the First Fleet*, Cassell, Sydney.

CLAY, J. (2001) *Maconochie's Experiment*, John Murray, London.

CLUNE, F. (1965) *Bound for Botany Bay, Narrative of a Voyage in 1798 Aboard the Death Ship, 'Hillsborough'*, Angus and Robertson, Sydney.

COBLEY, J. (1983) *The Crimes of the First Fleet Convicts*, Angus and Robertson, Sydney.

COLDHAM, P.W. (1992) *Emigrants in Chains: A Social History of Forced Emigration to the Americas 1607–1776*, Alan Sutton, Stroud.

CORDINGLY, D. (2003) *Billy Ruffian*, Bloomsbury, London.

COSTELLO, C. (1987) *Botany Bay : The Story of the Convicts Transported from Ireland to Australia, 1791–1853*, Mercier, Cork.

CRITTENDEN, V. (1981) *A Bibliography of the First Fleet*, Australian National University Press, Canberra.

CURREY, C.H. (1963) *The Transportation, Escape and Pardoning of Mary Bryant*, Angus and Robertson, Sydney.

DAMOUSI, J. (1997) *Depraved and Disorderly: Female Convicts, Sexuality and Gender in Colonial Australia*, New York: Cambridge University Press.

DANIELS, K. & MURNANE, M. (1980) *Uphill All the Way: A Documentary History of Women in Australia*, University of Queensland Press, St Lucia.

DUFFIELD, I. & BRADLEY, J. (eds) (1997) *Representing Convicts: New Perspectives on Convict Forced Labour Migration*, Leicester University Press, London.

FIELD, M. & MILLETT, T. (eds) (1998) *Convict Love Tokens: The Leaden Hearts of the Convicts Left Behind*, Wakefield Press, Kent Town, Australia

FLYNN, M. (1993) *The Second Fleet: Britain's Grim Convict Armada of 1790*, Library of Australian History, Sydney.

FROST, A. (1993) *Botany Bay Mirages*, Melbourne University Press.

GIBBINGS, R. (1956) *John Graham, Convict: An Historical Narrative*, Dent, London.

HARVIE, D.I. (2002) *Limeys*, Sutton, Stroud.

HASLUCK, A. (1959) *Unwilling Emigrants: A Study of the Convict Period in Western Australia*, Oxford University Press, Melbourne.

HAWKINGS, D.T. (1987) *Bound for Australia*, Phillimore, Chichester.

HOLDEN, R. (2000) *Orphans of History: The Forgotten Children of the First Fleet*, Text Publishing, Melbourne.

HUGHES, R. (2003) *The Fatal Shore*, Vintage, London.

JONES, D.J.V. (1999) *The Last Rising: The Newport Chartist Insurrection of 1839*, University of Wales Press, Cardiff.

KEMP, P. (1970) *The British Sailor: A Social History of the Lower Deck*, Dent, London.

KENT, D. & TOWNSEND, N. (1996) *Joseph Mason, Assigned Convict 1831–1837*, Melbourne University Press.

KENT, D. & TOWNSEND, N. (2001) *The Convicts of the 'Eleanor': Protest in Rural England, New Lives in Australia*, Merlin Press, London.

KING, J. (1982) *The First Fleet: The Convict Voyage That Founded Australia, 1787–88*, Macmillan, Melbourne.

McLACHLAN, N. (ed) (1964) *Memoirs of James Hardy Vaux*, Heinemann, London

NICHOLAS, S. (ed) (1988) *Convict Workers*, Cambridge University Press.

NICHOLSON, I. (1991) *Log of Logs: A Catalogue of Logs, Journals, Shipboard Diaries, Letters and All Forms of Voyage Narratives, 1788–1993, for Australia and New Zealand, and Surrounding Areas*, 2 vols, Roebuck Society/I. Nicholson, Yaroomba, Australia.

OXLEY, D. (1997) *Convict Maids*, Cambridge University Press.

PALMER, R. (ed) (1974) *A Touch on the Times: Songs of Social Change 1770 to 1914*, Penguin, Harmondsworth.

PALMER, R. (1979) *A Ballad History of England, from 1588 to the Present Day*, Batsford, London.

PALMER, R. (1988) *The Sound of History, Songs and Social Comment*, Oxford University Press.

PIKE, D. (ed) (1968) *Australian Dictionary of National Biography 1788–1850*, vols 1 and 2, Melbourne University Press.

POTTLE, F.A. (1938) *Boswell and the Girl from Botany Bay*, Viking, New York.

REECE, B. (ed) (1989) *Irish Convicts: The Origins of Convicts Transported to Australia*, University College, Dublin.

REES, S. (2002) *The Floating Brothel*, Headline Review, London.

REID, T. (1822) *Two Voyages to New South Wales and Van Diemen's Land*, Longman, London.

RICKARD, S. (ed) (2001) *George Barrington's Voyage to Botany Bay*, Leicester University Press, London.

RIGDEN, R. (1976) *The Floating Prisons of Woolwich and Deptford*, Borough of Greenwich, London.

ROBSON, L. (1994) *The Convict Settlers of Australia*, Melbourne University Press.

RODGER, N.A.M. (1988) *The Wooden World*, Fontana Press, London.

RYAN, R.J. (1983) *The Third Fleet Convicts: An Alphabetical Listing of Names Giving Date and Place of Conviction, Length of Sentence and Ship of Transportation*, Horwitz Grahame, Sydney.

SALT, A. (1984) *These Outcast Women: The Parramatta Female Factory 1821–1848*, Hale & Iremonger, Sydney.

SHAW, A.G.L. (1998) *Convicts and the Colonies*, Irish Historical Press, Dublin.

SHORE, H. (1999) *Artful Dodgers: Youth and Crime in Early Nineteenth Century London*, Boydell Press, London.

SILLARD, P.A. (1901) *The Life and Letters of John Martin, with Sketches of Thomas Devin Reilly, Father John Kenyon and other Young Irelanders*, James Duffy, Dublin.

SMITH, B. (1988) *A Cargo of Women: Susannah Watson and the Convicts of the Princess Royal*, New South Wales University Press, Sydney.

STURMA, M. (1983) *Vice in a Vicious Society: Crime and Convicts in Mid-Nineteenth-Century New South Wales*, University of Queensland Press, Brisbane.

TOBIAS, J.J. (1974) *Prince of Fences: The Life and Times of Ikey Solomons*, Valentine, Mitchell, London.

WEBSITES

There are many websites dealing with convict history. These include large genealogical sites, national archives, local archives and those that offer general and specific information. Particularly useful ones include:

Ships arriving in Australia—excellent for data on certain ships.
http://members.iinet.net.au/~perthdps/convicts/index.html

First Fleet Online—contains a good database.
http://cedir.uow.edu.au/programs/FirstFleet/

Fremantle Prison—a convict database of about 10,000 men between 1850 and 1868.
http://www.fremantleprison.com

Medical pioneers—a database of over 3,000 pioneer doctors plus ships' surgeons.
http://www.medicalpioneers.com

Old Bailey online—An excellent website containing over 100,000 trials.
http://www.oldbaileyonline.org

Index

AUTHORS' ACKNOWLEDGEMENTS

We were fortunate enough to be commissioned to write this book by the National Archives (formerly the Public Record Office) and we have been able to base it largely on the wealth of material that is open to the public and housed at Kew in South West London. Researching these documents has been an extremely rewarding experience and we hope that readers of this book will be encouraged to consult the National Archives online or, in our opinion a more rounded-out and rewarding experience, to visit Kew themselves, where they will find the staff extremely helpful.

Anyone who attempts to write on such a big topic is indebted to the help, advice and perseverance of many people. We record our gratitude to Wendy Bloomfield from Western Australia who gave us permission to use information on her ancestor who sailed to Van Diemen's Land as a boy convict in 1842. We wish to thank the National Archives for asking us to write this book and then giving us such generous access to their material. Jane Crompton initiated the idea and helped us through the early stages. Many of the staff at the National Archives gave enormous support. Our thanks also go to Paul Carter and Jane Brown for drawing our attention to the rich seam of material in the Home Office records on Judges Reports on Criminals 1783 to 1830 (HO 47 and HO 13). Ken Wilson created the design for the book. Deborah Pownall brought her expertise to exploring and providing many fascinating illustrations. Janet Sacks and Rosie Anderson, through their meticulous editing and proofreading, spotted many inconsistencies. The index was compiled by Indexing Specialists (UK) Ltd. We are especially indebted to Catherine Bradley, who worked tirelessly and made many positive comments and suggestions. Any surviving errors of fact rest with the authors.

Reading, researching and writing are time-consuming activities and necessarily involve much work of a sedentary and isolated nature. Gratitude must therefore extend to relatives and friends who have not only tolerated our preoccupations but also positively encouraged our efforts.

ALAN BROOKE & DAVID BRANDON 2005

PICTURE ACKNOWLEDGEMENTS

Cover Mitchell Library, Sydney; p. 61 National Library of Australia; p. 85 Timothy Millet Collection; p. 138 Private Collection; p. 161 National Library of Australia; p. 192 Private Collection; p. 220 Mitchell Library, Sydney; p. 237 National Library of Australia: all Bridgeman Art Library

Back cover, frontispiece, pp. 28, 124, 217, 224–5 National Library of Australia, Canberra

p. 17 John T. Smith *Vagabondia* (1874)

p. 21 Collage/Corporation of London

pp. 33 (Add.31360), 48 (19492.aaa.16), 56 (Add.13880), 213 (Add 13880) British Library/Images on line

pp. 49, 149, 201 Art Archive

pp. 52 (top), 104 National Maritime Museum

pp. 52 (bottom) *Life and Adventures of John Nicol* (1822)

pp. 92, 101 Knapp and Baldwin's *Newgate Calendar* (1825)

pp. 105, 109 Mary Evans Picture Library

p. 126 Charles Dickens' *Oliver Twist*

p. 172 Mitchell Library, Sydney

p. 189 Wellcome Trust

p. 253 The National Archives Library

The remaining illustrations are from the National Archives.

Name	Where Convicted		Crime
	County	Town	
Gardner Francis	Middlesex	London	Felony
Garth Edward	Middlesex	London	Felony
Garland Francis	Devon	Exeter	Return from Transportation
Garth Susannah alias Grath			
Gabel Mary	Surry	Southwark	Felony
Gascoygne Olive	Worcester	Worcester	Burglary
Gearing Thomas	Oxford	Oxford	Burglary
Gess George	Gloucester	Gloucester	Horse Stealing
George Ann	Middlesex	London	Felony
Glenton Thomas	York	Northallerton	Grand Larceny
Gloster William	Middlesex	London	Felony
Gordon Janet	Southampton	Winchester	Felony
Goodwin Edward	London	London	Felony
Goodwin Andrew	Middlesex	London	Felony
Gould John	Devon	Exeter	Felony
Gray Charles	Surry	Southwark	Felony
Griffiths Samuel alias Briscow alias Butcher	Gloucester	Gloucester	Sheep Stealing
Greenwell Nicholas	Middlesex	London	Felony
Green John	Berks	Reading	Grand Larceny
Griffiths Thomas	London	London	Felony
Granger Charles	Devon	Plymouth	Felony
Grace James			
Green Hannah			
Groves Mary	Lincoln	Lincoln	Felony
Green Mary	London	London	Felony
Green Ann	Middlesex	London	Felony
Greenwood Mary	Middlesex	London	Felony
Gunter William	Bristol	Bristol	Felony